THE COMPLETE
ASCENSION MANUAL
HOW TO ACHIEVE ASCENSION IN THIS LIFETIME

JOSHUA DAVID STONE, Ph.D.

THE EASY-TO-READ ENCYCLOPEDIA OF THE SPIRITUAL PATH

Volume I

The Complete Ascension Manual

How to Achieve Ascension in this Lifetime

Joshua David Stone, Ph.D.

ISBN 0-929385-55-1
Published by
Light Technology Publishing
P.O. Box 1526, Sedona, AZ 86339

Cover design by
Fay Richards

Printed by
Mission Possible Commercial Printing
P.O. Box 1495, Sedona, AZ 86339

The Complete

ASCENSION MANUAL

How to Achieve Ascension

in this Lifetime

Joshua David Stone, Ph.D.

Dedication

I would humbly like to dedicate this book to four wonderful spiritual beings. The first and most important is my lovely wife, Terri. She has been a constant source of love, support, and inspiration. She has had an enormous impact on my life, and I would not have written this series of books in the form they are in if it had not been for Terri's help on spiritual, mental, emotional, and earthly levels. She has truly been the source of a tremendous amount of Light and love in all areas of my life.

Secondly I would humbly like to thank Rags, our cat. Rags is also known as Muffin, Sweet Pea, and Pink Belly. Rags has faithfully and devotedly kept me company on my desk and in my office during the long hours of typing and research. Her selfless devoted service, in my opinion, has earned her the right to be an "Ascended Master Kitty."

The third person I would like to thank is the Ascended Master Djwhal Khul, who I am honored to call my spiritual teacher, friend, and brother in the Light. His continued support, guidance, and teachings have been the true source of inspiration behind these books.

I would also like to thank Marc Norelli, who in a most selfless and dedicated manner diligently proofread the many volumes of material whenever this service was needed. I am also honored to call him my friend and fellow brother in the Light.

Lastly, I would like to dedicate this book and give a very, very special thank you to my dear friend and colleague, Raney Alexandre. Raney has, with total selflessness, dedicated herself to the task of typing on her computer all four volumes of *The Complete Easy-to-Read Encyclopedia of the Spiritual Path*. She has helped me with graphics, editing, spiritual ideas, research books, and feedback when I have gotten off track.

Without her help these books would have been delayed years in coming to full fruition. Her dedicated, selfless service allowed me to put my full and total concentration on writing, while she did the truly hard part of putting the book together logistically. She has truly been an "angel" sent to me by God to free me up for the work I needed to do.

Contents

Introduction

Every person who incarnates into this physical world has a particular mission or purpose in God's plan which he is here to fulfill. The particular mission and humble gift that God has graced me with is twofold in function.

The first is the ability to consolidate vast amounts of practical, useful, and very interesting spiritual information in an easy-to-understand form. The second is the ability to garnish and harvest the essential kernels from this vast amount of spiritual information and leave the rest behind.

My mission in writing this book and the three books that follow it was, in essence, to save people time. This book is the first of a series of four books which I have collectively called *The Easy-to-Read Encyclopedia of the Spiritual Path*.

What I have attempted to do is present to my reader four easy-to- read books that cover the entire field of spirituality and religion on Planet Earth. I realize that most people do not like to spend time reading, studying, and researching as much as I do. My service to humanity is the ability to take the information in the Alice A. Bailey books, *A Course in Miracles*, Theosophy, the Great Masters, the Edgar Cayce material, the world's great religions, spiritual psychology, and the extraterrestrial movement and make these books and subjects easy to understand.

The Alice Bailey books, for example, are, in my opinion, some of the most profound books ever written on Planet Earth. The problem is that they are so difficult to read that most people will never take the time to completely study them. Most people do not have the time or the inclination to research and study the thousands of books, teachings, religions, and mystery schools that grace our planet.

My service to humanity is, in essence, to provide a shortcut. Stated in another way, this spiritual encyclopedia could be likened to the Cliff Notes of the spiritual path. I have most joyously done the vast amount of research for you and have brought to you the pearls from the oyster. This will give my reader a solid introduction to religion, spirituality, and the teachings of the Spiritual Hierarchy and Ascended Masters that govern this planet.

Please do not be intimidated by the word encyclopedia, for this collected work does not read like what we normally consider an encyclopedia. It is easy to read, filled to the brim with practical, extremely useful, and absolutely fascinating information.

The books are also written with dynamic enthusiasm that comes from a deep and profound love for God and great love for what I have been commissioned to share. These books, though easy to read and a type of Cliff Notes, are still incredibly comprehensive. The information has been accessed through both intuitive and didactic means and I have attempted to integrate the entire field into one synergistic, unified whole.

The religions of the future will be more universal in nature and will honor and respect all paths to God. This series of books will, hence, serve as a type of networking vehicle. It will allow people to be introduced to the many pathways to God, and as they are guided by their souls, they may read other books and get involved with organizations I have referenced.

It is my humble prayer that these books may serve to accelerate your path of initiation and your realization of your unity and oneness with God.

Joshua David Stone, Ph.D.

1

The Story of Creation

Mind is the Builder
Edgar Cayce

The following story of creation is quite an amazing and often unbelievable story. I just want to qualify this chapter by saying that I didn't
make any of this up myself. All of this information comes directly out of
the Universal Mind channelings of Edgar Cayce and other sources such as
Djwhal Khul, Ruth Montgomery, The Tibetan Foundation, and other similar types of channelings. The amazing thing is that all these different
sources tell a basically similar story, so I know that I am very much on the
mark, although some of it may be quite surprising to some readers.

In the beginning was one source of Light, the one presence, called God.
God, in His great joy and love, had a desire to create, to express Himself.
From this undifferentiated state God created suns, moons, galaxies, universes, and He liked what He had created. Something, however, was
missing: companionship. God wanted to create self-conscious beings who
could share His joy of creation. Out of the infinity of God came trillions of
sparks of Light made in His image.

Out of this expression also came Amilius, the Light, the first expression of the Divine mind, the first manifestation of spirit. All souls were
created in the beginning and all souls were androgynous. The unique thing
about our creation was the aspect of free choice.

In our creation we went jetting out into the universe, creating as God
creates, with our minds, and extending God's kingdom. We were perfect,
and this was the Edenic state. In our travels through the infinity of God,
we discovered the physical, or material, universe and we were intrigued,
for in the beginning we didn't have physical bodies, just spiritual bodies.

Then we began projecting a part of ourselves into, let's say the Earth, to explore the beauty of matter. There was, in actuality, nothing wrong with this, for the entire infinite universe was a playground of sorts. We began projecting a part of ourselves into a tree to see what a tree was like. Then we would project ourselves into a rock to see what that was like, then into an animal to experience what it was like to eat grass and interrelate with other animals.

In each case we would do this and then we would leave and project ourselves back into the spiritual planes. We would also, then, with the incredible power of our minds, create thought forms of animals through the power of our imaginations. These thought forms would begin to densify and we would inhabit these thought form creatures just as we would an animal that had already been created.

This was all fine until that moment in creation which the Bible refers to as the fall of man. It was in this moment that we forgot who we were because of our over-identification with the material universe. We got caught in the density of matter and thought we were the animals or thought form animal creatures we had created.

Falling under the illusion that we were material instead of spiritual in identity began the downward spiral of creation. In this moment, "ego" began, ego being a thought system and philosophy based on the illusionary belief in separation, fear, selfishness, and death.

This phenomenon of souls' getting more and more deeply caught up in the illusion of matter continued at an alarming rate. Amilius (an incarnation of Jesus) and other higher beings who had not fallen knew that something had to be done to help their fellow brothers and sisters, for man was continuing to create a conglomeration of monstrosities to satisfy his out-of-control desire.

He created cyclopes, satyrs, centaurs, unicorns, animal bodies with human heads, beings with hooves, claws, feathers, wings, and tails. Man had become trapped in the grotesque bodies that were not suitable for sons and daughters of God. Man even created the first female, whose name was Lilith and who was the forerunner of Eve. This projection was created again to satisfy his selfish carnal desires.

The plan that God and the Godforce created to rectify this situation was the creation of five physical races on the five continents of the planet. Each race had a different skin color. No skin color was better than another, but each was for a different climate condition. Certain skin colors were better for certain climates.

The plan was that all those souls who had gotten caught up in matter would use these more perfectly fitted human bodies to incarnate into, bodies that were more fitting for sons and daughters of God. So man did not descend from monkeys, as the evolutionist would suggest; we were created.

After the creation of the five races there were one hundred thirty-three million souls on the Earth. The red race lived in Atlantis and America, the brown race in the Andes and Lemuria, the yellow race in the Gobi Desert of East Asia, the black race in the Sudan and upper West Africa, and the white race in Iran along the Black Sea and in the Carpathian Mountains of central Europe.

The basic plan that God created was reincarnation: souls would incarnate into these human bodies rather than into animal bodies to reawaken to their true identity as God-beings and learn to demonstrate this on Earth, hence beginning their ascent back to the Creator.

This act of creation occurred ten and a half million years ago. The animal influences created by the fall and the initial thought form projections of animals didn't completely disappear from the Earth until around 9,000 B.C. Remnants of these pathetic creatures were later depicted in our mythology and in Assyrian and Egyptian art.

Another factor that involved the grotesque animal creations was that in the earliest of times, human beings were able to procreate with the animal species and with the grotesque beings. After human souls were separated into male and female, God imposed Divine laws making it impossible for human beings to produce offspring with another species.

Man was able to live up to one thousand years in the same body until another Divine law was implemented to change this because of the need for souls to be able to reflect more on the inner plane about the purpose and reason for incarnation.

Amilius (the first incarnation of Jesus Christ) himself descended into matter and became the first Adam at the time of the creation of the five first root races. Adam was the first of the perfected race, the first of the sons of God, as opposed to what the Bible refers to as the daughters of men. Adam was an individual but also a symbol of all five races, as was Eve.

The Seven Root Races

The graph on page five shows the seven root races that make up what is esoterically termed the manvantara or world cycle. These root races, seen in column one of the graph, make up a period of time of from eighteen and a half million years ago to our present day.

Sanat Kumara, our Planetary Logos, incarnated into this planet at this time. We are currently living in the Aryan root race. This term was completely distorted by Hitler and Nazi Germany, so please don't think of it in those terms. The Aryan race has been in existence for over a million years and will continue for some time more.

The Meruvian root race is just beginning to come into play, so there is kind of an overlapping of root race going on. The name of the seventh root race is the Paradisian.

I would also like to add that Djwhal Khul has told me that the first two root races, the Polarian and Hyperborean, are often referred to as the Pre-Lemurian root races, which is also how The Tibetan Foundation has referenced them. This is because the first two races were not completely physical as we understand physicality.

The continents on which these root races began and thrived are listed in the second column. The third column lists the specific type of psycho-spiritual attunement each root race had. The fourth column lists the chakra each root race was working on developing. The fifth column lists the type of yoga each root race was practicing.

Tara, the continent for the final root race, is a continent that will emerge from the ocean floor in the distant future.

The members of the Polarian, or first, root race had huge filamentous bodies and were more etheric than physical. They were also totally sexless. They multiplied by a process of what scientists refer to as fission, or budding. For this reason they were basically immortal. They have been called the "archetypal race." Their bodies were basically gaseous in nature.

The members of the Hyperborean, or second, root race were similar to the first; however, they slowly but surely began the process of materializing more. Djwhal Khul and The Tibetan Foundation have often just called these two root races pre-Lemurian, because they weren't totally physical-ized as the members of the Lemurian, or third, root race were. Human beings as we know them began with this third root race.

When human life first manifested on Earth in these first two root races, the only dry land was at the North Pole. The rest of the Earth was covered with water. This polar continent looked like a skull cap on the head of the Earth. This is the only continent that will never submerge under water in the entire manvantara, or world cycle, of all seven root races. One other interesting point is that Lemuria was called the "land of Shalmali" at the time it existed.

It is also important to understand that the seven root races all have seven subraces. This makes a total of forty-nine subraces in a manvantara. An example of this can be shown by our present Aryan root race: the Hindu began sixty-two thousand years ago, the Arabian forty-two thousand years ago, the Iranian thirty-two thousand years ago, the Celtic twenty-two thousand years ago, the Teutonic twenty-two thousand years ago; the sixth and seventh subraces of the Aryan root race are evolving in America and on a continent that will be arising in the Pacific Ocean. To make God's plan even more intricate, every subrace race has seven family races, which I am not going to get into.

The Seven Root Races

Root Races	Continent	Attunement	Chakra	Yoga
1. Polarian	The Imperishable Sacred Land	Physical Attunement	1st Chakra	Hatha Yoga
2. Hyperborean	Continent of Hyperborea	Physical Attunement	1st Chakra	Hatha Yoga
3. Lemurian	Continent of Lemuria	Physical Attunement	2nd Chakra	Hatha Yoga
4. Atlantean	Continent of Atlantis	Emotional Attunement	3rd Chakra	Bhakti Yoga
5. Aryan	Europe, Asia Minor, America	Mental Attunement	4th Chakra	Raja Yoga
6. Meruvian	North America	Personality Integration	5th Chakra	Agni Yoga
7. Paradisian	Tara	Soul Attunement	6th Chakra	Unknown

Pre-Lemurian History

There were two great Avatars who came to Earth in the early pre-Lemurian times. The first Avatar focused on the Earth an energy of spiritual attunement. He came forth as a scientist, through a highly developed civilization. His message was to blend the scientific and the spiritual understandings. Humanity didn't accept his message at the time. They weren't ready for it. So this great teacher left. He has since returned into that full-fledged cocreator state.

Another great Avatar was sent to Earth at a later pre-Lemurian time. He was a very tall man and he was fond of wearing a silver robe. He was the first great teacher who really made an impact on the Earth. His name was Lo Chi. Lo Chi anchored courage, wisdom, and love in their beginning stages. He took a war-torn civilization and began to build a spiritual community with temples all over the land. At the end of his reign a mass ascension took place.

The next great teacher who came changed his approach and stressed the emotional qualities and occupations rather than the scientific, as the first Avatar had. Some of the greatest art was produced; however, the scientific side of society began to shut down. In a sense, a pendulum-swing took place, from a more masculine to a more feminine society. Great strides were made in art, music, and dance, but the mental creativity and potency were not there because of this pendulum-swing. This began to change over a long period of time and society became more balanced. Then another mass ascension took place.

Vywamus has called these two previous mass ascensions periods of spiritual harvesting. He says that we are again approaching a harvesting time in this century. This has to do with the Planetary Logos. Sanat Kumara, in his cosmic evolution, has reached another plateau. Each time he reaches one of these plateaus it is time for the harvesting of souls, or mass ascension.

We are currently completing a six-thousand-year, a twelve-thousand-year and a thirty-six-thousand-year cycle. Each time two or more cycles come together, that period is extremely important. We are in that period now. This harvesting window is approximately one hundred years long. The end of this hundred-year cycle is from 1995 to the year 2000. The closer to the end of this hundred-year cycle, the greater the harvesting. To be incarnated at this time in history is a very great opportunity!

The Electrical Wars

It was also in this pre-Lemurian period that Planet Earth was attacked by the "Electrical Ones," a group of beings from another planet who wanted to take it over. Humanity began to defend itself, and this war lasted for five hundred years. Earthlings eventually won this battle. The Electrical Ones were not really evil but simply scientists looking for a new place to live. They came from a very great distance. This war is part of the fear of spaceships that still exists to this day in the race consciousness, for these Electrical Ones took people and animals aboard spaceships and did painful experiments on them. A lot of our present-day fixations and patterns of attack/defense programming stem from this period in the Earth's history.

The Electrical Ones were actually seeking to bring their technology of Light to the planet to aid in the trip back to the Source. Humanity and the Earth, however, were moving toward greater material density. This was not a negative thing on the part of the Earth. The Earth and humanity were saying that they wanted to learn everything they could within the densest part of physicality.

A truce was finally declared after five hundred years of war and many of the Electrical Ones left, promising to return when the Earth was ready. Some stayed in specific areas given to them. The Electrical Ones stimulated an impatience for this downward materialistic cycle.

Lemuria

Lemuria, or Mu, was a landmass lying in the Pacific Ocean and extending from the United States all the way to South America. The Lemurian stage of existence had to do with the race consciousness learning the lesson of physical attunement. Humanity as a whole progresses in stages, and physical attunement was the key lesson during this period of history.

The Lemurians were very philosophical and spiritual people, much more so than the Atlanteans who were much more technologically advanced and focused.

At this period of history great dinosaurs roamed the Earth and because of this the Lemurians, to a great extent, had to live underground. They lived in caves, hiding from the dinosaurs except to hunt for food. They would beautifully and artistically decorate their caves. The Lemurians were rather small, physically: men were five feet tall and women a few inches shorter. The survival rate of children was not very high. They lived on grain, berries, and fruit.

Atlantis

Atlantis was in the north Atlantic Ocean. It compared in size to Europe and Russia combined. The eastern seaboard of the United States, then mostly under water, comprised the coastal lowlands of Atlantis, which extended from Mexico as far as the Mediterranean Sea.

As mentioned earlier, dinosaurs roamed the Earth, and many of them were carnivorous. Many of the Atlanteans lived in great walled cities to protect themselves from these beasts.

Also still existing in Atlantis were the grotesque animal-like humans that I spoke of earlier in this chapter. By certain segments of the society they were called "things" and treated as slaves and beasts of burden. There were two groups of people in Atlantis: those who served the Law of One and those called the Sons of Belial.

The Sons of Belial were the followers of Beelzebub. They were the lords of materialism, the selfish, materialistic, and egotistical group. These were the people who enslaved the "things," or animal-humans that had hooves, claws, feathers, wings, or tails on human bodies.

Those people who served the Law of One tried to help the "things" both spiritually and physically by taking them to the great temples of healing in Atlantis. Using advanced technologies of crystals, Light, and sound they were often able to do surgery to remove these ungodlike appendages that no longer manifested the Adam Kadmon perfect design that God had created for the perfected human body.

In 52,000 B.C. a council of wise men of the five races was convened to discuss ways to get rid of the dinosaurs. A plan to use super-potent chemical forces to poison the dinosaurs in their lairs was discussed. This plan was implemented and began to work.

The first of a series of three continental Earth change catastrophes occurred about 50,700 B.C. This first catastrophe occurred as a result of the use of chemicals and explosives to annihilate the dinosaurs. Huge and numerous gas pockets were blown open in the lairs of the animals, which precipitated volcanic eruptions and earthquakes. The magnitude of the disturbances was so great that it caused the axis of the Earth to shift, bringing the poles to their present positions and causing the last great ice age.

The continent of Lemuria was completely destroyed but strangely enough, Atlantis was not affected that much in terms of its landmass. Lemuria's entire continent sank to the bottom of the ocean as a result of the pole shift. Atlantis then became the premiere civilization on the planet. As mentioned earlier, Atlantis was very technologically advanced but much less spiritually advanced, much like the United States is today. As a matter of fact, many of the same souls who lived in Atlantis are reincarnated and living in the United States today.

The great cataclysm destroyed most of the dinosaurs because of the landmass transformation and the change in climate conditions. Atlantis, being now the premiere civilization on the planet, began to thrive. It was during this period that extraterrestrials visited Atlantis and introduced them to advanced crystal technology.

The Atlanteans used crystal energy to run almost every aspect of society. They had one great crystal which was the major energy source for the entire continent. It ran cars, ships, submarines, and airplanes, providing all the energy needs of society. Science was more and more becoming the new god, and people became less and less interested in the presence of God.

The Sons of Belial and negative extraterrestrial influences began to take more and more control over Atlantean civilization. The crystal energy began to be used for warfare and to control the people. One fateful day, Atlantean scientists tried to use the great crystal to send some kind of energy beam through the Earth's crust for some evil purpose. This precipitated a massive explosion, the likes of which had never before been seen on this planet. This occurred in approximately 28,000 B.C. and resulted in the submergence of Atlantis into three islands. This account was alluded to in the Bible story of Noah's ark and the great flood.

A period of building began in Atlantis after this great catastrophe, but Atlantis never returned to its original glory. Atlantis became more and more decadent as time went on. There were great advancements in electricity, atomic power, and the harnessing of the sun's energy; however, in 10,700 B.C. the country reached its depths of moral and spiritual decline. Human sacrifice and sun-worshiping were prevalent, as were adultery and corruption.

The sun crystals were crudely adapted as a means of coercion, torture, and punishment. The common people called the many sun crystals the "terrible crystals." Gigantic Earth changes rocked Atlantis around 9,500 B.C. and Atlantis vanished from the face of the Earth. The explosion was one million times greater than that at Hiroshima.

Those Atlanteans serving the Law of One listened to God and the prophets and fled before this catastrophe occurred. They went to Egypt, and they later became known as the Mayans in the Yucatan and as the Iroquois Indians in America. In all these civilizations the influence of Atlantis was felt in the building of pyramids.

All of the secrets of Atlantis are stored in the Hall of Records in the Great Pyramid. These records are mystically protected. Paul Solomon and Edgar Cayce, in their source channelings, have said that a great initiate who is now living on the planet, by the name of John of Penial (who is the reincarnation of John the Beloved, the disciple of Christ), will be the great one who will travel to Egypt and release all these records.

In the exodus from Atlantis to Egypt they took with them a great spiritual teacher whose name was Thoth. For several thousand years Thoth was incarnated in Egypt, which was a civilization of great spirituality. The pyramids were actually temples of initiation.

Vywamus has said that Egyptian history lasted as long as one hundred thousand years, not just the four thousand or five thousand years that modern historians speak of. Egypt had a great deal of extraterrestrial involvement. The concept of the pyramid came from other planets. The Egyptian civilization was the blending of consciousness from several other planets.

Plato has referred to the sinking of Atlantis in his writings. It is quite amazing to me that our modern history books are so limited in their scope. Edgar Cayce predicted that Atlantis would rise again and emerge off the eastern coast of the United States around 1968 or 1969. The Bahama Islands are remnants of the peaks of Poseidia, one of the islands that was left after the second Atlantean earthquake. Divers found underwater temples and ruins sixty feet below the water in 1968, just as Cayce predicted.

The Bermuda Triangle, according to three different sources of information I have found in my research, is actually the great crystal I spoke of earlier that has sunk to the bottom of the ocean. At certain times when the sun shines upon the ocean floor at a certain angle in relationship to the moon, this great crystal is activated. Anything that passes through its energy vortex during this activation is turned into antimatter—is disintegrated. This is why the Bermuda Triangle effects occur only on specialized occasions and not all the time.

The United States is now going through a testing period very similar to that of Atlantis fifty thousand years ago. The question is whether our development of science and technology is going to cause us to lose sight of our true reason for being here, which is a more spiritual one.

The Cosmic Day and the Creation of the Planet Earth

In this chapter about the story of creation, I have been focusing on the creation of human life on this planet. The chapter, however, would not be complete if I did not speak of the creation of Planet Earth herself. This gets into the understanding of the meaning of the Cosmic Day or a day in the life of Brahma (God).

One day in the life of Brahma equals four billion three hundred twenty million years. One night in the life of Brahma equals four billion three hundred twenty million years.

One twenty-four hour day in the life of Brahma equals eight billion six hundred forty million years. Three hundred sixty full days make up one year of Brahma which equals three trillion one hundred ten billion four hundred million years.

One hundred years constitute the whole period of Brahma's age (Maha Kalpa), three hundred eleven trillion forty billion years.

Monads

According to Djwhal Khul, God created sixty thousand million monads in our planetary system. Each monad creates twelve souls, and each soul creates twelve soul extensions or incarnated personalities. Multiply sixty thousand million times one hundred forty-four and you have the number of people working through this school. Djwhal has also stated that of these sixty thousand million monads, thirty-five thousand million monads are of the second ray of love, twenty thousand million monads are of activity, or the third ray, and five thousand million monads are of power, or the first ray.

More of the Life of Brahma

This next little chart from the Alice Bailey book on Cosmic Fire shows more of what goes on in the life of Brahma. It is interesting that a solar system lasts for one hundred years of Brahma. The rest I don't fully understand myself; however, it is interesting to get a right-brained intuitive grasp of the infinite beauty and cyclic nature of God's creation.

a.	One hundred years of Brahma	An occult century; the period of a solar system
b.	One year of Brahma	The period of seven chains, where the seven planetary schemes are concerned
c.	One week of Brahma	The period of seven rounds in one scheme; it has a chain significance
d.	One day of Brahma	The occult period of a round
e.	One hour of Brahma	Concerns interchain affairs
f.	One Brahmic minute	Concerns the planetary centers and therefore egoic groups
g.	One Brahmic moment	Concerns an egoic group and its relation to the whole

At the end of one Cosmic Day, all of creation for that particular source is consumed and called back into Source. Then there is a cosmic night before the impetus of the creation of another Cosmic Day.

You will be interested to know that in the Cosmic Day of which Earth is a part, 3.2 billion years have already gone by. We need not worry. We still have 1.2 billion years left in our present Cosmic Day. Human life as we know it has existed on Planet Earth in its present physical form for only 10.5 million years. We still have 1.2 billion years left.

This whole process, on a cosmic scale, is known as the in-breath and out-breath of Brahma. Later in this book I have written a chapter by this title; it signifies a smaller cycle that the Earth is experiencing within the larger cosmic understanding of these cycles of the in-breaths and out-breaths of God.

2

The Monad, the Soul, and the Personality

There are sixty thousand million monads working through our planetary system

Djwhal Khul
as channeled by
Alice A. Bailey

In the beginning God created sons and daughters in the spiritual state. He created what are esoterically called "monads" or individualized spiritual sparks of the Creator. It is the monad that has also been called the "I Am Presence." That was our first core intelligence and our first individualized identity.

This divine spark, also called spirit, is our true identity. The monad, or spiritual spark, decided with its free choice that it wanted to experience a denser form of the material universe than it was living in.

Each of our monads, with the power of its mind, created twelve souls. It is as though the monad puts down twelve fingers of fire, and at the end of each finger are the twelve individualized souls. Each soul is a smaller and partial representation of its creator, the monad. The soul has also been referred to as the higher self, the superconscious mind, and the higher mind.

What we have here so far is that God created infinite numbers of monads, or spiritual sparks, and each monad then created twelve souls to experience a denser form of matter than previously experienced. Each soul, then desiring to experience an even denser form of the material universe, created twelve personalities or soul extensions who incarnated into the densest material universe. We on Earth are personalities, or soul extensions, of our soul, just as our soul is an extension of a greater consciousness which is our monad. Our monad is an extension of an even greater consciousness which is God, the Godhead, the Father and Mother of all creation.

So each of us on Earth has a soul family, so to speak, of eleven other soul extensions. The eleven other soul extensions could be incarnated on the Earth or on some other planet in God's infinite universe. Our other soul extensions could also not be incarnate in a physical body at this time but could be existing on one of the other spiritual planes of existence.

Our eleven other soul extensions or personalities could be looked at as our immediate soul family. Extending this metaphor further, we also then have an extended monadic family. Each of us has twelve in our soul group and one hundred forty-four in our monadic group.

Ascended Master Djwhal Khul has stated that there are sixty thousand million monads working through our earthly planetary system. If we multiply sixty thousand million by one hundred forty-four we have the number of soul extensions, or personalities, involved in the process of reincarnation on this planet.

A Personal Story

To make the understanding of the monad, soul, and personality even easier to understand I would like to share my own experience as to how this theory has related to my personal evolution as a soul extension.

In my research into how this all related to myself, I found out that of my particular soul group, four of my soul extensions were still in incarnation and eight others were back on the inner plane. Of the four still in incarnation, I was the only soul extension still on Earth. One of my soul extensions was a female in the Pleiades, and two others were on planets in this galaxy whose names I had never heard of.

In respect to my one hundred and forty-four soul extensions, three-quarters of them were no longer in incarnation and one-quarter were still incarnated in the material universe. When one achieves certain levels of initiation it is a common practice for the soul to begin to call some of its soul extensions back to the spiritual world.

The soul extensions could be looked at as businesses. Let's say that four of them were doing really well in Los Angeles, Tokyo, Paris, and Brussels, and the other eight were losing money. A good businessperson might close down the eight businesses that weren't doing well and channel all her/his resources into the four businesses that were very active and successful financially.

This metaphor is exactly how the soul looks at its twelve soul extensions.

The twelve soul extensions are all working for the evolution of the soul, just as the ten fingers on your hand are working for your physical body. In my case, four of my soul extensions were more active and successful, spiritually speaking, so the other eight soul extensions have been called back to soul and are channeling their resources into the four successful spiritual businesses, so to speak.

The same thing is going on in the larger context of my one hundred and forty-four soul extensions. All my twelve souls are at a stage of spiritual evolution and initiation where all resources are being channeled into the successful soul extensions. Just as the fingers of your hand don't compete with each other and all work for the same goal, ideally, all soul extensions work for the evolution of the soul and later of the monad.

To make my personal story a little more interesting, I was told by Ascended Master Djwhal Khul that I was an oversoul, or teacher, for the other soul extensions of my soul group. Because of my dedication to my spiritual path, my other soul extensions on the inner plane had been greatly helped by my presence and consciousness. At the time I heard this, it was news to me, because I had no conscious recollection of my contact and involvement with my other soul extensions. A lot of this involvement occurs on the inner plane while we sleep.

Djwhal Khul also told me that there was some codependency going on, however. I said, "Codependent?" I couldn't believe it, because I saw myself as one of the least codependent people I had ever met. Djwhal told me that I was not codependent with people of the Earth plane, but rather with my other soul extensions. In other words, I was running their karma through my physical body.

Djwhal told me that the Spiritual Hierarchy and Great White Brotherhood wanted me to use this physical body for service and not run it down by taking on too much karma from my other soul extensions as a service for them. I knew intuitively that what he was saying was true. In my zeal for spiritual growth I had a total knowingness that I had unconsciously been doing this. I immediately told my other soul extensions that I loved them but that the buck stopped there, and that they would have to be in charge of discharging and releasing their own karma from now on. I set the appropriate boundaries just as I always do with people on this plane of existence.

One last fascinating story that relates to this whole process is the story of how I met my wife, Terri. About two years ago a friend of mine told me about a day-long workshop called "The Monadic Anchoring." All the information she had about it was this title. I had always been incredibly intrigued by the concept of the monad, but I found it almost impossible to find information about it. When I heard the word monad, I said to myself, "I am going to that seminar."

Upon arriving at the seminar I found, to my great surprise, that Terri was channeling Djwhal Khul. Synchronistically, I had just begun rereading all the Alice Bailey books which Djwhal Khul wrote. I was very impressed with her channeling, and the workshop had to do with a special process, which the Great White Brotherhood was doing in one hundred forty-four groups around the country, of anchoring the monad into the physical body.

This had never been done before and was kind of an experiment which the Hierarchy was doing to see the effect. The workshop was very powerful and at the end of it I went up to Terri and asked her if she ever did private channeled readings with people. Terri lived in Alabama and said she would be happy to do some readings for me over the phone. To make a long story short, I worked with Terri professionally for a period of time.

I was intensely studying the Alice Bailey material and I would ask Djwhal a lot of questions concerning this most advanced material. It was during this time that Terri and I started having dreams about each other in which we were involved romantically. We both were not really looking for a relationship. However, the dreams kept coming and we finally decided to check it out. Lo and behold, it was a match made in heaven!

Approximately three or four weeks after our initial, super-profound bonding, I had a dream one night. In the dream, Djwhal Khul was talking to me. He told me that Terri and I come from the same monad. Upon waking from the dream I was amazed, for that is the way I had felt inwardly; but it was such a confirmation to get this occult piece of information so clearly. I immediately called Terri in Alabama. We confirmed this fact with Djwhal also through her channeling.

We later did some deeper exploration of this and we were also told that Terri and I were the only soul extensions from our monad on Earth. So, in other words, all the other one-quarter soul extensions of our one hundred forty-four were incarnated on other planets, a whole cluster of them, apparently, in the Pleiades. So Terri and I are not from the same soul, but from the same monad. Terri is one of my other one hundred forty-four soul extensions, so we are what might be termed "monadic mates." What was also so remarkable was that we had initially met at the anchoring of the monad workshop.

The Seven Planes of Our Solar System

Our solar system is made of seven planes, or dimensions, of reality. On the very densest level we have the physical plane. Above that, the astral or emotional plane. Above that, the mental plane. Above that, the Buddhic or intuitional plane. Above that, the atmic or spiritual plane. Above that, still, the monadic plane, and finally the Divine or Logoic plane.

In the process of evolution and initiation it is necessary to master and evolve through these planes. Our monad is anchored in the second plane downward which is the monadic plane. The soul is anchored two planes downward into the Buddhic plane. Lastly, of course, the soul extension, or personality, is anchored in the seventh plane which is the dense physical plane.

The Seven Cosmic Planes

The seven dimensions I have just mentioned are the seven planes of this solar system. There are, however, seven cosmic planes, as well. Each of the planes I have just mentioned has a cosmic counterpart. In other words, there is a cosmic physical plane, a cosmic astral plane, a cosmic mental plane, a cosmic Buddhic plane, a cosmic atmic plane, a cosmic monadic plane, and a cosmic Logoic plane. The seven planes of our solar system are the seven subplanes of the cosmic physical plane.

In other words, once we evolve through these seven subplanes, then we will have completed just the cosmic physical plane. Then we will eventually evolve through the six higher cosmic planes. The Ascended Masters that we have such enormous respect for are really only masters of the cosmic physical plane. They have not really even begun their cosmic evolution yet. This is in no way meant as a criticism but rather as a statement showing the incredible vastness and magnitude of God's creation.

Vywamus has said that the spiritual path can be likened to a ten-inch ruler. The Ascended Masters such as Jesus, Buddha, Saint Germain, Kuthumi, Lord Maitreya, El Morya, and so on, have attained only one inch on this ten-inch ruler. As these great souls continue to evolve they will eventually leave this planetary system and move on to their cosmic evolution. We here on Earth will continue to evolve and ascend and take their places in the Spiritual Hierarchy. We are all destined to evolve back to the cosmic Logoic plane, or back to the Godhead on cosmic levels. Vywamus has termed this state of consciousness the Creator level.

The Spiritual Constitution of Man

The spiritual constitution of man can be divided up into three levels:

I.   Monad, spirit, mighty I Am Presence, Father in heaven
    A.   The three aspects of the monad are
        1.   Will or power—which is the Father principle
        2.   Love/wisdom—which is the Son principle
        3.   Active intelligence—which is the Holy Spirit principle
II. Soul, higher self, superconscious mind
    A.   The three aspects of the soul are
        1.   Spiritual will
        2.   Intuition—love/wisdom, Christ principle

  3. Higher mind
III. Personality, or soul extension
  A. The three bodies of personality are
   1. The mental body
   2. The emotional body
   3. The physical body and the etheric body

The Three Levels of Self-Actualization

As the above outline indicates, there are three distinct levels of our spiritual constitution, and hence there are three distinct levels of self-actualization.

The first level of self-actualization has to do with self-actualization of the personality.

There are many, many, many people on this plane who have achieved this level. This would mean that they are psychologically self-actualized, but not necessarily spiritually self-actualized. A person who comes to my mind as an example is Tom Cruise, the famous movie star. Here is a person who is very successful as a movie star. He has made it to the top in an earthly sense. Whether he is soul-awakened, I do not know because I don't know him personally, but he has definitely self-actualized his personality.

Another example might be a famous psychologist who has not yet explored his spiritual life but is helping a great many people psychologically.

The second level of self-actualization would be self-actualization at a soul level. This would not occur until the third and fourth initiations, which will be explained in great detail in a later chapter. A self-actualized person at this level has become one with the soul and higher self and is living this reality in daily life. This would be a state of consciousness of living in unconditional love for self and others, desiring always to be of service, recognizing the inherent oneness of all creation, recognizing our true identity as God-beings, Christs, Buddhas, and as sons and daughters of God.

The third level of self-actualization is self-actualizing at a monadic, or spiritual, level. This does not fully occur until the fifth and sixth initiations. People at this level of self-actualization are masters of wisdom and lords of compassion. They have now merged even beyond soul to merge with the monad and I Am Presence. They have become one with the monad spirit on Earth. They must have become Ascended Masters, completely limitless and free of all planetary karma, truly self-realized beings.

The Three Stages of the Spiritual Path

 I. The Hall of Ignorance
  A. Identification with the material world and use of outgoing organs of perception

    II. The Hall of Learning
        A. Restlessness and a search for the knowledge of the self or soul
    III. The Hall of Wisdom
        A. Realization, expansion of consciousness, and identification with the spiritual self

Spiritual aspirants, upon entering the "path of probation," are in the stage of the Hall of Learning. Upon taking the first initiation, they move into the Hall of Wisdom.

3

The Path of Probation and the First Five Initiations

Each of us is recognized by the brilliance of our Light

Djwhal Khul
as channeled by
Alice A. Bailey

The path of probation is best described by Ascended Master Djwhal Khul in the Alice Bailey book, *Initiation, Human and Solar*, when he says, "The probationary path precedes the path of initiation and marks the period in the life of a person when he definitely sets himself on the side of the forces of evolution and works at the building of his own character. He takes himself in hand, cultivates the qualities that are lacking in his disposition, and seeks, with diligence, to bring his personality under control. He is building the causal body (soul body) with deliberate intent, filling any gaps that may exist and seeking to make it a fit receptacle for the Christ principle."

The probationary path might be likened to the nine months of gestation prior to the birth hour. The birth hour would mark the beginning of the first initiation. The person on the probationary path is taught principally to know himself, to ascertain his weaknesses, and to correct them. The spiritual aspirant is taught the basics of Divine wisdom and is entered into the final grades in the Hall of Learning.

Each spiritual aspirant is known to a Master and is in the care of the disciples of that Master. Classes are held by initiates of the first and second degree for accepted disciples and for those on probation between the hours of ten and five every night in all parts of the world. They gather in the Hall of Learning, and the method is much the same as in the big universities. Classes at certain hours, experimental work, examinations, a gradual moving up and onward as tests are passed. All are graded and charted. Each of us is recognized by the brilliance of our Light. We are graded, therefore, according to the magnitude of the Light, the rate of vibration, the purity of the tone and the clarity of the color of our aura.

A great deal of training is given to a probationer without his really recognizing it consciously. The probationer usually does recognize three things:

    1.   Increased mental activity,

    2.   Increased responsiveness to ideas and increased capacity to envision the plan of the Spiritual Hierarchy,

    3.   Increased psychic sensitiveness.

Only those disciples who seek initiation because of the added power to help and bless others will find a response to their desire. Selfish motive must not enter into it. Many people who are regarded as initiates are only endeavoring to be initiates. They are not, however, real initiates; they are those well-meaning people whose mental understanding outruns the power of their personalities to practice.

The First Initiation

The first initiation is the first step into the spiritual kingdom. The disciple has left the Hall of Ignorance and the Hall of Learning and entered into the Hall of Wisdom. The key lesson of the first initiation has to do with mastery of the physical body and vehicle.

Control over the physical body must have reached a high level. The sins of the flesh must be dominated. Gluttony, drink, and licentiousness must no longer control the disciple. The first initiation stands for commencement. A certain structure of right living, of thinking, and of control has been attained. Very little soul control other than this need be evidenced when the first initiation is taken.

This initiation indicates simply that the germ of the soul life has been vitalized and brought into functioning existence. The throat center, or chakra, is related to the first initiation. The first initiation is regarded by the Masters as signifying admission to the path. In the life of Jesus this initiation is signified as the birth of the Christ, or the birth of the Christ life. The lives of initiates of the first initiation are beginning to be controlled by the Christ consciousness, which is the consciousness of responsibility, unconditional love, and service. Lord Maitreya, the head of the Spiritual Hierarchy is the Hierophant for this initiation. One-fourth of the physical body is composed of atomic matter after this initiation.

The Second Initiation

The main lesson of the second initiation has to do with mastery of the astral and/or emotional body. Djwhal Khul has said that this is usually the hardest initiation for people to pass, and it often takes many, many lifetimes. Once, however, the second initiation has been taken, the third and fourth usually follow in the same lifetime or the succeeding one.

This initiation has to do with the sacrifice and death of desire. The lower nature is rapidly being controlled. The astral elemental is controlled and the emotional body becomes pure, limpid, and serene.

In the life of Jesus Christ this initiation is referred to as the baptism. The three keynotes for the second initiation are dedication, glamour, and devotion.

Dedication results in glamour, which is dissipated by devotion. The emotions are brought under control, and necessarily the factor of the mind assumes an increasing importance. Freedom is the keynote of the individual who is facing the second initiation. Lord Maitreya, again, is the Hierophant for this initiation. Much greater control of the selfish sensitivity of the lower self is attained. The physical body is now made up of one-half atomic matter.

The Third Initiation

The third initiation has to do with developing self-mastery over the mental body and hence over the threefold personality. This initiation is also referred to as the soul merge. It is at this initiation that the disciple becomes blended and merged with the higher self and becomes a soul-infused personality. The entire personality becomes flooded with Light from above. The disciple is no longer controlled by the lower mind or desire. The personality vibrations are of a very high order.

This initiation is considered the first major initiation. The mind is responsive primarily to ideas, intuitions, and impulses coming from the soul. The disciple is receiving energies from the soul, the ashram to which he or she belongs, and from the Spiritual Hierarchy itself. Accumulation of knowledge is unbelievably rapid. Energies from the causal body become available to the disciple.

The physical body is now made up of three-quarters atomic matter. The disciple begins receiving direct guidance from the monad, whereas up to this point in the disciple's evolution, all guidance was received only from the soul who has been functioning as the intermediary between the incarnate personality and the monad, or Father in heaven.

At this initiation the disciple has mastered the ability to manipulate thought matter and has learned the laws of creative thought-building. This initiation in the life of Jesus is referred to as the transfiguration. The third eye is the chakra that has been stimulated at this initiation and Sanat Kumara is the Hierophant.

At each initiation the disciple has become polarized to a higher level. At the first initiation the disciple was polarized in the physical body. At the second initiation the disciple became polarized in the astral and emotional body. In this third initiation the disciple has become polarized into the mental body. After this initiation the disciple has mastered, theoretically and practically, the laws of his own nature. The matter in the three bodies has become relatively pure. The soul itself now assumes the dominant position, not the material world. A terrific voltage of spiritual energy is passed through the initiate at this initiation under the direction of the Planetary Logos. The rod is used as the transferring agent in initiation and is held by Sanat Kumara.

The Fourth Initiation

The fourth initiation is referred to as the renunciation and/or initiation of crucifixion. It has to do with freedom from all self-interest and the renouncing of the personal life in the interest of a larger whole. Even soul-consciousness ceases to be of importance and a more universal awareness, one closer to that of spirit, takes its place.

The life of the person taking the fourth initiation is usually one of great sacrifice and sometimes suffering.

The initiate has laid all, even his perfected personality, upon the altar of sacrifice. All is renounced—friends, money, reputation, character, standing in the world, family, and even life itself. In passing the fourth initiation one has achieved liberation from the wheel of rebirth.

It is at this initiation that the causal body or soul body is burned up and the soul merges back into the monad. The initiate's main source of guidance from this point forward is the monad and/or I Am Presence. The soul, who has been the intermediary between the incarnated personality and the monad, is no longer needed.

At the fourth initiation the initiate is considered a master of wisdom and lord of compassion. The initiate is no longer a soul in prison. He has been lifted out of the three lower worlds. The initiate now works from above downward in service of the Divine Plan. The personality life of the soul through all its incarnations is over. The initiate is fully using the Buddhic vehicle and is operating on the Buddhic plane of consciousness.

The initiate is totally liberated, and future contact with the material world is totally voluntary. The initiate has become an unchanging permanent member of the Spiritual Hierarchy and the Fifth Kingdom. The initiate has turned his back on the physical, material world for eternity except for voluntary service. Sanat Kumara is the Hierophant again for this initiation. The initiate is admitted into closer fellowship in the lodge. He is rapidly exhausting all resources in the Hall of Wisdom. The initiate can contact his monad with more freedom than the majority of the population can contact their souls. Energies of the initiate's soul group become available for use for the good of planetary evolution.

The antakarana, or rainbow bridge, has been successfully completed to the soul, the spiritual triad, and the monad. The three lower centers reach a point of utter purification, with no energy of selfishness. The initiate is guided by intuition, pure reason, and complete knowledge illumined by love. The fifth initiation usually follows closely upon the fourth initiation. The initiate has completely crucified his lower nature. All knowledge, science, wisdom, and experience gathered in all past lives are now in possession of the spiritual man or woman. Jesus Christ took his fourth initiation upon the cross when he was crucified. Lord Maitreya, who overshadowed Jesus and in a sense shared his body during the last three years of his life, took his sixth initiation or ascension.

Another interesting point that Djwhal Khul has made in the Alice Bailey books is that when Jesus made that famous statement, "Father, why hast thou forsaken me?" what he was experiencing was his soul merging back into the monad. He was experiencing the loss of his soul as his guide, for it was now time to get his guidance directly from the Father or the monad, or the I Am that I Am.

The physical body is now made of 100% atomic matter. The initiate who passes the fourth initiation is referred to as an arhat. There is no pain or suffering for the master who has attained liberation.

The Fifth Initiation

The fifth initiation has to do with monadic merger, whereas the third initiation had to do with merging with one's soul or higher self. The fifth initiation has to do with merging one's consciousness with one's monad and spirit. The fifth initiation has to do with freedom from blindness, a liberation that enables the initiate to see a new vision.

This initiation has been referred to as the revelation or resurrection, in Christian terminology. A Master of the fifth initiation is referred to as an adept. The fifth initiation is the first cosmic initiation. It is a merger with the atmic plane rather than the Buddhic plane of the fourth initiation. The majority of Masters working with humanity preserve the body in which they took the fifth initiation; or they can build and manifest a new body.

Djwhal Khul was a fifth-degree initiate while writing most of the Alice Bailey books and he ascended in that lifetime. He preserved the body known as Djwhal Khul. Kuthumi, Djwhal's teacher, chose to build a new one.

To achieve the sixth initiation the adept must take a very intensive course in planetary occultism. This book, in combination with meditation and your own work that you do in life, can allow you to fulfill that requirement while you sleep. This book is an intensive course in planetary occultism. The energy of the fifth initiation allows for the energies of the planet to be made available for the adepts or for world service.

The first chakra is the one stimulated at this initiation. The adept fully realizes that the statement, "I and my Father are one." The adept's body is a body of Light. In essence, the man or woman has achieved a perfected state.

4

Ascension—the Sixth Initiation

Be ye faithful unto death and I will
give thee a crown of life

The Master Jesus

The sixth initiation is the achievement of one's ascension, becoming an Ascended Master. In essence, this initiation occurs when the adept and the Light of the monad merge on the physical plane. The adept's entire being, including the physical body and clothes, is turned into Light. The physical body just disappears and is replaced by the Lightbody. In the past, ascension meant passing on to the spiritual world; however, there is a new thrust of the Spiritual Hierarchy to have Ascended Masters remain on Earth and continue their service. There also has been a recent dispensation that has made ascension a little bit easier, in that it is no longer necessary to take along the physical body when one ascends. This is the choice of the adept.

Ascension is the attainment of the Christ. It is becoming a perfected Buddha. It is becoming a full-fledged Spiritual Master and realized being, not just a soul-realized being. The law of karma no longer has any hold over the Ascended Master. The adept has completely merged with the monadic plane of consciousness.

When a person ascends he fully inhabits his Lightbody. The Lightbody is a body created from the Light a person has manifested throughout all his incarnations. It is the body the Ascended Master travels in from that time forward. To ascend, an adept needs to balance fifty-one percent of his karma from all of his previous incarnations. Most people have an average of two hundred to two hundred and fifty past lives.

Another requirement for ascension is that a person complete his dharma or mission on the Earth plane. The consciousness of ascension is that of total joy, total unconditional love, and the complete, full recognition and realization that you are God and everyone else you meet is God walking on Earth.

It is also an ability to express on any plane of consciousness at any time, not just the physical plane. Ascension is the ability to materialize and dematerialize oneself at will. It is the ability to materialize what is needed and desired instantly. Ascension is a feeling of oneness at all times with God and one's brothers and sisters in Christ. It is a consciousness of being a world-server. It is the power to command one's life to be as one desires it by the power of one's word. It is an ability to bilocate and achieve physical immortality. There are great stories of Ascended Masters such as Saint Germain who lived for three hundred fifty years and Hermes-Thoth in Egypt who lived for over two thousand years in a physical body.

It is also important to realize that we on Earth now are ascending or descending every day. Every thought we think, every word we speak, every action we take, the food we eat, how we spend our time, everything is raising or lowering our vibrations.

Ascension is a very natural occurrence that we all will ultimately achieve. It is just a matter of time. The idea here is to shorten the need for time, and hence future incarnations, by applying and focusing our energies now on our spiritual growth as our only purpose for being here. The negative ego will try to take us on illusionary and glamorous side roads which are not where we really want to go.

One more very important point to understand in the process of ascension is that since, in truth, there is no such thing as time or space, there is an aspect of each of us that has already ascended. One of the keys to accelerating our own ascension process is to call this fifth-dimensional ascended self back into the present, and have him or her blend with our auras. This will help to raise our vibrations up to their already ascended level.

The spiritual body is already doing the work on those ascended levels and is patiently waiting for the rest of the six bodies to catch up with its vibration. It wants to blend with us here in the eternal now but must be asked to do so, for that is cosmic law.

The Relationship to Ascension of the Monad, the Soul, and the Personality

As the disciple develops on the path of initiation, the soul begins to focus its consciousness and energies on the soul extensions that are most highly developed spiritually. As I mentioned in a previous chapter, the soul begins to call back the soul extensions that are less active and focuses all its energy and resources on the spiritually active ones. In my case, I have four soul extensions still in incarnation.

What I have been told is that the soul chooses one soul extension out of the twelve soul extensions in the soul group with which to achieve ascension. In other words, only one soul extension can achieve ascension for a soul group. All twelve soul extensions do not have to ascend. When one soul extension ascends, he or she does it for all twelve, so there is no competition. The eleven other soul extensions ascend also.

I have been told, in my case, that I have been chosen by my soul and monad as the soul extension to ascend for the group, if I would like to do this. I have agreed to this arrangement. When it is a sure thing that I will ascend, my monad will pull up the other soul extensions and they will channel their resources and energies toward helping me ascend for the group. Ascension has a very uplifting effect on the other one hundred forty-four soul extensions of one's monadic group; however, only the soul extensions of one's soul group receive the full benefit of the ascension.

Now I have also been told that there is such a thing as a short path of ascension. It is not a complete ascension as I have just explained it above. What happens on the short path of ascension is that a soul extension ascends alone and not with the eleven other soul extensions. In other words, the eleven other soul extensions can remain in incarnation and do not ascend when one of the soul extensions does.

Vywamus has spoken of two periods in Earth's history when mass ascension has occurred. He referred to these periods in Earth's history as times of spiritual harvesting. Vywamus says that we are again approaching a spiritual harvesting time. This has to do with the Planetary Logos, Sanat Kumara. In his cosmic evolution he has reached another plateau. Each time he reaches one of these plateaus it is time for harvesting, or mass ascension. We are currently completing a six-thousand-year cycle, a twelve-thousand-year cycle and a thirty-six-thousand-year cycle. Each time two or more cycles come together, that period is extremely important in Earth's history. We are in that period right now. The actual "cutting of the wheat" occurs within a few years' time. This harvesting period is approximately one hundred years. The end of this cycle is 1995 to the year 2000.

Sanat Kumara is the overseer of the ascension ceremony. One of the questions I asked was whether marriage partners ever ascend at the same moment. Djwhal Khul told me that this was very rare, but has occasionally happened. When a person is ready to ascend there is no waiting or stopping the process.

After ascension we are no longer under the jurisdiction of the Spiritual Hierarchy, but are now transferred to the jurisdiction of Shamballa. Once ascended, the adepts stay entirely free and liberated from all aspects of planetary karma.

Before making our final decision about which of the seven paths to higher evolution we take, there is a meeting of all sixth-degree initiates. At this meeting we are asked to decide the measures the Hierarchy should take that will drastically and permanently affect the planet. The Ascended Masters are the group that makes the final decision in respect to human affairs, for they are the spiritual government for this planet.

In a later chapter I will discuss the twenty-two chakras that make up our entire being. The twenty-two chakras include the common seven we know about and the additional fourth- and fifth-dimensional chakras that most people don't know about. At the time of ascension the sixteenth chakra has descended down into the crown chakra. The fifteenth chakra has moved into the third eye chakra, the fourteenth into the throat chakra, and so on all the way down. At the time of ascension the fourth-dimensional chakras have been mastered and completed.

Ascension is a fifth-dimensional state of consciousness. Ascension, in essence, is the uniting of the soul extension, or personality, with spirit. It is the merging of the incarnated personality with the I Am Presence, or the monad.

A person does not have to be in perfect health to ascend. Many people with very serious illnesses have ascended. Secondly, there is something called a delayed ascension. A delayed ascension is when a person leaves the physical body, but in the first two hours after death the Masters work super-extensively with the adept to help him or her achieve ascension. This occurs when an adept was close to ascension but died before it occurred.

Once we ascend, our ability to serve will be greatly enhanced. When we ascend and remain on Earth we are no longer in our earthly physical bodies but rather in our glorified spiritual bodies. The physical body is changed in an instant by the total immersion in the great God-Flame.

The Ascended Master Serapis Bey, who is in charge of the ascension retreat in Luxor, lucidly describes the process of ascension in Elizabeth Clare Prophet's book on ascension when he says, "The blood in the veins changes to liquid golden Light, the throat chakra glows with an intense blue-white Light, the spiritual eye in the center of the forehead becomes an elongated God-Flame rising upward. The garments of the individual are completely consumed and he takes on the appearance of being clothed in a white robe, the seamless garment of the Christ. Sometimes the long hair of the soul appears as pure gold on the ascending one; then again, eyes of any color may become a beautiful electric blue or pale violet."

During our ascension we retain full consciousness of the entire ritual and, once ascended, become an instant emissary of the Great White

Brotherhood. The entire process of ascension and of turning our entire being into Light, Djwhal Khul has said, takes thirty minutes.

I also asked Djwhal what the difference was between merging with the Light after death in the first stage of the bardo (the after-death experience) and merging with the Light during ascension. He said they were basically the same, except that during ascension, when we merge completely with the Light we are still in physical bodies on Earth. When we merge with the Light in the first stage of the bardo, or after-death experience, we have left our bodies. Djwhal said that it is possible to achieve ascension by merging with the Light upon death of the physical body. I will go into the science of death and dying and the bardo in chapter 7.

We have been told that over one hundred thousand souls have achieved ascension in Earth's history, which seems like a lot to me. John the Beloved was the only disciple of Jesus who ascended in that lifetime. Djwhal Khul has called the ascension flame the "cosmic fire." He said that it is permissible, in an unascended state, to call forth the cosmic fire, but only a little bit. He said to call forth cosmic fire the size of a match flame. Too much cosmic fire too soon can actually burn out the physical body. It would be almost like spontaneous combustion. We can ask at night before bed to go to Djwhal Khul's retreats or Serapis Bey's retreats on the inner plane for preparation and training for our ascension.

Ascension is a fantastic achievement; however, I would remind you again that there are, in actuality, nine initiations in our planetary system, seven of which can be taken on the Earth plane. The passing of these nine initiations allows us to leave the cosmic physical plane and then begin working on the initiations of the seven cosmic planes. So I would say it is very hard to be anything but humble when we see how far we have to go to ultimately return to union with the Godhead. As I mentioned earlier, ascension is probably only three-quarters of an inch up a ten-inch ruler in terms of how far we have yet to evolve.

On the other side of the coin, the achievement of ascension, as compared to the evolution of the rest of humanity, is a very, very great achievement, indeed. It is always important to keep these two sides of the coin in perspective.

I would like to end this commentary on ascension by sharing a little story about a woman by the name of Analee Skaron. Analee was a Mormon. She was an elderly lady of great Light. She wrote a very beautiful book called *Ye Are Gods* which was really a channeling of her God-self. The Mormon church didn't like this most precious book and excommunicated her from her church even at her elderly age. She was very distraught over this, for she had spent her whole life serving the church. One day she told her roommate that she thought the angels would be coming for her soon so she wanted to put her things in order. Very soon after this, one night very late, her roommate woke up from a sound sleep and had the impulse to check on Analee. When she got to Analee's door she saw from under the door a brilliant white Light such as she had never seen before. Her intuition told her not to bother Analee at this moment so she went back to bed. In the morning she went to see Analee and when she knocked and opened the door, Analee was not there. Analee's false teeth were on the table, which was very strange because Analee never went anywhere without her false teeth. The entire day went by and Analee never returned.

The roommate called her family and they came over that night. The entire family was sitting in the living room when all of a sudden the door opened and Analee stood before them in tattered clothes. She immediately said to them, "Do you believe I have translated?" (Translated is another word for ascended.) They all said they did. Analee blessed them for their faith and immediately transformed herself into a beautiful robe of white Light. Her family stood there aghast as she disappeared right in front of them!

In my continuing research into the subject of ascension I have found out some absolutely fascinating new information. First, Vywamus told me that there are eight hundred physicalized Ascended Masters living on Earth. Of these eight hundred Ascended Masters, approximately 20% to 30% of them have female bodies and 70% have male bodies. Vywamus also told me that there are anywhere from eighteen hundred to twenty-five hundred if you count the etheric Ascended Masters on Earth. Many of these etheric Ascended Masters are members of the Ashtar Command.

The first wave of mass ascension for the planet begins in May of 1995 at the Wesak. I have been told that anywhere from four thousand to seven thousand people will ascend at that time. The majority of these people will ascend in a four-day period that surrounds the actual Wesak Festival of the full moon in May. There will be approximately one hundred (40% female, 60% male) in the group that will ascend within the two months previous to this large group. Of the people ascending in the first wave, 90% will ascend and remain on Earth in service.

The main period of mass ascension will be between the years 1995 and 2000; it will continue to occur after this, but with less frequency.

Vywamus also told me that the Light quotient needed for the actual ascension and sixth initiation is 80%. The seventh initiation requires a minimal Light quotient of 92% to ascend. The third initiation and soul merge need 56%; the fourth initiation needs 62%; the fifth initiation needs 75%.

There are basically three waves or stages that exist between the fifth and sixth initiations. The stages are initiated by Sanat Kumara, our

Planetary Logos. The first stage has to do with ascension activation; the second stage has to do with ascension integration; the third stage has to do with ascension declaration.

There are two types of body you can use for your ascension. You can raise your existing body into the ascended state or you can ascend in your Mayavarupa body. Of these two choices one is not better than the other; it is just a matter of preference and individual resonance. I, myself, have chosen to ascend in my Mayavarupa body. Djwhal has told me it is a little sturdier and, given the fact that I had some serious health lessons earlier in this incarnation, this path felt better for me personally. Master Kuthumi and Lord Maitreya chose this path. Djwhal Khul chose the path of raising the physical.

One of the abilities that comes with ascension or is available with a little training is teleportation. Before you ascend you can take teleportation classes on the inner plane to prepare you for this type of ability, along with bilocation and transfiguration. (Transfiguration is the ability to actually change into another person in order to do service work when you don't want to be recognized.)

After you ascend you don't have to eat food or get a haircut or shave and so on. However, many Ascended Masters will continue to partake in such activities because of the nature of their service work. Terri, my wife, and I have decided to continue in such activities so as to avoid making ourselves look better than or separate from others while performing our service work.

In the history of Earth, approximately one hundred thousand have ascended, Djwhal Khul has told us. There will be many waves of mass ascension. The second wave of mass ascension will occur in October of 1995 and this will also contain approximately five thousand to seven thousand people. The third wave of mass ascension will occur in the summer of 1996 around July and will again contain about five thousand to seven thousand people.

Four ways to build up your Light quotient have been given. The first way is to build up the physical and etheric nervous systems. The second way is to reabsorb the power and energy aspects of the soul that have been given away in past lives or in this life. The third way is to polish the rough edges of your character within the four-body system. The fourth way is to call on the Ascended Masters for help in building your Light quotient during meditation and sleep time. Later I will share some other extraordinary techniques for achieving this goal.

I asked Vywamus if psychic faculties open up after ascension and he said that they do in terms of clairvoyance, clairaudience, clairsentience and so on. One other very important aspect of purifying yourself in preparation for ascension is to make sure to have cleared out all elementals. They are a type of thought form that latches onto the aura, glands or organs and sucks energy away from them, much as an alien implant does. In meditation, you can call to Vywamus and other Ascended Masters and ask them to clear any unwanted elementals from your field.

At a certain point in your ascension process you will reach a point called spiritual ascension, which is a precursor to actual ascension. Spiritual ascension is a later stage of the fifth initiation. It is when you have really ascended on the spiritual level, but are now waiting for it to manifest on the physical level.

I want to make it clear here that other people will be ascending on an individual basis in between these waves of mass ascension I already spoke of. The waves of mass ascension are like planetary windows that, in a sense, make it easier. May of 1994 was also a very powerful time, for Wesak brought in very powerful pre-ascension energies that Vywamus told me were powerful enough to make people pass out because of their intensity.

An important exercise you can do to accelerate your ascension process is to ask in meditation to be connected up properly to your other eleven soul extensions, in both an electrical and an energetic sense. This is something you will need to ask the masters to help you with. Vywamus is especially good at this type of work.

I have always been curious about whether Paramahansa Yogananda ascended, because when he died his body was old and he left in a state of Mahasamadi, which is a "conscious exiting." Vywamus told me that Paramahansa Yogananda did indeed ascend before he left.

In terms of how old you will look after ascension, I am told it is usual to take on the age and look you had when you ascended. If you want to youth your body after this and change appearance, you can. Usually this is done slowly.

To my surprise, I discovered there will be children who will actually be part of the mass ascension waves; however, the majority will be adults between the ages of thirty and sixty. There will be some elderly ascensionists also, however.

After you ascend, the chakras are no longer separate individual chakras but rather one long chakra column with a golden-white flame in the third eye. The actual gateway for mass ascension will open as of December 12, 1994. It has been esoterically referred to as the 12:12. This is the next big spiritual event on the planet after the 11:11 that Solara made famous in 1992.

It also must be understood that you do not achieve your ascension without first passing the fifth initiation. You cannot skip steps in the initiation process. Since these times are so accelerated, these initiation steps can be moved through very quickly.

There will be many waves of mass ascension beyond the three that I have mentioned. They will continue on, especially through the year 2012 which, of course, is the end of the Mayan calendar and the pyramid prophecies. Ascensions will occur after this but at a slower rate.

After you ascend you still continue to develop and refine your abilities and skills. It is not as though you ascend and have no more to learn. Another interesting understanding I have come to about ascension is that there will be many different types of Ascended Masters. Some will be emotionally based, some more mentally based, some with more physical abilities or healing powers. There will be great variation in the abilities and potentials of the Ascended Masters. The tendencies you had before ascension will carry over after ascension. Individual skills will vary according to your soul and monadic blueprint.

It is strongly recommended that all of you interested in becoming full-fledged ascension candidates stand before Sanat Kumara in meditation and make this request.

I asked Vywamus one time if people ever ascended at night while they slept. He told me that this often was the case but that people always woke up once their ascension actually began to happen. He told me that there was only one case he knew of in which a person actually slept through his ascension. When this man woke up he thought he was still dreaming when in actuality he had ascended and didn't know it.

I asked Djwhal Khul what a person's actual ascension would look like to a third-dimensional person who might be watching. Djwhal said that the person would begin to disappear into kind of an ectoplasmic form and then rematerialize. A third-dimensional person would think his vision was going fuzzy or hazy for some reason. If you choose to ascend in your Mayavarupa body, the cosmic fire actually begins to pour in at your ascension and it literally burns up the physical vehicle. The Mayavarupa body, which is like a monadic blueprint body, then is rematerialized into a perfect body. When raising the actual physical body, a spiral motion is set forth and the physical vehicle is raised into Light rather than being burned up.

Those people going through the ascension process before the mass ascension waves might be referred to as prototypes. Each wave of mass ascension will make it easier for the ones who follow. Many who will be taking their ascension in these earlier waves will be taking their seventh initiation between the years 1995 and 2012.

Accelerating Your Path and
Building Your Light Quotient

Ascension Technique Number One

For my own knowledge as well as for the writing of this book, I have investigated my personal path of ascension and I have attempted to learn everything I could about the process and mechanics of ascension. One of the interesting things I have come across in my exploration on the inner plane is the existence of ascension seats or ascension chambers. There are many of them. I will share with you five that I have found to be the most powerful and effective. They are actual seats or tables or columns that you sit or stand on or lie down in. The Masters, through some kind of higher technology, pulse Light through the mechanism to raise your vibration. There is one on Commander Ashtar's spaceship. There is one in Serapis Bey's Ascension Retreat in Luxor. There is one in Telos, the underground city beneath Mt. Shasta. There is one in the Great Pyramid of Giza, in the king's chamber. My personal favorite is the one actually in Mt. Shasta which is an ascension chamber inside a gigantic pyramid. Ask in meditation or at night while you sleep to be taken to these ascension seats. You can switch around if you like and find your favorite. It is one of the best ways I have found to build the Light quotient and raise your vibration. You can feel the Light and energy being very gently pulsed into your body as you sit in meditation. I would also recommend calling upon Archangel Metatron for help in building your Light quotient. He is the Creator of all outer Light in the universe and seems to have special ability in this area.

Ascension Technique Number Two

Call to the Mahatma to integrate all three hundred fifty-two levels of the Mahatma into your being during every meditation. Also ask to receive the Light information of all three hundred fifty-two levels of the Mahatma. It will come through in what would look like Light packets, if you looked at it clairvoyantly. Ask to receive the Light information packets from the fifth, sixth and seventh dimensions of reality. This is actual spiritual information that will be programmed into your computer banks and that you will eventually use in your future mission. It also helps to build your Light quotient. You can also request to be a cosmic walk-in for the Mahatma on Earth. In doing this you are requesting to be subtly overshadowed by the Mahatma to help heal the separation among your personality, monad and soul, and also between you and the presence of God.

Ascension Technique Number Three

Call forth many times throughout your day for an axiatonal alignment and a spiritual integration and alignment. This will properly align your personal self with the cosmic energies.

Ascension Technique Number Four

Call forth to your monad and to the Masters for the construction of your personal merkabah, if you don't have one already. Ask in meditation that your merkabah be spun to raise your vibrations to the fifth-dimensional, Ascended Master frequency. Use your merkabah any time you want to do soul traveling in meditation or at night while you sleep. The spinning of the merkabah is part of the process of learning to dematerialize and rematerialize.

Ascension Technique Number Five

When meditating from now on, make a request for your eleven other soul extensions to join you in your ascension work. Don't order them, but rather give them an invitation to attend and ask your monad and maybe Vywamus for help in gathering them. In later meditations you may also want to invite all one hundred forty-four of your soul extensions. By doing this, you are doing your ascension work for twelve of you instead of just one of you. Remember, it is your whole soul group that is actually ascending through just one soul extension. I cannot recommend this ascension technique highly enough.

Ascension Technique Number Six

Call to Isis, Osiris, Serapis Bey and Thoth for the Ark of the Covenant to be used in the acceleration of your path of ascension during your meditations. The Ark of the Covenant was used by the great Ptahs and Egyptian masters of the past in their initiations and ascension work. You will experience a marked increase in the power of your meditations upon calling for it.

Ascension Technique Number Seven

Call forth, under the guidance of your monad, the anchoring and activation of your twenty-two chakras. Your chakras will actually descend into the body like bodies of Light. They will remain in your four-body system for a period of time and then leave. The consistent invocation of your higher chakras to descend will, over time, build up your spiritual battery. It will increase the wattage of the spiritual lightbulb that you are. It is essential that you do this under the supervision of your monad, so as not to burn out your body. This is not something that should be done all at once but slowly and gradually, to prepare your nervous system. Ask your soul and monad to supervise this process and you have nothing to worry about. I would recommend using the ascension meditation treatment in the back of this book for a period of time. Put it on an audio tape that you record yourself. Over time you will integrate the first sixteen chakras. Then you can begin calling forth the fifth-dimensional chakras sixteen through twenty-two.

Ascension Technique Number Eight

If you are ever feeling any discomfort in meditation, always immediately call in the MAP (Medical Assistance Program) healing team. This is a group of ascended beings made up of Pan, the overlighting deva of healing, the Great White Brotherhood Medical Unit and your soul and monad. Just call them in by name. They are especially trained to help with any medical or energetic blockages. I personally call on them in every meditation to help keep my physical body balanced while I'm meditating. For a total understanding of the MAP team, read the chapter about them in my second book, *Soul Psychology*.

Ascension Technique Number Nine

In every meditation, call forth the descending and anchoring of your monad, your Mayavarupa body, your golden solar angelic body, your solar body of Light, God and the Mahatma. These are all higher aspects of yourself (your multidimensional identity) which will merge with your four-body system and build your Light quotient, raising your overall vibration.

Ascension Technique Number Ten

In every meditation ask for the building of the twelve strands of DNA in your etheric physical body. Contrary to what most people understand about this, the twelve strands of DNA are built into the etheric body and do not really manifest into the physical until after ascension. Keep requesting this and over time this work will be completed. It is part of the work of preparing your ascended body.

Ascension Technique Number Eleven

Call forth an experience in meditation of the rapture. This is an experience of being taken up the pillar of Light or ascending the pillar of Light in meditation.

Ascension Technique Number Twelve

In every meditation call forth a special ascension blessing and acceleration from one of the Ascended Masters.

Ascension Technique Number Thirteen

In every meditation request a complete opening of your ascension chakra and a complete opening and activation of all of your brain centers. Your ascension chakra is a chakra that is in the back of your head where a pony tail would begin to come out. It is a soft spot on the top of your head, a little bit to the back. At ascension this chakra is fully open. Another key to ascension is fully activating your brain centers and achieving full brain illumination. Ask the Ascended Masters that you be given a divine dispensation of ascension keys and ankhs in your brain and heart. These function as miniature arks of the covenant or miniature merkabahs that spin and raise your Light quotient and contain ascension information. Ask for these to be placed within you during meditation and before sleep to accelerate your ascension process.

Ascension Technique Number Fourteen

Call forth Vywamus or other Ascended Masters for the preparing of your physical and etheric nervous systems for ascension. This is one of the keys to building your Light quotient and beginning to hold the higher Light frequencies.

Ascension Technique Number Fifteen

On a regular basis, do the ascension meditation and treatment at the end of this book. When not using this longer meditation, take notes from the ascension techniques section and try these different methods in different meditations.

Ascension Technique Number Sixteen

In meditation, go before Sanat Kumara and make your prayer-requests about your path of ascension. Also state what you have to offer the hierarchy and humanity in terms of service work you would like to do. Use this technique especially every Wesak festival, which is the full moon in May. This, in truth, is the holiest day of the year from the Spiritual Hierarchy's perspective.

Ascension Technique Number Seventeen

Call forth the greater flame to merge and blend with the lesser flame on Earth. Call forth the complete merger of monad, soul, and personality on Earth. Call forth the divine marriage of soul and spirit on Earth.

Ascension Technique Number Eighteen

Call forth to Helios, Metatron and Enoch to receive the fire letters and all relevant spiritual information from *The Keys of Enoch* in all five sacred languages. Ask that all this information be transmitted to you in meditation or in the sleep state. This concept is much like a foreign language tape that is played at night while you sleep, except at an infinitely more expanded level. The entire keys of Enoch and much more are literally programmed into your computer bank without your even reading these books. This is similar to Ascension Technique Number Two, calling in the Light information packets of all three hundred fifty-two levels of the Mahatma. The whole process does not take that long and all this material will be available to you in the future. It also helps to build the Light quotient.

Ascension Technique Number Nineteen

Have all your alien implants and elementals removed. This can be done by contacting my wife Terri and me, or by contacting any other qualified person in your community. It can be done over the phone and takes about one hour. Everyone on the planet has them and they are nothing to worry about. It is just another subtle refinement and purification that is helpful to accelerate your ascension. (For more information on this, read my book on the hidden mysteries; the second half of the book is a complete overview of the extraterrestrial movement and it gives a detailed explanation of this whole process.)

Ascension Technique Number Twenty
Call forth to Helios sepcifically to help build your Lightbody. Request also a complete anchoring of your soul and monadic Lightbodies into your four-body system and a full merger into your physical vehicle. Helios is especially proficient at this work since he is the Solar Logos and he embodies the sun energy which has its direct correlation to the Lightbody.

The Seventh Initiation
The seventh initiation is the highest initiation that can be taken on this plane. The seventh initiation is freedom from the hold of the phenomenal life of the seven planes of our planetary life. It is in reality a lifting out of or above the cosmic physical plane. It is a merger with the Divine or Logoic plane of consciousness. The will of the Master becomes perfectly merged with that of the Planetary Logos. The son or daughter of God has found his way back to the Father and to his originating source, that state of existence called Shamballa. The Master has become a concentrated point of living Light. He or she has the right to come and go in the courts of Shamballa. The Master's vision penetrates beyond the solar ring-pass-not. He controls all seven rays. (The science of the twelve rays will be discussed in a later chapter.) He wields the law in the solar system. He begins to see the plans and purposes of the Solar Logos. The Master is accorded a revelation of the quality of love/wisdom that expresses itself through all created forms. The Master has become divorced from all consideration of form. The crown chakra is the chakra that is stimulated at this initiation. This initiation is referred to in Christian terminology as the resurrection.

The Seven Paths to Higher Evolution
At the time of our ascension we are required to choose one of the seven paths to higher evolution. The seven paths from which we can choose are the following:
1.   The Path of Earth Service
2.   The Path of Magnetic Work
3.   The Path of Training for Planetary Logos
4.   The Path of Sirius
5.   The Ray Path
6.   The Path the Logos Himself Is On
7.   The Path of Absolute Sonship

Most of humanity chooses the path to Sirius because it is the university of which Shamballa is a part. It serves as a training ground from which one can transfer to some of the more advanced paths at a later time in one's cosmic evolution.

Djwhal Khul chose the path to Sirius, as did the Buddha. The first path is for those who want to continue to work with the Earth after they ascend. My wife has chosen that path and has made an agreement with Djwhal Khul to remain working with the Earth for four thousand years, although not necessarily will she remain physically on the Earth all that time.

I have chosen the Path to Sirius myself and am considering transferring possibly to the Path of Absolute Sonship at a later time, after my basic training on Sirius. I have also been told that I will remain on Earth for approximately twenty more years at which time I will be working in Djwhal Khul's ashram, before moving on to Sirius. Most nights while I am sleeping I travel to Sirius in my soul body.

For more information on these seven paths to higher evolution, I would recommend reading the Alice Bailey book called *Initiation, Human and Solar*. Djwhal Khul gives a brief synopsis of these seven paths. I will warn you in advance, however, that the information will need to be referenced more from your right brain than your left brain. I would recommend that you begin meditating about these seven paths of higher evolution even before you ascend. There is also some information about these seven paths toward the end of the Alice Bailey book *The Rays and Initiations*.

Because the information on the seven paths to higher evolution is so sketchy and hard to understand, I have dedicated an entire chapter to bringing this knowledge and information to the forefront in an easy-to-understand and clarified manner in the new book I am currently writing which is called *A Spiritual Autobiography of My Actual Ascension*. This book won't be available until late 1995 or early 1996. Until that time I would recommend reading this four-volume set of books.

5

The Building of the Antakarana

The building of the antakarana is like
laying a cable or bridge among three
great countries (personality, soul, monad)

The Master Kuthumi

The building of the antakarana, or rainbow bridge, is an absolutely fascinating subject. To be perfectly honest, I did not realize how very important it was until I did my in-depth research for this book. I have always had a vague understanding of the process; however, what I am going to share here is absolutely amazing.

The science of the antakarana will one day be taught in every school and classroom in the world. It is the true science of the mind; it uses mental substance for the building of a bridge between the personality and the soul, and as one evolves, between the soul and the spiritual triad and monad.

The spiritual triad, again, is the vehicle through which the monad works, just as the soul works through the personality on Earth. The monad works through the threefold vehicle which is made up of spiritual will, intuition, and higher mind.

The antakarana is the thread, and later the cord, often spoken of which the disciple creates through meditation, understanding, spiritual practices, and specific, focalized spiritual work. The disciple does receive help from the soul and later the monad in this process, but the first half of the work must be done by the disciple.

The monad already has a thread or cord of energy that extends from it to the heart chakra of the disciple on Earth. This cord of energy is called the sutratma, life thread, or silver cord. The soul has a thread or cord that extends from it to the pineal gland of the disciple which is called the consciousness cord. Knowledge utilizes the consciousness cord. Wisdom energy utilizes the antakarana when it is built.

In Lemurian times the sutratma or silver cord was the principal cord in operation. In Atlantean times the consciousness cord became more activated. In this present Aryan age it is now our purpose to build the antakarana, the rainbow bridge, and make it totally activated.

The antakarana is like a spiritual filament of Light that is built as a spider builds her web. This thread is spun by the disciple in life after life, and it is only that which is of a spiritual vibration that can energize it. The consciousness cord contains the mental qualities from the soul. The antakarana is constructed only of spiritual/mental qualities from the soul.

The sutratma and consciousness cord have been constructed since man's first arrival in the material world. The antakarana has grown very slowly because a person has to step onto the probationary path for this work even to begin.

The sutratma and consciousness cord work from above downwards. The antakarana works from below upwards. In the final stages of the building of this cord, at the fifth initiation and ascension, these three cords merge, integrate, and blend together, just as the personality, soul, and, later on, the monad merge. It is through the creation of the antakarana that this whole process is allowed to take place.

The creation of the antakarana is like laying a cable or building a bridge among three great countries, the personality, soul, and monad. This bridge-building occurs in stages. The first stage deals with integrating the personality and the four bodies. The second stage is then building the bridge from the integrated personality and four bodies to the soul. The third stage is building the bridge from the soul to the spiritual triad and then to the monad itself.

The building of the antakarana makes the disciple responsive in his brain's consciousness to intuition's guidance and to impressions from the higher spiritual realms and from the mind of God. It allows the soul at first and later the monad to use the disciple and later initiate for its service work on Earth. The personality has become a reliable vehicle for the soul to use for its purposes on Earth.

This process reaches total completion at the fourth initiation when the soul body or causal body, which stores all the virtue and good karma, burns up. Then the fire of the monad pours down the antakarana to the soul, who has been the mediator between the personality and monad, and the soul returns to the monad. The soul or higher self is no longer needed and has merged back into the monad so all that is left is the soul-infused personality and the monad who is now the guide.

The initiate has built the antakarana to the spiritual triad and monad at this point. Even though a strong antakarana has been built to the spiritual triad and monad, a complete merger of monad/spiritual triad and the soul-infused personality has not taken place. It is at the fifth initiation that these two aspects merge together in consciousness.

At the sixth initiation they merge not only in consciousness, but completely into the four bodies—physical, emotional, mental, and spiritual—and the entire monad-infused personality and bodies turn into Light. The initiate has become an Ascended Master at this, the sixth initiation. It is the antakarana that the disciple has built among the personality, soul, and spiritual triad/monad that has allowed this whole process to take place.

It is also at this point that the sutratma, the consciousness cord, and the antakarana have merged together, just as the monad, soul, and personality have merged together. This results in the immortality of the physical form. Just as God, Christ, and the Holy Spirit are three minds that function as one, we are three minds—monad, soul, and personality—that function as one. The microcosm is like the macrocosm. Spirit and matter, father and mother have merged.

The antakarana has been the bridge of Light or the lighted way on which the disciple has passed to the higher worlds. It is by means of this bridge and lighted way that he has attained liberation and ascension. This integration has also helped to bridge the Shamballa consciousness, Hierarchical consciousness, and human consciousness. Shamballa consciousness relates to the monad and the will aspect. Hierarchical consciousness relates to the soul and the love aspect. Human consciousness relates to the personality and the intelligence aspect.

The Master, at achieving this integration, has also helped to build the planetary antakarana. This is the antakarana for the entire Earth and for humanity as a whole. Each soul extension on Earth builds one thread of the planetary antakarana, which makes this whole process easier for the ones who follow.

The Stages of Building the Antakarana

In the beginning stages of the building of the antakarana there are three self-created lesser threads that are first created and that make up the antakarana. The first of these is a thread from the physical body to the etheric body. This thread passes from the heart to the spleen. The second thread is from the etheric body to the astral body. This thread passes from the solar plexus to the heart and then to the astral body. The third thread is from the astral body to the mental body. This thread goes from the third eye chakra to the head chakra and from there to the mental body. These three lesser threads help the soul extension to integrate the four-body system.

The second stage deals with building the antakarana from the personality on Earth to the soul. This process can also be described as building a bridge among the lower mind, the soul, and the higher mind. In other terms it can be called linking the brain/mind/soul. This bridge is built through the use of "mental substance." The stage of building the bridge from the soul to the spiritual triad and monad uses "Light substance."

This bridge from the personality to the soul creates a complete soul illumination of the personality on Earth. It is at this stage that the disciple sees himself or herself as a soul. In later stages the initiate sees himself or herself as spirit or as the monad itself. This bridge will allow the personality to release all sense of separateness and fear of death.

The purpose and goal of building this antakarana is to use it for self-realization and for service to humankind. By the third initiation this bridge from the personality to the soul is complete. The first great union has been achieved. This can be achieved only when the disciple has developed a strong mind and is not constantly overrun by the physical and emotional/desire bodies.

This bridge is built by learning to have a spiritual attitude in life rather than an egotistical attitude and also by learning to hold the mind steady in the Light. This means learning to keep the consciousness attuned to the soul and how it would have us think, feel, and act. The lower self, ego, carnal desires, other people, and environment will try to pull us away from this state of consciousness.

By our learning to own our power and stay in self-mastery, in the service of the soul, the antakarana is greatly helped in terms of its stabilization. It must be understood again that the soul does not pay much attention to the personality until the personality pays attention to the soul.

A soul extension can go through many, many, many incarnations without the soul's being involved in the life of the incarnating soul extension in the slightest. The importance of building the antakarana can clearly be understood after realizing this. The whole process involves intense mental activity. It also involves using imagination and visualization which will be explained at the end of this chapter.

The greatest danger for beginning students on the path is indolence or laziness. The antakarana is created over a long period of time, step by step. Those students who race out fast and then lose their momentum and fall into apathy will not reach the goal they seek. The only true desire is the desire for liberation and God-realization so we can be of greater service to humankind.

It is also essential for the disciple to be able to differentiate among the three threads of consciousness (the sutratma, the consciousness thread, and the antakarana). The sutratma, also called the life thread, is anchored in the heart and uses the blood stream as its distributing agent. Through the blood, life energy is carried to every part of the body. It is the life thread or life cord that keeps us alive.

The consciousness cord is the faculty of soul knowledge and is anchored in the pineal gland in the brain. It controls the response mechanism, which we call the brain, and activates awareness throughout the body by means of the nervous system. These two cords of energy are recognized by the disciple as being knowledge and life.

The disciple, in the initial stages, becomes aware of these three threads of life, knowledge, and creativity (antakarana) and utilizes these energies consciously upon the lower mental plane. When the antakarana has been completed from the personality to the soul, the disciple is then ready for a greater fusion and building to take place between the soul and the spiritual triad and monad.

The disciple begins to have monadic contact at the third initiation. It is at this stage in a soul extension's evolution that the monad and spiritual triad (spiritual will, intuition, higher mind) begin to become very interested in the aspiring disciple. The work of building and strengthening the antakarana moves much more quickly now than previously, in the initial stages of evolution.

This new bridge between the soul-infused personality and the spiritual triad allows the inflow of the will energy to become possible. Although the main initial work of building the antakarana is done by the disciple or personality on Earth, the soul and monad most definitely help in this process, just as the monad, in the creation of its twelve souls, projected a ray or finger of fire downward in the soul's creation.

In a similar manner the soul projected a ray of energy, or finger of fire, to create the twelve personalities or soul extensions for incarnation. In a very similar way, but in reverse fashion, the personality, in building the antakarana to the soul and monad, is projecting a ray of energy or finger of fire or bridge back to the soul and monad.

This action by the disciple on Earth at some point draws a response from the soul and monad, depending upon which level one is working on in the building of the rainbow bridge. Djwhal Khul, in the book *Rays and Initiations* by Alice Bailey, has given six steps in the building of the antakarana.

The Six Steps to Building the Antakarana

The six steps are "intention, visualization, projection, invocation and evocation, stabilization, and resurrection."

1. *Intention.*

The first step entails an understanding of the task to be carried out, a decision and determination to do so, and a right orientation to achieving the goal. This first step also entails the gathering of one's forces and energies into the highest point of mental/spiritual focus one can attain, and holding it there. This goes back to "holding the mind steady in the Light."

2. *Visualization.*

The second step involves the utilization of imagination and visualizing abilities in the building of the cord and bridge of Light. At the end of this chapter, visualization meditations that Djwhal Khul has given for this purpose are included.

3. *Projection.*

The third step involves the utilization of will, or will power, and the use of a word of power to send upon this line or bridge of Light substance. This action of sending a word of power using will power through the visualized cord with the highest possible intention extends the gossamer threads of Light toward the spiritual triad and monad.

4. *Invocation and evocation.*

This invocation by the disciple has now drawn an evocative response from the spiritual triad and the monad, or spirit. The father (monad) working through the thread created by the disciple moves to meet his son (soul extension). The monad, or father in heaven, sends forth a projection of Light substance itself that meets the projection that the disciple has created on Earth. The lower projection and the higher projection meet and the antakarana is built.

The tension created by the disciple evokes the attention of the monad and spiritual triad. Through practice this reciprocal cord or bridge of energy becomes stronger and stronger. It is a flame of Light. There is no longer a sense of the three separate countries of personality, soul, and monad but, rather, one being functioning on all planes through this path of Light.

5. *Stabilization.*

In the beginning the antakarana is very thin and thread-like. Through practice, meditation, and proper spiritual living on all levels of being it will form a cord that cannot be broken.

6. *Resurrection.*

This last step has to do with the strengthening of the antakarana cord, which then leads to the greater merger and blending and integration of the triplicity, which at the fourth initiation has become the duality. This duality at the fifth and finally at the sixth initiation, or ascension, becomes the oneness, or complete unification of the soul-infused personality and the monad that has been working through the spiritual triad. These two states of consciousness totally blend at the fifth initiation and blend fully into the four-body system at the sixth initiation which is ascension or resurrection. The four bodies (physical, astral, mental, spiritual) and the personality are merged into Light and become immortal.

Words of Power

Repeating the names of God, words of power, and mantras is so important to spiritual development and God-realization that I have dedicated an entire chapter to the subject (Chapter 24). The words of power one is drawn to will depend upon spiritual training in past lives, the ray type (see the chapter on exoteric psychology and the science of the twelve rays, Chapter 10) of one's soul and monad, and individual preference, intuition, feeling, timing in one's life's work, astrology and numerology, to name a few factors.

There are thirteen specific words or phrases of power that I would like to specifically recommend right now, which are a few of the most powerful I have found. These thirteen phrases or words of power are:

1.   The soul or monad mantra (see the next page)
2.   Elohim
3.   Aum
4.   Om mani padme hum
5.   I Am, I Am that I Am
6.   I am God
7.   I love
8.   Adonai (Lord)
9.   So Ham (I am God)
10. El Shaddai (God Almighty)
11. YHWH
12. Ram
13. Yod Hay Vod Hay (Divine Father)

These thirteen mantras or any of the other words of power one already uses or that are listed in Chapter 25 will also work. The idea of this meditation is to visualize a cord of Light extending from the personality up through the soul to the monad. One can actually visualize this cord as being as wide as the circumference of one's head or smaller in the beginning, if one so chooses.

The disciple should attune himself to this antakarana, visualize it in his mind's eye, and with full intention and will power, repeat the word of power out loud from three to seven times or for up to fifteen minutes as a type of mantra meditation. After chanting this mantrum one can sit silently in a receptive state and just feel the response from one's soul or monad, depending on which stage one is working on.

This is a very simple meditation; however, it is extremely powerful. It is essential to hold one's consciousness steady in the Light for the time period. It may be done for a very short period of time a number of times a day as a kind of centering process, also. This practice, along with other spiritual practices, will most definitely build the antakarana.

The Soul or Monadic Mantra

The soul or monadic mantra was released to the world by Djwhal Khul in the Alice Bailey writings. I can honestly say it is the most powerful mantra I have ever found. I recommend starting the day with it and ending the day with it. I recommend against doing any type of spiritual work without saying it first. This mantra activates the soul and soul star to do spiritual work. The words of the soul mantra are:

I am the Soul,
I am the Light Divine,
I am Love,
I am Will,
I am Fixed Design.

Those disciples at the fourth initiation and beyond may want to change the first line to "I am the Monad" instead of "I am the Soul," the rest of the mantra remaining exactly the same. This I have termed the monadic mantra. I urge giving this mantra a try in building the antakarana and also while doing everything else of a spiritual nature. I have never met anyone who didn't feel effects from using it.

The only line in the mantra that people sometimes don't understand is the last one, which refers to the plan of the soul for the current incarnation. This mantra is the beginning of all occult techniques, according to Djwhal Khul.

Even if one is working with another mantra, it is good to begin a meditation by saying the soul or monadic mantra three times and then meditating with the other mantra. This mantra is like an activation tool that signals the soul and the monad to go into action to do their part of the program in response to the invocation.

The Grounding Cord

Djwhal Khul has guided me to advise people to build the antakarana not only up through the soul and monad but also down through the chakra column to the base of the spine and then down into the Earth. In some metaphysical circles this has been called the grounding cord.

This can be visualized as going right down the legs into the center of the Earth, or if one is sitting it can be visualized as going right through the chair into the Earth. It should be wide, just as the antakarana going up the central canal is at least the circumference of one's head.

The Antakarana after Ascension

It is important to understand that the antakarana in actuality does not just stop at the monad. In reality it continues up all the way to the Godhead. The antakarana can be sent all the way to God even before ascension. The meditator will get a response from God, and He will meet you with His finger of fire, and/or thread of Light substance. So even the Ascended Masters are continuing to build their antakaranas, as they evolve into cosmic planes of existence.

The Soul Star

Approximately six inches above the head is an etheric star of Light that hovers over the head of every person on Earth. The brightness of this star very much depends on the evolution of the soul extension on Earth. The soul star is not the soul, but rather an instrument through which the soul does its work. The soul star is an extension of the soul. It is this soul star that becomes activated upon doing the soul mantra.

The understanding of the soul star is very important in terms of understanding how to do Djwhal Khul's other meditations. Upon the saying of the soul mantra the soul star lights up like a brilliant, shining star and is ready to go to work as long as the work is in the service of the soul.

After saying the soul mantra, the soul star will obey thought and creative visualization and will actually be able to move, expand, contract, or send out beams of energy in the direction of the personality, or soul extension. The understanding, aid, and usage of the soul star will become absolutely invaluable in building the antakarana and in all other areas of life.

The Central Canal

The central canal is a term that refers to the column of energy that extends from the base of the spine to the top of the head. It has sometimes been referred to as the chakra column, or sushumna. It is a part of the sutratma, silver cord, or life thread, which are all different names for the same cord.

One of the very important practices of the spiritual path is to widen the central canal and clear it of all psychic debris. Ideally, the central canal can be widened into a column of Light that is the size of the circumference of one's head. Most people's central canal is a very small tube and is very clogged, like a bathroom pipe that is not working effectively.

The following three meditations given by Djwhal Khul are for the distinct purpose of widening and clearing the central canal and building the antakarana. It is through the antakarana and central canal that the soul and spiritual energies can flow. A wide, clear, and well-built antakarana and central canal allow one to be filled with the Light of spirit at the slightest request. The importance, hence, of this work cannot be emphasized enough. A small amount of focused work will bring fantastic results. What is also quite interesting to experience after doing the soul or monadic mantra is that the soul and monad do half the work.

The first meditation by Djwhal Khul is the triangulation meditation.

The Triangulation Meditation

This picture is from the book *The Rainbow Bridge, Phase 1: The Link with the Soul.* This book and its sequel, by *Two Disciples,* are highly recommended to those who are interested in this work and want to learn more. This picture gives in visual form the exact process of the triangulation meditation. The meditation is as follows:

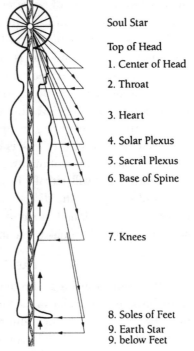

Soul Star

Top of Head

1. Center of Head

2. Throat

3. Heart

4. Solar Plexus

5. Sacral Plexus

6. Base of Spine

7. Knees

8. Soles of Feet
9. Earth Star
9. below Feet

1.   Say the soul mantra three times while concentrating on the soul star. Visualize the soul star as a brilliant star or sun.

2.   After saying the soul mantra three times, move the soul star with the power of your mind and imagination diagonally forward to a position one foot in front of your third eye. Then bring the soul star straight back into the center of your head and into the central canal and chakra column. Then bring the soul star straight upward through the entire central canal and back to six inches above the head where the soul star originally rested. Be sure to move the soul star very slowly and deliberately in its upward motion. The soul star is literally burning away hindering thought forms and psychic debris as it moves. This work is a cooperative effort of both the personality and the soul who is utilizing the soul star as its instrument. The soul is very excited to have this opportunity to work with you in this manner.

3.   Repeat this same process of creating the triangle with the third eye one more time.

4.   Repeat this same procedure now, but this time create your triangle down to your throat chakra, as the diagram indicates. Do this two times for the throat chakra.

5.   Repeat the same process for the heart chakra, solar plexus

chakra, sacral chakra, root chakra, knee chakras, the chakras in the soles of the feet, and for the Earth star which sits about one foot below ground. Do this triangulation method two times for each one of these centers and you are finished.

This meditation has helped you to clear your central canal and begin to build your antakarana. After completing this meditation and working with it for a while I suggest adding one more step. This last step is to build a triangle all the way to the soul itself, which is above the soul star. This part of the meditation will work on building the antakarana to the soul rather than focusing on the central canal.

If you feel it is appropriate you could also build a triangle all the way to your monad, or Mighty I Am Presence. I would do each of these three times, and upon completion you could chant your mantra, or word of power, while visualizing the antakarana and holding your mind steady in the Light. In a sense, here you would be blending the first meditation I taught you with this second triangulation meditation. This is very powerful, as you no doubt can see, feel, and intuit.

The Spiritual Whirlwind Meditation

Most people's auras (etheric, astral, and mental bodies) are filled with psychic debris, negative thought forms, and stagnant energy. The purpose of this next meditation is to clear all this unwanted material out of your auric field. Some of this debris, besides coming from normal daily living, also has come from the previous triangulation meditation you have just done.

The triangulation meditation has cleared the debris out of your central canal but has probably thrown it into your aura to a certain extent. There is a very simple process that the soul uses to clear out all this psychic debris. It is called the spiritual whirlwind meditation.

The idea of this meditation is to visualize a spiritual vortex or whirlwind coming down from the soul. Visualize it as you would a tornado, in the shape of a funnel. This spiritual whirlwind is made of the more refined energy substance of the soul. Even though you are visualizing it with your own mind, this spiritual vortex is a living psychic reality of your soul. If you are clairvoyant you can actually see it and watch it coming down from the soul, once it has been invoked. Please understand this is not just a visualizing exercise. This is a combined meditation experience of both the soul and the personality.

The tip of the lowest point of your funnel and spiritual whirlwind is in the antakarana, moving downward toward the central canal. As it moves down it picks up all the heavier bits of psychic debris. It rotates in a clockwise direction.

Let the soul decide the size, color, and speed at which it is moving.

The idea is to have this spiritual whirlwind move downward through your crown chakra and then through your entire auric field, cleansing away all psychic debris of a lower octave and taking it deep into the center of the Earth. At this point it drops the debris, ceases to move and disappears. Be sure to make the spiritual whirlwind very wide, so as to encompass your physical body and entire auric field.

Once the spiritual whirlwind gains strength and power it does not need the direction of the personality. At this point the soul and soul star are doing the work. A new spiritual whirlwind must be invoked each time you want to clear yourself. The initial spiritual whirlwind loses its energy once it moves into the Earth and unloads the psychic debris. I would recommend invoking anywhere from three to seven spiritual whirlwinds each time you do this meditation. I would recommend doing it to start your day, after work, and before bed to keep yourself clear.

I might add that it is a part of the Earth's work to handle the clearing of this sort of debris or negative energy. We are in no way polluting the Earth by working with her in this manner and the Earth is very happy to be able to serve in this way.

To invoke your spiritual whirlwind just follow these simple steps:

1. Say the soul mantra three times.

2. Visualize the spiritual whirlwind high above your head with its funnel tip in the antakarana, and say, "In the wisdom of the soul, I invoke the spiritual vortex."

3. Just watch it or visualize it moving down through your field and then into the Earth.

4. Call forth and invoke as many spiritual whirlwinds as you need until you feel clear. Usually three to five minutes is more than enough. If you ever feel off center or are in an emotional or psychological crisis, this process can be extremely helpful. These are simple techniques to let the soul and/or higher self help you in your life.

Corkscrew Meditation to Widen the Central Channel

In the first two meditations we have cleared the central canal and cleared the auric field of psychic debris. In this last meditation from Djwhal Khul, the purpose is to widen the central canal to the size of the circumference of your head. The central canal of most people is a very small, thin tube. This restricts the amount of Light and energy that can come in from the soul and monad.

There is a very simple meditation process for enlarging the central canal. It is similar to the triangulation meditation but uses only one triangle instead of a whole bunch of them. After saying the soul mantra, one triangle is created down to the Earth star beneath your feet as in the triangulation meditation.

As you begin to bring the soul star upward, visualize it as a corkscrew moving in a clockwise fashion up through the central canal, back to the soul star position about six inches above your head. Your central canal must be at least one inch wide but is preferably as wide as your head. In the beginning you may want to make yours a size somewhere in the middle as you build up to widening it as much as possible. Use your own discretion and intuition in this matter.

I would recommend that you do this meditation twice a day for three weeks. It takes three weeks to create a habit. Once it's widened, you are set for life. The exact process of this meditation as outlined by the Ascended Master Djwhal Khul goes as follows:

1. Say the soul mantra three times out loud.
2. Say the mantra of unification:

> The sons of men are one and I am one with them.
> I seek to love, not hate.
> I seek to serve and not exact due service.
> I seek to heal, not hurt.
> Let pain bring due reward of Light and love.
> Let the soul control the outer form of life and all events, and bring to Light the love which underlies the happenings of the time.
> Let vision come, and insight.
> Let the future stand revealed.
> Let inner union demonstrate and outer cleavages be gone.
> Let love prevail.
> Let all men love.

3. Build one large triangle down to the Earth star.
4. Move the soul star upward in the shape of a corkscrew moving in a clockwise direction, widening your central canal to the desired width.
5. End the meditation by saying The Great Invocation.

The Great Invocation

> From the point of Light within the mind of God,
> Let Light stream forth into the minds of men.
> Let Light descend on Earth.
>
> From the point of Love within the heart of God,
> Let Love stream forth into the hearts of men.
> May Christ return to Earth.

From the center where the will of God is known,
Let purpose guide the little wills of men—
The purpose which the Masters know and serve.

From the center which we call the race of men,
Let the plan of love and Light work out,
And may it seal the door where evil dwells.

Let Light and love and power restore the plan on Earth.

Some Last Thoughts

The building of the central canal all the way to the Earth star is very important. If the central canal isn't built in a uniform manner from the Earth and feet to the crown, then energy can become dispersed and congested, causing physical health problems, especially in the area of the torso. This issue speaks to the importance of proper grounding as well as attunement to the soul and monad.

Secondly, I would recommend moving slowly in the beginning, especially if a lot of this kind of work is new to you. Once the central canal is built and your four bodies are more purified and refined, you can move much faster. It is better to be like the tortoise instead of like the hare who races out fast in the beginning and burns himself out.

Thirdly, the doing of this most important work does help to build the planetary antakarana. It also helps to accelerate the reappearance of the Christ and the externalization of the Hierarchy, and it helps all those disciples who follow in your footsteps.

6

Glamour, Illusion, Maya

*The dweller on the threshold is like
a gigantic thought form of
glamour/illusion/maya that must be
dissipated prior to taking initiation*

Djwhal Khul
as channeled by
Alice A. Bailey

In Djwhal Khul's classic book, *Glamour, A World Problem,* he divided the levels of delusion into three categories. There is the delusion on the astral or emotional plane, on the mental plane, and on the etheric plane. Each of these planes has a unique form of delusion specific to its level, and each of these delusions has its unique remedy.

The form of delusion on the astral or emotional plane is called glamour. The form of delusion on the mental plane is called illusion. The form of delusion on the etheric plane is called maya.

The remedy for glamour on the astral plane is what Djwhal Khul termed illumination. The remedy for the mental-plane illusion is what Djwhal called intuition. The remedy for the etheric-plane maya is what is termed inspiration.

"The dweller on the threshold" is the term Djwhal has used to describe the sum total of all the delusion on all three levels that has remained unconquered and unsubdued and that must be cleared before initiation can take place. The dweller on the threshold is all that a human is, apart from his higher spiritual self. It is the sum total of the forces of the lower nature prior to illumination, intuition, inspiration, and initiation.

"The angel of the presence" is the term Djwhal has used to describe the spiritual self. The angel of the presence and the dweller on the threshold stand face to face in conflict. As the dweller on the threshold becomes subjugated and mastered, it eventually fades out in the blaze of glory that emanates from the angel of the presence.

The following chart summarizes the above-mentioned principles.

Plane	Problem	Remedy
1. Physical Brain Consciousness	Dweller on the Threshold	The Angel of the Presence
2. Astral	Glamour	Illumination
3. Mental	Illusion	Intuition
4. Etheric	Maya	Inspiration

The Problem of Delusion in Relationship to the Root Races

The second step in the understanding of this process is to take these same principles and apply them to the past root races on this planet.

The Lemurian root race's main lesson was attunement to the physical. The problem they were dealing with, hence, was maya. The etheric energies are intimately connected to the physical plane. The etheric body is the energy body of the physical body.

The Atlantean root race's main lesson was attunement to the astral and emotional level. This being the case, their main problem was that of glamour. The Aryan race, which we are now in, is attuned to the mental; hence, our main problem is that of illusion.

The yoga of the Lemurian race was Hatha Yoga, and they were dealing with the first initiation. The yoga of the Atlantean race was Bhakti Yoga and they were dealing with the second initiation. The yoga of the Aryan race is Raja Yoga, and we are dealing with the third initiation.

The chart on the next page summarizes the above information.

Race	Problem	Yoga	Goal
Lemurian	Maya	Hatha Yoga for aspirants Laya Yoga for disciples	First Initiation Inspiration
Atlantean	Glamour	Bhakti Yoga for aspirants Raja Yoga for disciples	Second Initiation Illumination
Aryan	Illusion	Raja Yoga for aspirants Agni or Ashtanga Yoga for disciples	Third Initiation Intuition
Future Meruvian Root Race	None	Ashtanga or Agni Yoga	Fourth Initiation Liberation from Wheel of Rebirth
Future Paradisian Root Race	None	Unknown	Fifth Initiation

Glamour

Glamour is astral in character and more potent than illusion because over 50% of the population are still run by their emotional bodies. Glamour veils the truth behind the fogs and mists of feeling and emotional reactivity and victim consciousness. Glamour is one of the main ways the "Dark Brotherhood" attempts to get well-meaning aspirants off the path.

When one finds oneself reacting with criticism, separativeness, and pride, it is a sign that glamour has a hold over one. When an aspirant can free himself or herself from these characteristics, he is well on the way to dissipating and relinquishing glamour. The best method for dissipating glamour is to act as a pure channel for the energy of the soul. This has to do with keeping a spiritual attitude toward life as opposed to an egotistical one.

A person who is caught up in glamour needs to learn how to become more polarized or more closely identified with the mental body. When a person is over-identified with the emotional body, he ends up being on an emotional roller coaster. Djwhal has termed this the glamour of the pairs of opposites.

As one develops and becomes more mentally polarized, he develops the path of the middle way, or even-mindedness and equanimity. As the disciple learns to develop right alignment to his soul, this results in increased Light that irradiates the mind and brain consciousness. This greatly helps in the development of spiritual perception as opposed to the ego's perception of reality.

Glamour prevents a person from seeing life truly or clearly and from seeing surrounding conditions as they truly are. The emotional type can be swayed by appearances and forgets what the appearance veils. In Lemurian times glamour and illusion were relatively unknown because the root race had only developed to the point of physical attunement. Humankind was more instinctual.

Glamour began to develop in the Atlantean times. It is interesting to point out that the other kingdoms of nature are relatively free of glamour and illusion.

On a world level, Buddha and his nine hundred arhats (fourth-degree initiates) struck the first blow in the dissipation of world glamour when he created his four noble truths. Christ struck the second blow with his teachings of individual responsibility and brotherhood. The third blow is now being struck by the New Group of World Servers acting under the direction of the Christ and his disciples.

Each human being has to deal not only with his own personal glamour, but also with family glamour, national glamour, and the glamour of the human race as a whole. The family glamour deals with the "desire life" of family in both the past and the present. The national glamour is the sum total of the desire life of the nation. The glamour of the human race is the sum total of all glamours of the human race combined in the consciousness or race mind.

The disciple who wants to dissipate glamour must do two things: He must stand in his spiritual being and he must keep his mind steady in the Light. This means keeping the consciousness and mind always on God, the soul or higher self, and on a spiritual attitude. No matter what happens, he must be vigilant for God and His kingdom.

The glamours that hold humanity are:

1. The glamour of materiality. This has to do with an over-identification with materialism, with the gluttonous desire for possessions and/or money.

2. The glamour of sentiment. This is pseudo-love based on attachment and addiction to loving or being loved.

3. The glamour of the pairs of opposites. Here the disciple swings back and forth between opposites without even- mindedness. The ideal is to remain even-minded whether one is experiencing profit or loss, pleasure or pain, sickness or health, victory or defeat, praise or criticism. This glamour has a lot to do with letting go of attachments, also. If one is not attached to things or people one does not suffer or experience pain.

4.   The glamour of devotion. This refers to people who fanatically follow a cause in an extremist fashion.

5.   The glamours of the path. The glamours of the spiritual path itself include working with the Ascended Masters from the negative ego's perspective.

It is essential to understand that the remedy for dissipating glamour is illumination. Trying to dispel glamour with intuition or inspiration does not work. It is the illumined mind, or Christ-thinking, that will get rid of glamour. The astral glamour needs the use of the illumined mind, just as the illusions of the mental plane need the next level above it which is intuition. The astral glamour needs hard, straight, correct thinking in the service of the soul's guidance. This is achieved through right analysis, discrimination, and right thought.

The following are some examples of the common glamours of the seven different rays as elucidated by Djwhal Khul in the Alice Bailey book, *Glamour, A World Problem.*

Ray 1:

The glamour of physical strength

The glamour of personal magnetism

The glamour of self-centeredness and personal potency

The glamour of "the one at the center"

The glamour of selfish personal ambition

The glamour of rulership, of dictatorship, and of wide control

The glamour of selfish destiny, of the divine right of kings personally exacted

The glamour of destruction

The glamour of isolation, of aloneness, of aloofness

The glamour of the superimposition of will upon others and upon groups

Ray 2:

The glamour of the love of being loved

The glamour of popularity

The glamour of personal wisdom

The glamour of selfish responsibility

The glamour of too complete an understanding, which negates right action

The glamour of self-pity, a basic glamour of this ray

The glamour of the messiah complex in the world of religion and world need

The glamour of fear based on undue sensitivity

The glamour of self-sacrifice

The glamour of selfish unselfishness

The glamour of self-satisfaction

The glamour of selfish service

Ray 3:

The glamour of being busy

The glamour of cooperation with the plan in an individual rather than a group way

The glamour of active scheming

The glamour of creative work without true motive

The glamour of good intentions, which are basically selfish

The glamour of "the spider at the center"

The glamour of "God in the machine"

The glamour of devious and continuous manipulation

The glamour of self-importance, from the standpoint of knowing, of efficiency

Ray 4:

The glamour of harmony, aiming at personal comfort and satisfaction

The glamour of war

'The glamour of conflict, with the objective of imposing righteousness and peace

The glamour of vague artistic perception

The glamour of psychic perception instead of intuition

The glamour of musical perception

The glamour of the pairs of opposites, in the higher sense

Ray 5:

The glamour of materiality, or over-emphasis on form

The glamour of the intellect

The glamour of knowledge and of definition

The glamour of assurance based on a narrow point of view

The glamour of the form that hides reality

The glamour of organization

The glamour of the outer, which hides the inner

Ray 6:

The glamour of devotion

The glamour of adherence to forms and persons

The glamour of idealism

The glamour of loyalties, of creeds

The glamour of emotional response

The glamour of sentimentality

The glamour of interference

The glamour of the lower pairs of opposites

The glamour of World Saviors and Teachers

The glamour of the narrow vision
The glamour of fanaticism
Ray 7:
The glamour of magical work
The glamour of the subterranean powers
The glamour of that which brings together
The glamour of the physical body
The glamour of the mysterious and the secret
The glamour of sex magic
The glamour of the emerging manifested forces

Illusion

Illusion is a soul activity and is the result of the mind aspect of all incarnated personalities in manifestation. When a person lets his ego interpret reality rather than the soul or the spiritual attitude system, he is lost in illusion. In the context of the four-body system, those people who are more intellectual than emotional in nature are more prone to illusion than glamour.

Deception is created by the misunderstanding of ideas and thought forms. The incarnated personality needs to learn to pour the Light of the soul through into the mind and brain. Only the intuition, and not illumination or inspiration, as Djwhal has defined them, can dispel illusion. It is in meditation and techniques of mind control that incarnated personalities will rid themselves of illusion. The mental plane is especially important during this particular period of history because we are now in the Aryan race which, again, is the attunement to the mental plane.

Illusion began to arise during the stage of the advanced humans in the later Atlantean times. Djwhal Khul, in the Alice Bailey books, has also defined illusion as "the reaction of the undisciplined mind to the newly contacted world of ideas."

There are various threads that lead to this distortion on the mental plane. They might be listed as the following:

1. The point of evolution the incarnated personality has reached;

2. The integration or lack of integration of the physical, emotional, mental, and spiritual bodies;

3. The degree of attunement and enlightenment achieved by one's soul;

4. The ray type of the mental body of the incarnated personality, which colors the incarnated personality's interpretation of ideas;

5. The level of development of the mental body;

6. The ray type of the soul which also colors the person's interpretation of ideas.

One of the absolute keys to dispelling illusion is to learn to "hold the mind steady in the Light." Most people in the world let their minds wander willy nilly and do not keep them focused. People have not been trained to own their personal power and to retain self-mastery at all times. People let themselves operate on automatic pilot and lose their vigilance. When this happens the ego or lower self becomes their director.

The aspirant must make a commitment never to let his mind leave the point of focus on God, his soul, and his spiritual attitude. If he does this, he will see his life absolutely revolutionized. This will become a habit after the initial battle with the subconscious mind and negative ego takes place. Keeping one's mind in the Light at all times will bring "a peace that passeth understanding."

The mastery of the mind will bring one to the third initiation and the soul merge. For remember, the first initiation is physical mastery, the second initiation is astral and emotional mastery, the third initiation is mental mastery and mastery of the threefold personality in service of the soul. Only one more initiation is needed after this for liberation from the wheel of rebirth. The fifth initiation will lead to monadic and spiritual merger and the sixth to ascension. The need to control the mind cannot be emphasized enough. God and the Ascended Masters will not do this for people. It is their job. The aspirant must never forget that it is his thoughts that create his reality.

The remedy for illusion is intuition. Intuition leads to a progressive understanding of the ways of God in the world on behalf of humanity and leads to the development of pure knowledge and pure reason. Djwhal has listed four types of people who are subject to revelation through the awakening of the intuition:

1. Those who are on the line of the world saviors,
2. Those who are on the line of the prophets,
3. Those who are on the line of true priests,
4. Those who are on the line of the practical mystics, or occultists.

Djwhal Khul has also stated that illusion usually demonstrates in one of seven ways:

1. The way of wrong perception,
2. The way of wrong interpretation,
3. The way of wrong appropriation,
4. The way of wrong direction,
5. The way of wrong integration,
6. The way of wrong embodiment,
7. The way of wrong application.

For a more in-depth discussion of these principles I would guide you to read *Glamour, A World Problem* by Alice Bailey, pages 57 to 65.

It also bears noting here that every bit of glamour dissipated and illusion recognized and overcome clears the way for those who follow and makes the path easier for one's fellow disciples. Those who have gone before have performed the same service for those who are here now.

It is also important to recognize that one has made great strides just by recognizing and owning the fact that one is even battling with illusion. There is a large grouping of the population that is not even aware that they are caught in glamour, illusion, or maya.

Maya

The first sense of glamour arose in the Lemurian times. Maya is experienced upon the path only when one begins the path of probation. The problem of maya deals with the world of vital forces. A person can be victimized by emotions, thoughts, and also just energy or vital force. Until one attains self-mastery, an aspirant can be swept around by all kinds of uncontrolled forces. It is for this reason that maya is predominately a difficulty of the etheric plane and etheric body.

These uncontrolled forces pour through the seven chakras producing reactions and effects that can be disastrous if not controlled properly. Maya is the term given to these uncontrolled energies, forces, and impulses which emanate from the world of prana and from the latent force of matter itself.

This mass of uncontrolled force can stem from the animal nature, the world, and/or the environment in which a person finds himself or herself. The bulk of humanity are governed by maya until they stand on the path of probation. People are governed by maya when they are controlled by any force or forces other than those energies that come directly from the soul.

When people are governed by physical (maya), astral, and mental forces they are usually convinced that these forces are right for them. This is exactly the problem of maya. It is the same as when people always think or feel that their opinions or perspectives are right, even though they may be completely egotistical and personality-based.

Djwhal Khul has stated about maya, in the Alice Bailey book, *The Problem of Glamour*, that many people, particularly the unintelligent masses, are solely inspired by desire—material, physical, and temporary. Animal desire for the satisfaction of the animal appetites, material desire for possessions and the luxuries of existence, the longing for "things," for comforts and for security—economic, social, and religious—control the majority. Man is under the influence of the densest form of maya, and the forces of his nature are concentrated in the second center when this is taking place.

In the case of glamour, the forces of a man's nature are stored in the solar plexus. Glamour is subtle and emotional, whereas maya is more tangible and etheric.

The two keys for the disciple are to bring all of the chakras under the inspiration of the soul and to transmute the forces of the lower chakras, which control the personality, into the energies of the chakras above the heart, which respond automatically to the inspiration of the soul. The remedy for maya is inspiration. Inspiration will devitalize and remove maya.

It is the first initiation that deals with physical mastery that is connected to the mastery of maya. Glamour, maya, illusion, and the expression "the dweller on the threshold" all stand for the same general concept or some differentiation of that same concept.

The Dweller on the Threshold and the Angel of the Presence

The dweller on the threshold is the one who stands before the gate of God and at the portal of initiation. The dweller is like a gigantic thought form of glamour/illusion/maya that must be dissipated prior to taking initiation. The aspirant is not even aware of the dweller until just prior to initiation.

The dweller on the threshold will arrive at full potency at the end of this Aryan cycle and in the lives of all initiates prior to taking the third initiation. Remember, it is the third initiation that has to do with mental mastery and mastery of the threefold personality, which cause the soul merge to take place. The third initiation is the mastery of the physical, emotional, and mental bodies, hence the mastery of maya, glamour, and illusion.

At the fourth initiation the initiate demonstrates the ability to produce complete atonement (at-one-ment) between the higher and lower aspects of the soul in manifestation, and hence the dweller on the threshold merges into the Angel of the Presence and disappears. The Light has absorbed the darkness.

At an earlier stage the dweller controls. The second stage is when the dweller, or the personality, is conflicted between materialistic desires and the desire for soul-realization and initiation. Then the third stage is when the personality has decisively chosen the path of the soul and has learned how to "hold the mind steady in the Light." This ability has enabled the disciple to control his or her lower nature and hence the dweller is gradually overcome, controlled, and mastered.

Summary

The disciple on the path of probation and initiation has three main tasks in the dispelling of glamour, illusion, maya and the dweller on the threshold:

    1.   To be able to distinguish the three distinct levels of distortion;

    2.   To discover what conditions in the environment or in the individual constitution cause these aspects to develop; and

3. To find out what methods are effective in obtaining mastery over their combined effect.

Each person can discover within himself or herself which form his own dweller on the threshold assumes. The key to this is to become more deeply aware of whether one is a physical, emotional or mental type, or a combination of any two, or all three. I would also recommend careful study of the first three levels of initiation in Djwhal's book, *Initiation, Human and Solar*, by Alice Bailey.

I also suggest a careful study of the Alice Bailey book *Glamour, A World Problem*. Djwhal Khul has written what I think is an absolutely brilliant, detailed study of this entire process.

As the final entry in this chapter I would like to add three pieces of information I have stumbled upon in my research of the Alice Bailey material which I think are quite interesting.

In this chapter we have been talking about the distortion factor in the three levels of our being (mental, emotional, etheric). The etheric body is intimately related to the physical body. Within the physical body are inherited instincts. When we think of the term "instincts" we usually think about animals having them but not so much about human beings having them. Djwhal Khul, in his writings, has given a detailed study of what the animal, human, and divine instincts are. I share this with you for your further study, meditation, and contemplation. I, personally, find the comparison of the three quite interesting.

Instincts within the Animal, Human, and Divine Kingdoms

Animal	Human	Divine
Self-preservation	Creativity Self-preservation	Immortality
Sex	Sex, Human Love	Attraction
Herd Instinct	Gregariousness	Group Consciousness
Curiosity	Inquiry: Analysis plus Self-Assertion	Evolutionary Urge

The Archetypes

Another factor in becoming clear and free from glamour, illusion, and maya is the understanding of archetypes. If I am not mistaken, this was a term that was coined by the famous Swiss psychologist, Carl Jung. My dear friend Marcia Dale Lopez, a spiritual teacher living in New York, has defined archetypes in a very clear and concise manner:

"Archetypes are underlying mythic themes that can be found in all races and cultures at all times. The archetypes are ageless roles or key stereotypes that portray different forms of behavior. In other words, the archetypes are universal role models or personifications of perennial themes. They can be identified as the main characters found in legends, fairy tales, Shakespearean dramas, and Bible stories."

The following are twelve of the basic, most well-known archetypal forms. In my personal opinion, the purpose of these archetypes, as of any roles, is to play them if it is appropriate to one's life and spiritual path and, most of all, to play them consciously. The danger comes when these universal roles and archetypes play the disciple instead of the disciple's playing them.

The second key point is the danger of living out one particular archetype that might make one psychologically imbalanced. This can be a type of glamour of the opposites of which I spoke earlier in this chapter. For example, a person may live out the martyr archetype; however, one of his spiritual lessons might be also to learn to be spiritually selfish.

The wise one archetype may need to learn to be the fool in order to find balance. Every subpersonality has an opposite subpersonality. An archetype, being a type of universal mythic subpersonality, may need to be balanced also, as long as in doing so one is not serving the negative ego and lower self.

Many people find themselves identifying with a large number of these archetypal roles and patterns, and that is fine, too. There is no right or wrong, there is just what is appropriate for one's spiritual path and mission in this lifetime and the issue of being whole and balanced in life. Within the framework of the bigger picture, it is essential to master and integrate all twelve of the basic archetypes.

In a similar sense, one has to master all twelve signs of the zodiac and the ten sephiroth on the Tree of Life. This doesn't mean that one has to do this all in a single lifetime. There is also the possibility of another soul extension's being stronger in certain archetypes, while being, oneself, stronger in others.

It is a good idea to allow oneself to role-play these different archetypes during this life so as to gain the greatest sense of wholeness one can possibly have. Many of these archetypes have been lived out in past lives and so don't have to be lived out in this life.

The bottom line is to let the guidance of one's soul and monad lead one to the appropriate application of these universal states of consciousness. Thinking and meditating upon these twelve archetypes can be quite interesting.

The Archetypes

Destroyer
Change-maker
Enemy
Betrayer
Evil-doer
Mischief-maker
Devil
Rascal
Smartass

Fool
Risk-taker
Clown
Flake
Lunatic
Madman
Madwoman
Philanderer
Scatterbrain

Innocent
Artist
Child
Youth
Harmless One
Lover
Trusted One
Wonderer

Magician
Fairy Godmother
Merlin
Priest/Priestess
Shaman
Sorcerer
Trickster
Warlock
Witch
Wizard

Martyr
Great Soul
Saint
Savior
Loser
Struggler
Unfortunate Victim

Patriarch
Ancestor
Father
Mother
Old One
The Great Father
The Great Mother

Ruler
Aristocrat
Emperor/Empress
Judge
Prince/Princess
Queen/King
Superior

Seducer
Deceiver
Enchanter
Lover
Philanderer
Tempter/Temptress

Seeker
Adventurer
Explorer
Hermit
Hunter
Monk
Pioneer
Pursuer
Wanderer
Wonderer

Servant
Assistant
Attendant
Person Friday
Right-Hand Person
Slave
Subject
Subordinate
Worker

Warrior
Fighter
Gladiator
Hunter
Knight
Rival
Soldier
Survivor
Struggler
Teacher
Thinker

Wise One
Guru
Holy One
Master
Mystic
Oracle
Philosopher
Prophet
Sage

Psychic Development and the Senses

Just as each person has five physical senses, each person has five subtler senses that are spiritual counterparts to the five outer ones. The chart on the next page shows the progression of the senses and supersenses as one travels up the first five dimensions of reality as Djwhal Khul has described them in the Alice Bailey books.

The lack of understanding of this is a source of great glamour in the psychological and spiritual fields. In my development and progression on the spiritual path, it has been very interesting to me to have met people who are often extremely psychic and yet not spiritual. This has been hard for some people to understand. How can they be so psychically developed yet often not even believe in God?

The psychic senses are often coming from what Djwhal Khul has described as the "astral senses," and many times people get stuck at this level. Another example might be a person who channels but is channeling astral entities that aren't very evolved. This chart presents a type of map of some of the higher senses in the causal, Buddhic and atmic planes that many people may not be aware of.

There is absolutely nothing wrong with developing one's astral senses. It is just important to use them in the context of the understanding that there are seven dimensions of reality and seven levels of sensory apparatus. The chart on the following page depicts the first five dimensions of reality, taking one up to the doorway of ascension and/or merger with the monadic plane.

The Senses and the Supersenses

All knowledge Perfection Realization Active service Beatitude	Atmic senses	Atmic Plane
Idealism Intuition Divine vision Healing Comprehension	Buddhic senses	Buddhic Plane
Spiritual telepathy Response to group vibration Spiritual discernment	Higher mental senses	Astral- Emotional Plane
Discrimination Higher clairvoyance Planetary psychometry Higher clairaudience	Lower mental senses	
Emotional idealism Imagination Clairvoyance Psychometry Clairaudience	Astral senses	Physical- Etheric Plane
Smell Taste Sight Touch, feeling Hearing	Physical senses	

7

Death, Dying, and the Science
of the Bardo

*Where you go when you die is
determined by the last thought in your
mind before death*

Bhagavan Krishna
in the *Bhagavad-Gita*

Death and dying, from the soul's perspective, are quite different from the perspective of death of current Western thinking. The view of modern-day science is a half-truth. Its premise is that all that is real is what can be seen with the physical eyes and sensed with the five physical senses. This most limited approach causes adherents to interpret death from a totally materialistic viewpoint which sees the death of the physical body as the death of the person, for they have not yet come to the realization of the existence of the soul.

The second theory of death is one of conditional immortality. In this theory, immortality is available but there are certain conditions that must be met. One must first accept Jesus, join a church, and let Him absolve one of all sin. If one doesn't do this one will either go to hell or there will be no existence after the death of the physical body.

The third view is that of reincarnation. This is a view held by the majority of people on Planet Earth, but much less so in the Western world than in the East. This is because the church higher-ups took all references to reincarnation out of the Bible at the Second Council of Constantinople in 553 A.D. This has been documented in the minutes of that meeting that appear in our modern-day history books. The church authorities didn't like the concept because it took away their control of the people.

Reincarnation is, of course, a fact. We are soul extensions of our soul who keep reincarnating over and over again in our quest to realize our true identities as sons and daughters of God. In reality there is no such thing as death. Death is an illusion of the negative-ego thought system.

By definition, the ego is that thought system which is over-identified with matter. When we believe we are physical bodies rather than souls living in physical bodies, we then think death is real. Death is nothing more than a transformation from one state of consciousness to another. We have been taught to look at it as the ultimate terror when in reality it is the ultimate release and liberation.

In this society we have it all backwards, as we do most things. The ultimate terror should be being born, not dying. As free spirits, when we are born we have to come into a tiny baby's limited physical body and be at the mercy of our physical parents. That's scary!

Death allows us to be free from the illusion of form and to return to our spiritual home. Coming into incarnation is like donning a diving suit and then trying to get around underwater in it. Death is the freedom from this most limited state of consciousness.

The real death that has taken place in so many of our incarnations has been the death of the soul. I do not mean this in a literal sense, but rather in the sense that we, as soul extensions, come into matter, become over-identified with it, and fall asleep to our true identity. In that sense we die to our true identity, which is soul.

We also die every night when we go to sleep. We die to physical consciousness, translate into our spiritual consciousnesses and bodies, and travel.

In beginning our discussion on death and dying I would like to list some of the other ways we experience death on the spiritual path.

1. Physical death. We each have experienced it between two hundred and two hundred fifty times. We are experts at it.

2. Death of the negative ego and/or personality. This occurs at more advanced stages of a soul extension's evolution, usually at the third initiation.

3. Death of desire. This also begins to occur at the second initiation and comes into full death at the third initiation.

4. Second death. This is an occult term that refers to the burning up of the causal body, or soul body, at the fourth initiation. At this initiation we die to the body of the soul and to the soul itself, who merges back into the monad.

5. We experience death again at the ninth initiation. At the ninth initiation we leave or die to the cosmic physical plane itself. All contact with the physical plane is severed and we move on to the

higher cosmic planes.

6. Death of the etheric, astral, and mental bodies. We die to the etheric body in every incarnation, and we die to the astral and mental bodies also, after certain stages of the spiritual evolution.

Spiritual Evolution

From this discussion you can see that we die all the time, and it is something we are quite familiar with. With every death also comes a corresponding rebirth. The process of initiation is nothing more than death to a certain stage and level of consciousness and rebirth to a more expansive and liberating state of consciousness. It is painful only when we are attached to the level or stage we have been experiencing.

Death: Not Necessarily an Unhappy Occurrence

In this society we are taught that death is a very unhappy and sad event. In India, when people die there is actually a celebration because everybody there recognizes that the soul has been released from the confines of the physical vehicle. They feel joyously happy for that soul. When a soul extension is suffering in a broken-down, disease-ridden physical vehicle, death becomes a beneficent friend.

Western medicine tries to keep people alive at all costs. This materialistic identification is not always in line with the soul's purpose. People must realize that continuance of life in a physical body is not the highest possible goal.

When people die, their individualities are not lost. They are the same people on the other side as they were on this side. The only difference is that they are minus their physical and etheric bodies. Most soul extensions, when they die, inhabit their astral bodies and hence find themselves in the astral world. Soul extensions who are more advanced spiritually and who are mentally rather than emotionally polarized will find themselves in their mental bodies and on the mental plane. Esoterically, this plane of existence has been called Devachan.

Initiates of an even more advanced state of consciousness will find themselves in their Buddhic, atmic, and/or Light, or ascended, bodies. Where people go when they die is totally determined by their development in all their past lives and in the life just concluded. When people die they are attracted like a magnet to the level of consciousness they have achieved, but not until after they have gone through the three-day bardo experience. (The bardo experience will be discussed in much detail later on in this chapter.) This is why it is so important for people to achieve as much spiritual growth as possible while still in this physical body.

Krishna, in the *Bhagavad-Gita*, said that "where you go when you die is determined by the last thought in your mind before death." This is true, and so one's whole life is a quest, in reality, to die with the thought of God on one's mind.

This same process happens when one goes to sleep at night. Where one goes during sleep is determined by the last thought in the mind. If one watches the news before bed, one will probably end up wherever the current "hot spot" is on the planet. If one spends time before bed meditating, praying, or reading spiritual material, then one will probably end up on the celestial planes of existence.

Paramahansa Yogananda, the great saint from India, said that peoples' passing, or dying, will be a wonderful experience if they have the slightest bit of spiritual belief and purpose in their lives. It is only those people who are completely cut off from their souls and who are completely materialistic and egotistical who vibrate to the lower astral planes.

The Average Person versus an Initiate

For the average person, interestingly enough, the soul does not play a big part in the death process. When a soul extension is not very evolved, the soul does not play a big part in the soul extension's life on any level of existence, including death.

The only part the soul plays is the determination to end the cycle of incarnated life when the physical vehicle has broken down and has been overcome by disease. The person, or soul extension, usually dies when the will to live is lost, and the will to die in conjunction with the disease process has taken over. For the average person, this is an unconscious process.

The initiate's death becomes a deliberate and fully conscious choice to release his vehicles. The initiate does this through an act of soul-will. In some cases, a highly developed initiate has a pre-vision of the exact day of his death.

Sai Baba, in India, is currently (in 1993) sixty-five years old. He has said that he will live until he is ninety-six and then he will pass on to the spirit world. Sai Baba is an extraordinary example, for he not only knows his time of death, he also knows the body he is going to be born into in his next incarnation.

Paramahansa Yogananda, when he died, knew his time of death and exited consciously. He gave a lecture to a large group of people, and when he had completed the lecture, he just consciously left his body. There was so much Light in his body after he died that it remained in a perfect state of preservation for almost three weeks. The mortuary people said they had never seen anything like it.

The Life Thread, the Consciousness Thread, and the Antakarana

The life thread has also been termed the silver cord and the sutratma. This is the cord of Light that extends from the monad through the soul, down to the soul extension, or personality, on Earth and into the heart. The consciousness thread is a separate cord of Light that extends from the soul down to the soul extension's pineal gland in the brain. The antakarana, or rainbow bridge, is the cord of Light the initiate builds from the personality on Earth to the soul, and, eventually, after the fourth initiation, to the spiritual triad and monad.

I bring these cords or threads of energy to your attention for they play an important part in the death process. During normal sleep the consciousness thread is pulled up through the soul, which causes sleep or unconsciousness. The consciousness of the soul extension is hence focused on the inner plane.

During death both the consciousness thread and the silver cord are withdrawn. This causes the vitality to cease penetrating through the blood stream, heart, and brain. These threads will be discussed more fully later.

Cremation versus Burial

Djwhal Khul, in his writing, has most strongly recommended cremation over burial in the Earth. It is recommended that at least seventy-two hours be allowed before this is done to allow the soul extension to complete the bardo (after-death) experience. By the use of fire, all forms are dissolved. The more quickly the human vehicle is destroyed the more quickly its hold upon the withdrawing soul extension is broken. Some of the reasons for choosing cremation which Djwhal has given are that

1. It hastens the release of the subtle vehicles from the etheric body, thus it will occur within a few hours rather than a few days;
2. It purifies the astral plane;
3. It stops the downward-moving tendency of desire;
4. It prevents the poisoning of the Earth.

Djwhal Khul has called cemeteries unhealthy psychic spots. He has predicted that before too long, burial in the ground will be against the law, and cremation will be enforced as a health and sanitation measure. Just think about it. When we bury a diseased body that has cancer, let's say, in the Earth, we are poisoning the Earth with the cancer. If the body is cremated, the Earth Mother is saved this misery. We must never forget that the Earth is a living being, just as we are.

Some Other Interesting Thoughts about Death

One very interesting thought that I just learned about is that when a soul extension dies in, let's say the month governed by the sign of Sagittarius, when the soul comes back into incarnation in its next lifetime, if that is necessary, it will be born in the sign of Sagittarius. The soul extension picks up the thread of experience exactly where it left off.

One other interesting idea is to think about death in terms of our Planetary Logos, Sanat Kumara. He will also physically die when all the units, cells, or soul extensions in his physical body, which is the Earth, achieve liberation and ascension. He will die and move on to his next level of cosmic evolution.

Another important concept to understand in relationship to death is that of physical immortality since, in reality, we are God-beings and limitless. Death and old age are beliefs of the collective mind of this global consciousness we call Earth. Physical immortality is the belief that if we really unhooked ourselves from the mass negative hypnosis or belief that we had to age, we wouldn't. This statement becomes a total reality when we ascend.

A great deal of our aging and the breakdown of our physical bodies comes from our minds. The subconscious mind runs the physical body and does whatever it is programmed to do. It is as happy to create perfect health as it is to create cancer. It has the ability to create either one. The only problem is that it doesn't have the reasoning to choose on its own which one to create. This is the job of the conscious mind of the soul extension who is inhabiting the three lower vehicles.

On lower levels of initiation, physical immortality may not be a possibility, although aging more slowly is a most definite possibility. At higher levels of initiation, physical immortality is not only a possibility but a total reality.

Physical immortality is exactly what happens at the sixth initiation, which is ascension. The monad and/or spirit fully inhabits the four-body system (the physical, emotional, mental, and spiritual bodies). When this takes place all are transformed into Light.

An Ascended Master can live indefinitely on the physical plane. This is no idle fantasy. This is a total reality which each and every one of us will experience either in this lifetime or one soon to come. As mentioned in other chapters, Hermes, also known as Thoth, lived for over two thousand years in the same body, and Saint Germain did so for three hundred fifty years. When we ascend, if we choose to, we can remain on the earthly plane and continue our service.

The Science of the Bardo

The science of the bardo deals with the three days that follow the actual death experience of the physical body. This chapter may be one of the most important of this entire book. The science of death and dying is not understood in the Western world or even in most of the rest of the world, for that matter. Much of the information I am about to share with you comes from the Master Kuthumi and Djwhal Khul, most of it from the archives of the Spiritual Hierarchy dealing with the "Manual on Death."

Death, in reality, is life's greatest challenge and its greatest spiritual test and initiation. There is an art to dying, just as there is an art to living. Most people don't realize this and hence miss the greatest opportunity of their lives. Every soul extension, whether prepared or not, will face the transformation called death.

The First Phase of the Bardo

In the first phase of the bardo just prior to the moment of death, the soul extension will see before himself or herself the dazzling, blinding, clear Light of God. The soul extension will see this regardless of its level of spiritual evolution. It is of the utmost importance in this moment to allow oneself to merge with this Light. To merge with this Light is to allow oneself to merge with God.

The merging with this Light is very similar to that of ascension, at the sixth initiation, the only difference being that during ascension one merges with this Light while still in the physical body. During the bardo one merges without the physical body.

Remember what I said earlier about the famous statement of Krishna in the *Bhagavad-Gita*: where we go when we die is determined by the last thought in the mind before we die. We must let the last thought in our minds be only to merge with the Light, to merge with God. For some, this can be a death-bed salvation and liberation.

Remember, in the story of Jesus on the cross, the two other thieves who were also being crucified. One of the thieves was unrepentant. The other said that he deserved what he had gotten, but Jesus had no sin. Then Jesus said, "On this day, you will be with me in paradise." Even though he was a thief, in God's infinite mercy and forgiveness, He gave the thief the opportunity to return to paradise. The moment just prior to death is the ultimate moment of the soul extension's entire incarnation.

Now here comes the problem. The problem is that most people in the world are not educated about the art and science of death and dying and do not know about the clear Light of God; hence they miss this momentous opportunity. Why do they miss this opportunity? For many reasons. The first is that they don't know they are supposed to merge with the Light, so they don't do it. The second reason is preconceived religious notions or fear of the Light. Third, many people, when they die, are too drugged by medical doctors. Other people are so materialistically identified that God is the furthest thing from their minds. Other people are too preoccupied with their families or matters of estate and other assorted worries and concerns. There are probably infinite numbers of reasons, but the biggest one is lack of education about this most important science.

In the future this science will be taught in every school, church, temple, and hospital. Missing this opportunity is most unfortunate, for the soul extension will not get another opportunity until the completion of its next lifetime on Earth.

The merging with the Light can possibly mean liberation from the wheel of birth. God, like the story of the prodigal son, always welcomes us home, no matter what sins we have committed in our pasts.

The Second Phase of the Bardo

In the second phase of the bardo, if the soul extension has missed the opportunity to merge with the initial clear Light of God, it is given a second chance. This secondary Light is toned down a bit and not quite as bright, so may be more comfortable to some seekers. The merging with this Light still enables one to advance in spiritual development.

The Third Phase of the Bardo

In the third phase of the bardo, the first two opportunities have been missed and the soul extension usually spends a three-day period reviewing his/her life. This third phase has often been called the "valley of judgment." This is not a judgment in the ego sense of the word but rather, as one reviews one's life, it is seen with a spiritual clarity that the soul extension probably did not have prior to the bardo experience.

The reviewing process is not like just watching a movie; it is more like actually reliving the key moments of one's life. The unique thing about this experience is that one has the opportunity to reenact and improve upon missed lessons. This third phase of the bardo is a spiritual test, just as living on the Earth plane is a spiritual test. How one performs in the third-phase bardo test will determine what dimension and level one gravitates to after leaving the bardo experience.

God is not judging the personality; the soul extension is judging himself. The third phase of the bardo is the enforced realization of the significance of the soul extension's own misdeeds. In a sense one is seeing one's own dweller on the threshold. During the bardo, that which was desired most during life becomes active in a type of dream state that seems totally real.

The Mechanics of Death

As the death process begins, a number of things take place, not necessarily in this exact order:

1. The removal of the life thread, or silver cord;
2. The removal of the consciousness thread;
3. The exit of the three permanent atoms. They are the recording devices in the solar plexus, pineal gland, and heart. They are called the astral seed atom, the mental seed atom, and the heart seed atom;
4. The exit of the etheric, astral, and mental bodies;
5. The rising of the kundalini and the exit of the soul extension, or personality.

This last occurrence is absolutely fascinating in that the soul extension and kundalini exit from the chakra that the person focused on the most in that lifetime. The ideal would be to leave out of the crown chakra or at minimum, the third eye. However, the soul extensions, or personalities, that were very astrally focused in that lifetime will leave out of the solar plexus chakra. If they were love-focused they will leave out of the heart chakra. If they were will- and communication-focused in that lifetime they will leave out of the throat chakra. If they were focused on spiritual sight as their main interest they will leave out of the third eye. If they were God-focused they will leave out of the crown.

Which chakra the personality leaves out of will also affect the bardo experience and possibly which plane it will magnetize toward after the bardo.

This understanding is an integral part of the science and art of dying. In the following section I have listed some of the absolutely key points for insuring that the kundalini and soul extension exit through the higher chakras, preferably the crown. Everything that has happened in one's entire life is really a preparation for this moment.

Preparation for the Exact Moment of Death to Insure the Highest Spiritual Passing

1. The burning of an orange light in the room is important. The orange light stimulates the brain centers which causes the kundalini to be magnetized to flow upward.
2. Sandalwood is the incense of the first or the destroyer ray. The soul is in the process of deserting its habitation. It is essential that this be the only type of incense that is burned. The scent of sandalwood has the metaphysical effect of breaking down the old energies. This quality of energy is exactly what is needed at the time of death.
3. The dying person must be guided to merge with the clear

Light of God and to not focus on anything else.

4. Death-bed confession to a friend, family member, or priest is valuable. As much as possible of one's personal karma should be resolved to insure the highest passing.

5. The body should face eastward because the spiritual current is the strongest when facing in this direction. (This direction is also recommended for meditation.) The feet and the hands should be crossed.

6. Prayers should be made to God and Masters for help just prior to death.

7. All drugs should be avoided just prior to death. Drugs can cloud a person's consciousness to the point where he or she might possibly miss the opportunity to merge with the clear Light of God.

8. Make sure a will is complete and all affairs of estate are in order to ease the dying person's mind of material concerns. The will could include a statement to the effect that the person does not want to be forcibly kept alive by a machine.

9. If the last thought on a person's mind before death is of God, that is where she or he will go.

10. Loved ones should have been bidden farewell so the soul extension is ready for the next step on its journey.

11. Everybody should have been forgiven.

12. Spiritual music in the background is helpful.

13. The chanting of mantras or the repetition of the name of God by the person dying is very valuable. (See the chapter on words of power, mantras, repeating the name of God.) A tape recorder softly playing in the background is an option.

14. The playing of an actual bardo tape especially designed for the dying process is of particular value. The Mystery School of Astara (Earlyne Chaney) has one, and I am pretty sure the Rosicrucians do, also. A little research might reveal that many churches, spiritual groups and mystery schools have such a tape as well.

15. Guidance should be provided to the soul extension so that it will exit through the crown chakra when it leaves.

The Death Hormone

At the time of death the heart seed atom begins releasing into the blood stream atomic particles and images of one's approaching death. As the blood reaches the glands, it causes the glands to create a mysterious substance called a "death hormone." This is a natural way that God has created to prevent us from suffering in the physical body once the soul has chosen to die. This death hormone usually frees the physical body from pain so drugs in those final hours before death are not needed.

There are two drugs physicians have recommended that are reported to block pain but not to block the soul extension's experience of death in full consciousness. One is called the "Brompton cocktail" and the second one is Zeneperin. Obviously, a doctor should be consulted before these drugs are used.

Death is Very Similar to Birth

When a person is physically born, the physical body travels through the birth canal and out into the world. During death the soul extension and kundalini rise up through the sushumna (the chakra column, or silver cord) out through the "birth canal" opening which is the crown chakra. At the moment when the kundalini arrives at the crown chakra, it strikes the pituitary and pineal centers in the brain, which causes the third eye to open. (This is also what happens when the kundalini is raised during meditation.) It is at this moment that the first phase of the bardo is experienced, and the clear Light of God is seen and, it is hoped, merged with. It is usually the astral seed atom that leaves first, then the mental seed atom, and lastly the heart seed atom. When the emotional and mental seed atoms leave, one is no longer conscious on the Earth plane. When the heart seed atom leaves, the silver cord then breaks, releasing the soul extension completely. The heart seed atom will leave rather quickly in an initiate, but may remain in the physical body for three days in the case of a less evolved soul extension.

More Thoughts on the Second Phase of the Bardo

If the first phase of the bardo has been missed then there still is the opportunity to merge with the clear Light of God in the second phase of the bardo. There are some things that the soul extension needs to be aware of, however, so as not to get confused.

Since the kundalini has risen, the third eye will be open. This will cause a person to be very psychic and possibly to see all kinds of images and figures and possibly to hear music. The most important thing is to keep one's focus on achieving the highest level of God-realization possible and to be most concerned with merging with the Light.

Many of the images and people one may see, although seeming totally real, are really just thought forms. Dreams seem totally real; in a sense, the second phase of the bardo is a phase of dreaming.

The bardo experience is a spiritual test and an opportunity for greater spiritual initiation. More enlightened soul extensions may see Ascended Masters or angels or dieties of some kind. A less evolved soul extension who left out of the solar plexus chakra or even the second chakra may see images of naked women dancing. It is possible, in this bardo state, to interact with these images and become involved with them.

It is of the highest importance to avoid being seduced by "false gods," so to speak. What a person puts first in life is in reality the god that is worshiped. Anyone who truly wants liberation, initiation and God-realization, must not get seduced by any images or thought forms of real or imagined people other than God and the clear Light. As Jesus said, "Be ye faithful unto death, and I will give thee a crown of life."

Which Body One Is in After Death

After death, the physical body and the etheric body die. The average soul finds itself in its astral body. The level of evolution will determine whether it will gravitate to the lower, medium, or higher levels of the astral plane after the bardo experience.

Those soul extensions who are disciples and initiates and are more polarized and/or are identified with their mental bodies will find themselves in their mental bodies after death. This results in a higher-level passing. This dimension of reality dealing with the mental plane of reality has been called Devachan. Those initiates and Masters who are yet even more evolved will find themselves in their spiritual bodies—the Buddhic, atmic, or glorified Lightbody.

At each initiation one dies to another body and inhabits the one that is next most refined in vibration. It is at ascension that one inhabits the glorified Lightbody and hence operates on the monadic and logoic dimensions of reality. Did not Jesus say, "In my Father's house there are many mansions"?

The astral and mental bodies are actually released and let go of at these higher levels of mastery and initiation. The higher the dimension one magnetizes to, the higher level of heaven it is and the more beautiful and wonderful life is. This is why it is so important to strive to gain as much spiritual growth and realization of God as possible in the current lifetime and to understand the principles of the art of dying; that way, the highest possible passing can be achieved.

Death and the Withdrawal of Energy from the Four Bodies

In the process of death, the soul or higher self first withdraws the energy from the physical body. The second stage of death is the withdrawal of energy from the etheric body. The third stage is the withdrawal of energy from the astral body. The fourth stage is the withdrawal of life force from the mental body.

After the death hormone is released, a kind of psychic tremor occurs within the four-body system which loosens and begins breaking the connection between the nadis (the etheric nervous system) and the physical nervous system. The etheric body then leaves through the chosen point of exit. The etheric body gradually becomes dispersed and dies.

In the advanced initiate this dissolution of the vital body can occur very rapidly. It is a slower process in the less evolved soul extension. After the astral, mental, and spiritual bodies exit, the soul extension will find itself in the body that is appropriate for its level of spiritual evolution, as discussed earlier.

In cases of sudden death through accident, suicide, murder, unexpected heart attack, war, and so on, the process of death occurs much more rapidly.

8

Between Lifetimes

A saint is a sinner who never gave up

Paramahansa Yogananda

In the last chapter I went into great detail on the subject of death and dying and the science of the Bardo. This chapter deals with what happens after the three-day bardo experience—where people go and how they spend their time before deciding to incarnate again. This is a monumental subject. It is like trying to write a single chapter about Earth life. I could write a thousand books just on one city on Earth, let alone the entire Earth and material universe.

In this chapter I am going to attempt to give a glimpse of what goes on on the astral, mental, Buddhic, atmic, monadic, and logoic planes of consciousness after the death of a soul extension. Where a soul extension goes after death is determined by how it has lived throughout all its past lives, including the most recent past life, and how it dealt with its bardo experience. It will gravitate like a magnet to the plane that is most appropriate to its soul development.

Each of the above-mentioned dimensions of reality can also be divided loosely into subdivisions. The choices for a soul extension first entering into the spiritual world are:

1. A quick return to Earth life,
2. Hell regions,
3. Purgatory,
4. Lower astral plane,
5. Middle astral plane,
6. Upper astral plane,
7. Lower mental plane,

8. Upper mental plane,
9. Buddhic plane,
10. Atmic plane,
11. Monadic plane,
12. Logoic plane.

These twelve states of consciousness, or regions of consciousness, are where all soul extensions will go. There is no real dividing line between them like a line on a map. However, they can be loosely described in the following ways.

A Quick Return to Earth Life

For the average person who has attained even the smallest level of enlightenment, an immediate return to incarnation on the Earth would be unthinkable. The average person gravitates to the middle astral plane. Paramahansa Yogananda said that if a person has the slightest degree of a spiritual belief in life, his passing would be a pleasant one.

Occasionally, however, soul extensions of a not very evolved nature will choose to reincarnate almost immediately without taking much time for any kind of a review. Part of the reason for the creation of reincarnation as a system of spiritual growth by God and the Higher Forces was to allow soul extensions to have a resting and review period between lifetimes. It is usually only the lower impulses of Earth life that draw a soul back for immediate rebirth without some kind of review and assessment period. This path is not followed very often.

Hell Regions

There is a lot of confusion as to whether there is actually a hell region. The more fundamentalist religions say there is, and that if you don't accept Jesus Christ as your Savior you will burn there forever. Some metaphysical schools of thought say there is no hell region, it is just a state of mind.

In my opinion the truth is somewhere in the middle. Hell is most definitely a state of mind. It is also a location, but it is not as the fundamentalist religions describe it.

People are in hell when they are run by the negative ego, by material and astral desire, and hence are cut off from their own souls. There are plenty of people who are living in hell on Planet Earth right now. Hell, however, is not a place of eternal damnation. It is really just the very lowest level of the astral plane. Some have referred to it as outer darkness. Soul extensions such as Adolph Hitler have gravitated to this region of consciousness.

The hell region is like an extended third stage of the bardo, where the faces and forms people have wronged rise before them, accusing and reminding them of their cruelty. Soul extensions will stay there indefinitely until they begin to take responsibility for their actions, or until they can't take the torture of their own deluded consciousnesses any longer and cry out to God for help.

Each time they cry out to God for help, a guardian angel will come and offer some aid and assistance. Over time, such a soul extension will begin to emerge out of the darkness. There is no eternal damnation in God's plan or consciousness. God, in His infinite mercy and forgiveness, gives all soul extensions, no matter how deluded, a chance to return home. Hitler will have to meet all the negative karma he set in motion, however, for this is the law.

Purgatory

The term purgatory is also a term that has been confused by the fundamentalist religions. It has a very negative connotation and has been associated with hell, but this is not true. Purgatory is a region where soul extensions go who are not evil like those in the hell regions, but rather just misled and not educated properly on Earth. They are those who have been misled in their education through unsound religious practices, those who have been overtaken by bad habits, those who are atheists, those obsessed with material desire and attachments, those who have gone insane, and so forth. This would be a lower astral region. It is often very difficult to awaken such people to their spiritual path. There is a great mass of humanity living in this region of consciousness.

Earth Life as Compared to Life after Death

It must be understood now that life after death looks not much different from life on Earth. The astral and mental and higher planes have a whole thriving life with cities, beaches, mountains, homes, streets, concerts, libraries, social halls, clubs, churches, and temples just like we have on Earth.

Many soul extensions, when they pass over, do not even realize they are dead. They are in their astral bodies which look just like their previous physical bodies. The unique thing about life after death is that astral bodies travel with the mind. If they want to go to the beach, they just think "beach," and they are immediately there. There is no need to get in a car, train, or airplane to travel.

Very often when soul extensions pass over like this, they will think of the family they have just left and they will immediately be with a given family member. What they don't realize is that they are in another dimension, and their family members can't hear or see them. This can be quite confusing for people who haven't realized that they have died.

There are some soul extensions who are so attached to the material world that they don't allow themselves to go through the tunnel to the other side and are stuck on the earthly plane even though they are in their astral bodies. These are called "Earth-bound souls." They may continue to live in the same house they lived in before death. They don't realize that it is their own consciousness that is keeping them stuck on Earth and not allowing them to continue their spiritual evolution.

There are some soul extensions who are able to get hold of some vital force and play tricks on people who are still in earthly bodies. These have been referred to as "poltergeists." The Hollywood movie of this title played up this phenomenon in a rather demonic Hollywood fashion, but the concept was based on truth.

Many people, when they die, stick around and watch their own funerals before passing on to the astral plane. Those soul extensions of a more evolved nature will gravitate to the higher astral realms and possibly to the mental realm. Many soul extensions, when they pass over, sleep for a long time before awakening on the inner plane. This is especially true of those who have experienced lingering illness or uncontrollable grief and of those with a strong desire to continue life in the physical body.

When a person dies he or she is usually met by friends and relatives from Earth life who have passed on previously. There is usually a celebration and a resting period. Just as no one makes a person do anything in earthly life, no one makes a person do anything in the spiritual world either. But the average person begins to get bored with just having fun or resting and begins to get back in touch with the soul's urge to grow.

A process of examining one's previous life ensues, and the soul extension usually begins going to classes and seeing advanced counselors to determine how it may best use its time and find ways to be of service to others.

When a person passes to the other side he is at the same level of consciousness as he was when he died on the earthly plane. This is why people who channel need to make sure they are channeling someone who is truly more advanced than themselves.

A person in an astral body can move right through physical objects on the earthly plane as long as he believes he can. If he believes he can't, he can often run into a wall of his own thought creation. Readjusting to the laws of the astral and mental worlds takes some practice. Houses are built by thought as everything else is. A person can either build a house himself with his mind or have others build his house. A hammer and nails, or even a lumber yard, for that matter, are no longer necessary. It does take some ability and training to be able to focalize and train the mind.

The same is true with growing flowers. With the proper training of the mind, a person can manifest an entire garden. Nature on the other side is even more exquisite and beautiful than on this side. The higher one goes in dimensions of reality, the more exquisite the beauty. Astral bodies contain all the senses of the physical body and more. This is why, in dreams at night while asleep, one is able to see, hear, taste, touch, and smell, even though the physical body is sleeping.

Suicides

It is against universal law to take one's own life. There is no judgment from God for doing this. However, one does miss the opportunity to merge with the clear Light of God during the initial stages of the bardo. The soul extension that kills its body is just putting off meeting that same lesson until a future life and incarnation. The person who commits suicide is the exact same person with the same state of consciousness and the same lessons after he dies, so he really hasn't escaped very much by checking out.

The Process of Reincarnation

When a soul extension has spent the needed amount of time resting and reviewing the recent life, he will begin planning for his next incarnation. He chooses his parents, brothers and sisters, educational opportunities, male or female body, country, skin color, and the astrological configuration to be born into. This is all decided upon by the soul extension, the soul, and higher teachers and guides.

Very often there can be many soul extensions desiring one particular mother. When there is this type of conflict, there is a kind of heavenly computer that immediately decides which soul extension is best suited and best able to achieve its appointed goals.

The true trauma is not death, but birth. A free spirit has now come back into the confines of a physical body that is not even developed yet. Death is a piece of cake for anyone who has the slightest inkling of spiritual belief. A crib death occurs when the soul extension comes into the physical body and then changes his mind for some reason and returns back to spirit. The more obstacles the soul extension has chosen, the greater the opportunity for spiritual growth and to pay off karmic debts.

The Prebirth Bardo Experience

There is a second type of bardo experience that every soul extension goes through and this has to do with the period of time just prior to being reborn into a new physical body, before reincarnating. The first preparation before reincarnating is getting in contact with one's spirit guide or guardian angel. The spirit guide, in conjunction with one's own soul and/or higher self, helps in the process of choosing the appropriate parents. This choice, again, is determined by a combination of free choice and the karma that one is still working out from all past lives.

Once the appropriate parents have been chosen, and the cosmic computer and one's future mother have agreed upon it, there is a reviewing of all one's past lives. One examines, in a nonjudgmental way, all failures and successes in past missions to Earth.

Upon gaining this wisdom, one will then fully examine the future lifetime in detail, determining, with the help of guides, that lifetime's mission and goals, its specific lessons, soul qualities to be developed, and lower-self qualities to be overcome.

Upon completion of these processes, one's soul and guardian spirit will cause a deep, hypnotic sleep to come upon the soul extension. In this state the extension is projected downward into incarnation. During this sleep state, post-hypnotic suggestions are given to the subconscious mind to spark the consciousness to move in the right direction after one has grown up in the new physical body that one is about to enter.

Basically one enters the physical body through the crown chakra just after birth. The type of physical, astral, and mental bodies one has will be determined by the three permanent seed atoms which are, again, the recording devices of the physical, mental, and emotional karma from all past lives.

Genetics plays a part mainly in physical looks, and even they are affected by these seed atoms as one develops. These seed atoms attract the atoms and molecules that will make up one's new bodies, depending on vibrational level, karma, and soul evolution. The more one refines, purifies, and develops the bodies and seed atoms in this lifetime, the less one will have to do in the next lifetime.

Visiting Others

In the astral, mental, and higher planes one is able to visit others by just thinking about them. The only exception to this is if the other person is busy and does not want company. One is not able to invade another's space. It is kind of like this: if the person picks up the telephone that is ringing, then one is instantly there; if there is no answer, the other person doesn't want to be disturbed.

Temples of Wisdom

For more advanced soul extensions and disciples there is the opportunity to study in the great temples of wisdom. In these temples the secrets of the universe are taught. Advanced training in meditation, philosophy, prayer, spiritual psychology, and God-realization are disseminated. Each soul extension draws from it according to his or her needs.

Age

Each soul extension, when he passes over, is at the prime of life, regardless of at what age he has passed over. Whatever age he feels he looked his best is how he will look on the other side. There is no disease or illness or pain.

Very often, when a soul extension passes over, he begins to remember past lives, as well. Children who pass over are often met by angelic helpers who are specially trained to help children. In reality, all soul extensions are adult souls, and they are gradually and lovingly retrained to come back to this awareness.

Often people or children who died a traumatic death are taken to rehabilitation centers on the inner plane to help in their recovery. In the spiritual world there is no exchange or need for money. People help and serve others because that is the only way to grow, evolve, and find peace and God-realization.

Murder

When a murderer passes over to the spiritual world, he is most likely to gravitate to the lower astral plane. When a soul such as this finally begins to wake up, he is appalled at what he has done, the lifetime of opportunity he has wasted, and the karma he has created for himself.

In some cases the murderer will have an opportunity to meet the person he murdered. This can be an incredible moment of truth for the soul extension. More often than not, the person who was murdered has evolved and will forgive the murderer, for this is the only way to God-realization. This act of forgiveness may uplift the murderer to the point where he may gradually be able to take his rightful place in soul consciousness and begin his long road back to realizing God.

In other cases the murderer may cry out to God in anguish from the hell regions and spiritual guides will come and begin the slow process of rehabilitation and growth for this person.

Bad Habits

It is of the highest importance to conquer bad habits now instead of waiting until one passes on to the inner place. It is much harder to get rid of them there because there is no physical body or physical environment to practice with. Alcoholics who die often hang around drunks, enjoying the fumes and sensations and the bars they hang around in on the Earth plane.

Heavy smokers, drug addicts, and sex addicts all do the same. If one is a slave to one's astral and desire bodies on this side, one will be the same on the other side. Character flaws are carried to the other side, and there is no advancement until the flaws are released.

Spiritual growth on the inner plane is much slower than growth on the earthly world, the reason being that there are no physical temptations to overcome. This is why birth into a physical body is at a great premium. If people knew how hard it is to obtain one, they might not take the ones they are in for granted, as so many people do.

Drug addicts, when they die, will actually be looking for heroine and morphine on the other side, even though they no longer have a physical body. This not being a possibility, the spiritual guides will finally cause the person to fall into a deep sleep for a long time until he finally wakes up and asks God for help.

Often drug addicts are taken to a type of sanitarium or hospital drug clinic. This type of soul extension gradually regains his strength and determination never to let this happen again and then, when ready, reincarnates, determined to stay clear. Some of the energy of the bad habits does fade out over time because of lack of ability to feed the habit.

Traveling to Other Planets

Very often, soul extensions are given the choice of either reincarnating or traveling to other planets as a means of spiritual growth. All soul extensions do this at some point in their spiritual evolution between lives. The visiting of these planets is not done in a physical sense, but rather in a spiritual sense.

Each planet in this solar system embodies spiritually a certain quality of energy. If soul extensions, in their consciousnesses, have worked out the lessons that each planet embodies, then they have a very pleasant experience. If they haven't, they are in for a very hard time.

One of the softer planets is Venus, for it embodies the quality of perfect love. This has to do with love of God and love of brothers and sisters in God. When soul extensions project themselves into the atmosphere of Venus, they are quite comfortable if they have worked on their lessons in giving and receiving unconditional love. If they haven't, their consciousnesses will clash with the spiritual atmosphere and they will feel quite uncomfortable. A person who was not soul-connected might feel uncomfortable with the spiritual rapture of this type of love.

When a person projects himself to Mars he must learn to burn off any fiery temper and warlike manner. On Mars he pits himself against the dislikes he has for others, the dislikes people have for him, and how he deals with them. It is a test for all that is the worst in human nature. A soul extension must learn to withstand its harsh, simmering atmosphere and the buffeting and turmoil and learn to remain calm and even-minded. Then, remaining in this atmosphere helps to cleanse the soul of these harsh qualities of anger and war, preparing it for the next stage of consciousness. Going to Mars is not many soul extensions' favorite experience, for to clash in consciousness with this spiritual atmosphere can be quite uncomfortable.

On Uranus, a soul extension learns to form a truce and a peace treaty and not focus upon resentments, indignation, or righteous anger. By learning to put one's attention elsewhere, one allows these negative feelings to drain off from the spiritual body. By doing this the soul extension comes to realize that the negative energy that was being created was all created by his own faulty thinking.

Arthur Ford, in Ruth Montgomery's book *A World Beyond*, tells a story of going to Uranus after an incarnation in Florence where he died with savage resentment. On the inner plane he went in a rage to Uranus. He completely clashed with the atmosphere of Uranus and became helplessly entrapped in the planet's energy matrix in ever tightening bonds that were in reality his own rage being wrapped around him. Uranus torments us with deeds left undone.

Neptune has a more beneficent and tranquil energy. In the atmosphere of Neptune one may lay down his burden and feel totally devoid of cares. It is a resting state and also a testing ground. On Neptune one experiences a feeling of nothingness. Many soul extensions are tempted to stay there too long because of its peacefulness and the feeling of being devoid of cares and worries. This can be a seduction if not kept in the proper perspective.

Jupiter is rather a pleasant experience if one will become introspective and assess his short comings. Jupiter helps to build restraint and the determination to achieve spiritual mastery. It is an expansive energy that permits no ego. Whenever a soul extension brings a superiority complex to Jupiter, the atmosphere will remind the being that after pride cometh the fall. Here the ego will meet its much greater match.

Mercury is a state of consciousness in which one is able to review all of one's preceding past lives and determine the positive or negative direction of one's behaviors and actions. It is a good place to do some attitudinal healing of one's motives and direction and to gain the golden nuggets of wisdom from each incarnation. For some people, visiting Mercury can be a heavy lesson, for they are reviewing all their past mistakes from all their incarnations.

Pluto is a minor stop that deals with ways of improving one's determination to succeed. It is a type of reevaluation station on the spiritual path. Pluto is quite a wonderful experience for those who are truly on the path of God-realization. If a person thinks of any other thought except union with God on Pluto, then he finds Pluto disappearing.

Saturn represents a state of consciousness of spiritual upliftment. It is usually reserved by most soul extensions until the other planets have been visited first. It is a blissful atmosphere that is filled with the adoration of God. It also represents the ultimate testing of the soul.

The reason for going to these planets is to meet self. It serves as a leveling process to refine the consciousness. People go to rid themselves of ego so they can more quickly realize God.

An Astrological Understanding of Visiting the Planets between Lifetimes

A more concise understanding of the visiting of the planets can be understood by looking at the meaning of the planets from an astrological perspective. These qualities will be experienced and worked with during sojourns between lifetimes.

Sun	The quality of individuality and self-expression through the ego
	The most powerful influence in ordinary human life
Moon	Instinct and feelings
	The subconscious carrying the past
	The unfamiliar self
Mercury	The quality of mind that analyzes and categorizes
	The rational mind or intellect that governs the mentality and common sense
Venus	The personal values and quality of emotions, particularly love
	Magnetism and harmony
	The social personality, with an emphasis on beauty and grace
Mars	The quality of energy—physical, creative, and spiritual
	The active will
	Strength
Jupiter	The higher mind, higher knowing
	Idealism and philosophic conception through the quality of expansion
Saturn	The contraction and quality of limitation that balances the expansiveness of Jupiter
	The power of purity as disciplinarian
	The lesson-giver
Uranus	Abstract mental principles or the greater mind that shatters structure, depersonalizes, and brings revolution of ideas

Neptune	The collective level of feelings
	The visionary or mystical aspect, bringing a sense of oneness, governing both illusion/delusion and dreams/visions
Pluto	Reform through death/the underworld, bringing preparation for regeneration and rebirth

The Astral Plane

The astral plane and the astral body, from the point of view of the Ascended Master, are figments of the imagination created through the uncontrolled use of the creative imagination. When a soul extension has not stepped upon the path of discipleship, the astral plane is very real. As a disciple evolves, he experiences what is called metaphysically a second death. This is the ultimate death of the astral body and hence of the astral-plane involvement.

In actuality, this death process will ultimately occur with the mental, Buddhic, and atmic bodies also. As one evolves one keeps dying to another level and plane of consciousness and keeps being born to a higher one.

The Seven Levels of Initiation and Death

Where a person goes when he dies can also be indicated by his level of initiation. The soul extensions of the first and second initiations will probably go to the upper astral regions. The third degree initiate will go into the higher mental plane regions. The initiate of the fourth degree will go to the Buddhic plane of consciousness. The initiate of the fifth degree will go to the Atmic plane of consciousness. The Ascended Master lives on the monadic plane of consciousness. The seventh degree initiate operates on the logoic plane.

Death and Prayer

Soul extensions who pass on to the spiritual world are very much helped by the positive thoughts and prayers of those on Earth. John F. Kennedy, after he was assassinated, probably would have slept for a long time; however, the prayers of the people of the United States and the whole globe lifted him up in quite a beautiful manner.

In the reverse sense, people who grieve excessively and hold onto their loved ones in an attached and addicted manner are also affecting their loved ones, often causing them to not let go and continue their mission and further education in the spiritual world.

The Dying and Spirit Guides

Sometimes soul extensions will return to Earth after a short stint of training in the spiritual world to function as spirit guides for loved ones still on the Earth. It is also important to realize that during the sleep state people on Earth visit friends and relatives who have died. Some of the dreams we have about the dead are actually real-life visitations. The key point here is that death is an illusion. There is no such thing as death. There is just the transferring from dimension to dimension.

One interesting personal story: My grandfather died about ten years ago, and both my sister and I were very close to him. My sister, especially, had a unique and wonderfully special connection. She was quite devastated when he passed away.

About three years later I went to see a psychic for answers to some personal questions. The psychic volunteered, without my asking, that my sister was about to get married and have a child. This was, in actuality, quite true even though the psychic did not know my sister. The psychic went on to say that my grandfather wanted to be the soul extension to come into Judith's new baby! We were all blown away, but it made total sense.

Death and the Law of Attraction

The first thing a soul extension wakes up to after dying is a world of his own creation. If the person has lived selfishly then the people around him will be selfish. A person who has spent his life chasing material desires will wake up in poverty-stricken surroundings. A person's home and environment and clothing all will reflect the state of soul consciousness or lack thereof.

The Astral Plane and Freedom

Many people, when they pass on to the astral plane, don't realize the new-found freedom they have because of not being in a physical body. They often think that they still need food, money, automobiles, a job, and so on.

One example of this is eating food. Once we physically die, we no longer, in reality, need food. When people first die they often spend great amounts of time preparing and eating food, when in actuality, this is just an illusionary remnant of physical-plane existence.

Another example might be a person building a house for himself, stone by stone, nail by nail, when in actuality he or other people could build it in an incredibly short amount of time with the power of the mind.

Possession

On occasion, when a soul extension is totally earthbound, he or she will try to latch on to another person's physical body and consciousness. This can happen only if the person on Earth is very weak psychologically, an alcoholic, or on drugs.

It is essential to remember that if a person chooses to be a victim in life to his subconscious mind, negative ego, emotional body, mental body, physical body, or inner child, he can also be victimized by an evil or deluded spirit. Many people who commit crimes in our society today are being told to do so by dark and unconscious spirits.

If a soul extension stands in his personal power, in service of love and God, he has nothing to worry about in terms of this kind of thing. If one of these dark spirits ever does come around he can just immediately claim his power and, with tough love, tell it to leave, immediately saying some prayers, chanting a mantra, or repeating the name of God. These dark spirits can enter only a very weakened and low vibration.

Homes on the Astral and Mental Planes

Every soul extension is provided with a home on the astral plane. The fascinating thing about this process is that the homes reflect the characters of those who live in them. A person who is poor in spirit will have a house and environment that reflect his or her character.

The houses are somehow mystically created from the spiritual substance that the soul extension has achieved. The more one evolves, the more beautiful one's home and environment become. Every act of kindness, love, service to one's fellow man can be instantly seen in some improvement in his environment and home.

The homes in the spiritual world do not crumble or decay. Time has no effect on them. They will last as long as the beings living there need them. When the beings leave and the homes no longer have a purpose, they will disappear. As I have mentioned many times in this book, "As within, so without; as above, so below"; this is so clearly seen in operation here.

The same process I have mentioned with the homes also occurs in terms of the clothes people find themselves wearing. Everyone has clothes and people have a choice of wearing what they wore on Earth or wearing clothes more fitting to the city and district they live in there.

There is some magical process that occurs in which the more evolved a soul extension becomes, the more beautiful the quality of the clothes and fabrics he finds on his body. A person's stage of evolution can be immediately seen in both his clothing and his home. Again I am reminded of the biblical saying, "So what that you gain the whole world, but lose your own soul." In the spiritual world true riches are not money but spiritual realization, love, and service to one's fellow man.

Rejuvenating and Singing Waters

In the upper astral planes and above them there are what have been referred to as "singing waters." They are not really waters yet they flow like a stream on Earth. There is no sense of wetness when one submerges oneself in them, yet these waters bring an incredible sense of healing and of the recharging of one's energies.

Most homes in the middle astral planes and above have them. Maybe a better term would be a liquid Light shower. As this fountain of liquid Light rises and falls it also seems to emit actual musical notes.

Flowers

Old flowers never die, they just fade away if one wants to change a floral arrangement. There are no weeds or changing of seasons. The flowers will live as long as one needs them. There are also birds of all different kinds with plumage far more beautiful than birds have on Earth.

Cities

Cities in the middle and upper astral are more beautiful than on Earth because there is no need for cars, pollution, industry, or traffic. Cities are often planned and built outward from a hub, like a wheel. In one such city there is a Temple of the Seven Spheres in the center, which is a church of all faiths.

Masters come from the higher planes. There are buildings devoted to the arts, and there are halls of learning. The higher one goes the more beautiful the cities and outlying areas become. The outlying homes eventually become beautiful mansions and estates with landscapes beyond description. On these higher planes it is spiritual success, not material success, that is the goal of all soul extensions.

In one of the more advanced cities on the upper mental plane, the central building in the city is a gigantic, pure white pyramid that is seven stories high. The bottom floor is a social hall for the citizens of the city. The second floor of the pyramid is dedicated to symphonies, concerts, operas, drama, ballet, and motion pictures. The third floor is an art gallery depicting the finest art pieces of both Earth and the higher mental plane. The fourth floor is a museum of the finest sculptures in the world. The fifth floor is a library that defies anything found on Earth. The sixth floor is focused on teachings of meditation, psychic development, and self-realization. The seventh floor is the sacred hall of worship. Lectures also occur there, with great spiritual Masters from the higher planes coming to teach.

Every home on these higher planes has a private spiritual room for contemplation and meditation. Every person in these cities is both a teacher and a student. There is no dust, there are no unclean floors, dirty clothes, bugs, heating or cooling, or fear of burglary.

There is a Master soul who is in charge of each city and who is like a governor. This Master usually lives near the center or the hub of the city.

There is a large staff of people who work under him, just as he takes orders from a higher intelligence above himself.

There is also a bureau of vital statistics in each city that is governed by highly developed spiritual beings. This organization has all the spiritual information about each member of the society. They know the problems of the newly arrived and hence can appoint the appropriate guides and teachers. They also advise the appropriate members of the community when a loved one is about to arrive from Earth.

Each city has a hall of records which is also a networking center. The hall of records gives news flashes of important news coming from Earth, like Bill Clinton's having been elected president of the United States.

Many people will be happy to know that their pets can go with them to the afterlife in the upper planes for a period of time. At some point the animals will need to continue their evolution and possibly reincarnate back onto the earthly plane, just as people will if they haven't yet achieved liberation from the wheel of rebirth.

People in these different astral and mental cities often congregate according to their religious beliefs. Those of the Islamic faith, for example, might share a certain district. This is especially true when one first passes over. It is not uncommon in the astral plane to find whole communities still practicing their old religious rituals that they shared on Earth. These rituals still may include prejudices and distorted and twisted spiritual beliefs. As I have mentioned before, just because people are on the other side doesn't mean that they have attained any form of enlightenment.

These soul extensions know they have died but think their present life is a form of heavenly reward, when in actuality they don't know what they are missing. Teachers come from higher realms to enlighten them, but just as on Earth, people can be rather stubborn and fixed in their ways. God never forces the truth on anyone. He comes and sends His messengers when He is asked, for everyone has free choice.

What I have said here applies to all the religions, not just the example I gave of the Islamic faith. The higher one goes, the less this process of religious isolation takes place.

Life on the Lower Astral Planes

There is a type of borderland zone that is above the purgatory and hell regions and that actually superimposes itself on Earth life. Here are good people who have found what they consider to be contentment in areas close to the Earth. This particular area is like an astral counterpart that duplicates life on Earth, except it is still in the astral plane. Life is so much like that of Earth it is often hard to realize that one has even left. At some point these soul extensions begin to yearn for something better.

Methods of Communication

In the spiritual world people communicate telepathically, for the most part. Vocal speaking is not given up entirely, however. In the lower astral planes the art of telepathy does take some training, but comes quite easily to those on the upper astral and mental planes. On the higher planes people can instantly understand each other even if they speak different languages.

Occupations

The list is endless in terms of opportunities for study and development. Some people paint, play music, sculpt, build homes with their minds. There are gardeners, scientists, inventors, teachers, counselors, and healers.

Many scientists work to implant their ideas within the consciousnesses of people on Earth. Many counselors work with people who have just died, helping them to adjust. There are endless opportunities for both learning and serving others. People who want to travel can travel all through the world they live in or around the earthly world if they so choose.

Some counselors and teachers travel to the lower planes to help awaken their brothers and sisters to the higher life that is ahead of them. Writers on the higher planes can use a machine that actually writes the book as they talk into it. Researchers can read books in a way that is more like seeing a movie than actually reading. In these higher planes one can go into a library and review the history of Earth in pictorial movie form right before one's eyes.

Wouldn't it be fascinating to go into the library and actually look at what happened at the crucifixion and resurrection of Jesus Christ in 3-D movie form? Another possibility would be to go back and look at the civilizations of Atlantis and Lemuria in 3-D. All the information in the universe is available when we reach these higher levels of consciousness.

Some occupations do vanish from the spiritual world, such as lawyers, beauticians, morticians, and politicians. This sounds pretty good, doesn't it! Painters actually learn to paint with their minds instead of with a brush.

Charts that are used for teaching purposes unroll in a picture that surrounds the students like moving scenery. It reminds me of the exhibit at Disneyland in which there is a movie that surrounds people on all sides. This is even more realistic because it looks like the real thing, not just a movie. There are also classes for teaching those who wish to review their past incarnations.

Summation

This chapter has been a summation of just the tip of the iceberg of the things going on in the spiritual worlds after death. I hope that it has provided a taste, a flavor of some of the infinite possibilities and wonders that await each and every one of us as we evolve and realize our divinity.

The last point that I would like to make in this chapter is the incredible importance of staying focused and on target in terms of one's present life on Earth. As much growth as is possible should be made on the spiritual path now. There are so many temptations and seductions in the world in which we now live that can take us off our path.

I would challenge all readers to totally reclaim their power in this moment, and for the rest of their lives focus it on the only valid desire, which is liberation and God-realization. People can let go of all material desire, for it holds nothing for them. Let their focus always be on unconditional love, forgiveness, and service to humankind. If they do this, they will find themselves to be truly rich in their present lives and even wealthier in a more obvious way when they pass on to the spiritual world!

9

The Soul

*Matter is the vehicle for the expression of
the soul on this plane, just as on a higher
plane the soul serves as an expression
vehicle for spirit*

Djwhal Khul
as channeled by
Alice A. Bailey

There are many ways to define and understand the soul. To begin with,
one could say the soul is the intermediator between the incarnated
personality on Earth and the monad or spirit in heaven. For all one's
incarnations up to the fourth initiation, that the soul is the guide and
teacher for personality. It is at the fourth initiation that the soul body, or
causal body, is burned up in some mystical fashion and the soul returns up
into the monad, its purpose and function for all the many incarnations
throughout the ages over. The monad or spirit now becomes the guide and
teacher for the soul.

Matter is the vehicle for the expression of the soul on this plane, just
as on a higher plane the soul serves as an expression vehicle for spirit. The
soul is neither spirit nor matter, but is the relation between the two. It is
the middle link between God and form. The soul is another name for the
Christ aspect.

The soul is also the quality that every form manifests. It is that subtle
quality which distinguishes one element from another. In the plant kingdom it determines whether a flower or a carrot becomes manifest. The soul
serves the same function in the animal kingdom. Everything that has been
created has a soul. Man's self-conscious soul is in rapport with the souls of
all things. It is an integral part of the universal soul.

The new wave of psychology in the future will eventually succeed in proving the existence of the soul. It is tragic that in the field of psychology 98% of the forms of psychology now taught do not recognize in their teachings the existence of the soul or spirit. Carl Jung, Abraham Maslow, and Italian psychologist Robert Assagioli are the only ones I can think of off the top of my head who integrate this spiritual aspect. There is a new form of psychology called transpersonal psychology that will eventually revolutionize traditional psychology. (Read any book on soul psychology.)

The process of soul contact begins when the aspirant first receives soul impressions; then more and more the soul is allowed to take control of the threefold personality. Finally, full identification with the soul is achieved at the third initiation, which is called the soul merge.

Another very interesting aspect in respect to the soul or higher self is that the soul does not really pay much attention to the incarnated personality until the incarnated personality begins to pay attention to spiritual matters. The soul is busy with meditation and other matters of service. Once the incarnated personality does show interest, the soul begins to take a very active role. The same concept can be applied to the monad in respect to the soul. The monad does not pay much attention to the soul until after the third initiation when monadic contact begins to take place.

The following table gives a synopsis of the monad, soul, and personality.

Monad	Soul	Personality
Father	Son	Mother
Spirit	Consciousness	Body
Life	Ego	Form
Divine Self	Higher Self	Lower Self
Spirit	Individuality	Personal Self
The Point	The Triad	The Quaternary
Monad	Solar Angel	Lunar Lords

The soul could also be defined as the attractive force of the created physical universe that holds all forms together so that God can manifest and express Himself through them. The physical, emotional, and mental bodies are the garment of the soul. Later in the evolutionary process they will be garments for the spirit of the monad.

The soul can also be described as the conscious factor in all forms. The phenomenon of crib death occurs when the soul and/or new soul extension (incarnated personality) decides not to stay in the body and leaves. When the soul extension leaves, the physical body dies. It is the soul that feels, registers awareness, attracts and repels, and keeps all forms in activity.

The soul can be described as the child of the Father God and Mother Earth who has come onto the Earth in order to reveal the nature of God which is love. The soul can also be described as the principle of intelligence that inhabits all forms. In the human kingdom this manifests as mind and mental awareness which demonstrate the power to analyze, discriminate, and be self-conscious.

It is also very important to understand that the soul and higher self are in a state of evolution. I want to make it clear here that when I speak of soul I am differentiating it from the incarnated personality on Earth, which is called the soul extension. The soul or higher self is, on its level, in the process of learning and growing. Not all souls or higher selves are at the same level of evolution. One of the main ways a soul evolves is through what the twelve soul extensions do in their material incarnations.

I was under the false perception for a long time that the soul or higher self was perfect. It is not. It is way more evolved than the incarnated personalities, but it is evolving just as we are. The same can be said of the monad on its level. All monads are not at the same level of evolution. Some are more highly evolved than others. This, again, has to do to a great extent with what their twelve souls and one hundred forty-four soul extensions have done in all their incarnations. It is important to see here that we depend on our soul and monad for guidance, and the monad and soul also depend on us.

The work of the aspirant is to learn to see himself as a soul and later in the initiation process to see himself as the monad, spirit, or God in incarnation. To fully realize this it is essential to learn to see this in others as well. What one sees in others is just a mirror of what, in truth, one is seeing in oneself.

The Soul of Humanity

The signs that the soul of humanity is being awakened can be seen in the following occurrences in our society:

1.   The growth of societies, organizations, and mass movements for the betterment of humanity;

2.   The growing interest of the mass of people in the common welfare;

3.   The great interest in humanitarian and philanthropic effort;

4.   The mass effort to educate children of all nations at a level never before achieved;

5.   The growing recognition that the man on the street is becoming a factor in world affairs.

The Appropriation of the Bodies by the Soul

It is often not understood that the soul takes possession of the physical, emotional, and mental bodies in a slow and gradual process. The soul comes into the body just before birth or just after birth. Djwhal Khul has said that it is usually between the fourth and seventh years that the soul makes contact with the physical brain of the child. The soul appropriates or takes hold of the astral body between the ages of seven and fourteen. The soul appropriates the mental body between the ages of twenty-one and twenty-five. Contact with the soul usually occurs between the thirty-fifth and forty-second years. The potential to contact the monad begins after the soul has passed the third initiation. This process can be gently accelerated, however. This is how Djwhal has described it in the Alice Bailey material.

Old Souls

All monads or individualized spiritual sparks were created in the beginning at the same moment. In that sense, all monads are the same age. The term "old soul" refers to how many lifetimes a soul has had in earthly or material incarnation. Djwhal has said that the average soul, with all its twelve personalities or soul extensions, has had around two thousand lifetimes. Older souls have had two thousand five hundred or even three thousand lifetimes.

Characteristics of the Soul

Unconditional love, inclusiveness, joy, happiness, the ability to be alone, Divine indifference, impersonality, detachment, freedom, serenity, inner calm, responsibility, wisdom, and intuition are all characteristics of the soul.

These are the qualities described by Djwhal Khul in the Alice Bailey material. Djwhal makes another very interesting differentiation among happiness, joy, and bliss. He says that happiness is a personality reaction. Joy is a quality of the soul. Bliss is a quality of at-one-ment with the monad.

The Light of the Soul

The attention of a Master is attracted to the incarnated personality by the brilliance of the indwelling Light of that individual. When the Light has reached a certain intensity, the aura a certain hue, and the overall vibration a specific rate and measure, the Master comes. The choice of the pupil by the Master is governed by past karma, past associations, and the ray on which the incarnated personality is found.

The Soul and the Hierarchy

The Spiritual Hierarchy is basically the world of souls. In respect to the soul there are three types of hierarchical workers.

   1.   Souls: Those initiates who have taken the fourth initiation and in whom the soul body or causal body has been destroyed. They are the custodians of the Plan.

   2.   Soul-infused personalities: Those disciples and initiates of the

first three initiations through whom the souls work in the carrying out of the Plan.

3. Intelligent aspirants: Those who are not yet soul-infused personalities but who recognize the Divine Plan and seek the welfare of their fellow man.

Early Stages in the Evolution of Incarnated Personalities

The earliest state of evolution consists in the opening of the line of communication from the personality to the soul so that the soul may be able to assert itself increasingly through the personality. As the soul extension develops, finally the soul is able to entirely dominate and control the personality so that it will have no separate thought or will.

The absolutely untrained person on Earth has practically no communication with the soul. Anyone who ever watches the news or sees people in the world must wonder how they are able to do the awful things they do. This is partly why. They have no connection to the soul, hence they are run by the personality or negative ego. They are cut off from intuition, conscience, and the will to do good and to love, which the soul embodies. Just as it is the evolution of the personality to learn to express only the soul, so it is the evolution of the soul to express only the monad. An undeveloped soul extension, or incarnated personality, forgets about this connection with his soul and feels quite independent and separate.

The soul involves itself in a whirlwind of activity on its own plane. If one wishes to attract its attention one must demonstrate to the soul that he can make the personality useful to it. The soul knows that certain parts of its evolution can be achieved only through its personalities on Earth. If one looks at many of the personalities here on Earth one sees soul extensions whose astral bodies are filled with negative emotions and whose mental bodies are interested in money, power, hedonism, and television. It is not difficult to see that the soul might not be that interested and is focusing on another one of its eleven other soul extensions.

The soul on its plane is so expansive it is not possible for it to fully manifest through one of its soul extensions. In the same respect, the monad on its plane is not able to fully manifest through one soul.

The Spiritual Triad

The spiritual triad is the threefold spirit through which the monad expresses. The threefold spirit includes spiritual will, intuition, and higher mind. The monad expresses through these principles, just as the soul expresses through the lower spiritual triad of the threefold personality, the physical, emotional, and mental bodies.

The Soul and the Monad

The disciple needs to learn to control and train his mind to receive communications from three sources:

1.   The ordinary material world;

2.   The soul, thus consciously becoming a disciple, a worker in one of the Master's ashrams;

3.   The spiritual triad (spiritual will, intuition, and higher mind) which acts as an intermediary between the monad and the brain of the incarnated personality on Earth. This takes place because at the third initiation the personality and soul have merged, so guidance can now come from the spiritual triad and monad. Duality has taken the place of triplicity, triplicity being the former soul extension, soul, and monad. The soul and soul extension have fused together, so a higher level of guidance is now possible.

The Soul and the Antakarana

At the fourth initiation the antakarana, or bridge for the line of communication, has been built from the incarnated personality through the causal or soul body and up to the spiritual triad and monad. The antakarana having been built, the causal body burns up and the soul merges back into the monad. (See Chapter 5 to understand the antakarana and how to build it.)

The Soul's Relationships on Its Own Plane of Existence

The soul on its own plane realizes consciously its relationship to the Master and seeks to send this awareness to the incarnated personality. The soul is not impeded by time and space. On the soul level, time and space do not exist in the same linear sense they do here on Earth. The soul on its own plane also has relationships with other souls, usually of the same ray. (The understanding of the rays is discussed in great detail in Chapter 10.) The soul works in a group formation and consciousness. The group consciousness is something that the soul would ultimately like to see exist on this earthly plane also. This will happen when the majority of soul extensions on this plane take their third initiations.

From the angle of the Master it is the ability of the soul to control its instrument, the incarnated personality, and to work through it that is of most interest.

The Soul and the Master's Ashram

Many of the Ascended Masters have ashrams on the inner plane. An ashram is an international group composed of souls who are both in and out of incarnation. The ashram is a combination of initiates of various degrees and of accepted disciples. The Master also has a group that is different from the ashram. Many people can be found in the Master's group, but those in the ashram are chosen out of the group. In the ashram only that is to be found which is of the soul. Nothing of the personality is allowed to enter. (By this I mean nothing of the lower self.)

So an ashram is basically formed of those who, through their devotion to the path, have worked their way out of the group into the inner center which is the ashram. They are groups of souls gathered together for the purpose of service.

The key for the disciple is to make his or her life of such a nature that it furthers the purposes of the group, enhances the group strength, and brings closer the objective for which the group was formed. The disciple is also trying to make himself useful in carrying out the Master's plans.

The Soul and Divine Will

When the attractive power of matter dies and desire is overcome, then the attracting power of the soul becomes dominant. Instead of the individual self being of importance, now the group goals and endeavors become most important. The soul attraction also now coincides with the attraction to the Spiritual Hierarchy and the Ascended Masters' work. When this shift or polarization has taken place, which occurrence I am sure all who are reading this book can relate to, the dynamic pull of the "will aspect of Divinity" can be felt and comes into play.

The Soul and the Dark Forces

Dark brothers are souls who are confused and have chosen the left-hand path instead of the right-hand path, the left-hand path being that of serving self instead of serving God and the unity of all existence. The dark brother (needless to say, I am not talking about race here) sees other people not as fellow souls or gods, but rather as objects to exploit and use for his own selfish gain. He doesn't care about the suffering or hurt he may cause. The job of all others is to protect themselves from these confused souls, both on this material plane and on the inner plane. The laws of karma will catch up with them ultimately and the pain and suffering they will go through will make them seek truth once again at a later time.

One other very interesting fact about the dark brothers is that if an incarnated personality carries on in this deluded way for too long, he can bring upon himself a destruction that is final for what Djwhal Khul has called the entire manvantara, or cycle. Somehow in the process the "physical permanent atom" becomes totally destroyed and the lost soul loses touch with the higher self for eons of time.

Alignment of the Soul with the Personality

The ideal for the incarnated personality is to align the three vehicles or bodies with the higher self or soul. When this alignment is achieved, the mental body will be calm and peaceful, the emotional body stable, even, and joyous, and the physical body healthy, with good, even energy throughout the day.

A higher level of alignment also exists for the disciple. It has to do with

    1.   the alignment of the soul and personality with the appropriate ashram, resulting in a conscious relationship with the Master of the ashram;

    2.   the alignment of the initiate of a higher degree with the spiritual triad, which results in conscious recognition of monadic energy;

    3.   the alignment of all the chakras in the etheric body of the disciple.

The Soul's Path of Progress

There is no limit to the amount of growth an incarnated personality can achieve in a given lifetime. It is all up to one's ability to stay focused and disciplined, totally committed to the spiritual ideal. Very often, soul extensions who make great progress are doing so because of what has been already gained in previous lifetimes.

Even though growth seems super-accelerated for some, even they are just preparing for a new period of slow, careful, painstaking growth. This slow and often laborious effort is the consistent method of all who evolve on the spiritual path, no matter what their levels of spiritual evolution. There are no shortcuts. Moment by moment, hour by hour, day by day, one's goals are achieved. It is very often the small things—a smile, a hug, a helpful hand—that are the most significant.

The Soul and Discipleship

There are three main objectives to which the disciple must be pledged above all else:

    1.   To serve humanity;

    2.   To cooperate with the Plan of the Great Ones;

    3.   To develop the powers of the soul and become obedient to the soul, not to the dictates of the three lower bodies and the negative ego.

Spiritual Impressions from the Inner Plane

There are four sources of spiritual impressions of which the spiritual aspirant and disciple must be cognizant:

1. Impressions from the disciple's own soul;
2. Impressions from the ashram with which the disciple is affiliated;
˜ 3. Impressions directly from the Master;
4. Impressions from the spiritual triad and monad via the antakarana.

The Soul and the Sutratma

The sutratma is the silver cord that extends down from the monad, through the soul, and into the incarnated soul extension on Earth. The soul dominates its form through the medium of the sutratma, also known as the life thread. The antakarana is a cord of energy that those on Earth have to build to the soul, spiritual triad, and monad.

The sutratma is there from birth. It is the line of energy back to the Father in heaven. It is the spiritual pipe, so to speak, that sends us our energy and keeps us alive. This life thread vitalizes our physical, emotional, and mental bodies and sets up a communication with our brains.

10

Esoteric Psychology and the Science of the Twelve Rays

Know Thyself

Carved above the gate of the Oracle of Delphi

The seven rays are the first differentiation of God in manifestation and they provide the entire field of His expression in manifested form. The seven rays are embodiments of seven types of force which demonstrate seven qualities of God. These seven qualities have a sevenfold effect upon matter and form in all parts of God's infinite universe. The seven great rays are embodiments of seven great beings. These are:

1. The Lord of Power or Will
2. The Lord of Love/Wisdom
3. The Lord of Active Intelligence
4. The Lord of Harmony, Beauty, and Art
5. The Lord of Concrete Knowledge and Science
6. The Lord of Devotion and Idealism
7. The Lord of Ceremonial Order or Magic

The rays are, in truth, quite a complex subject and there are many ways of and frames of reference for understanding them. The study of the rays is almost an unknown science in our world. I am a serious student of the field and have been involved with just about every religion and mystery school on the planet, but it was only when I read the Alice Bailey books on esoteric psychology that the profound significance of the rays came to my awareness. The rays are even more important than astrology, yet what I am going to share with you in this chapter is not talked about by those involved in 99.99% of the spiritual paths on Earth. The understanding of the rays may be the single most important spiritual science for understanding oneself and the world as a whole. It is these rays that govern all of creation.

The Rays of Aspect and the Rays of Attribute

Djwhal Khul, in his writings, has divided the seven great rays into two categories called the rays of aspect and the rays of attribute.

Rays of Aspect:

1st ray of Power, Will or Purpose
2nd ray of Love/Wisdom
3rd ray of Active, Creative Intelligence

Rays of Attribute:

4th ray of Harmony through Conflict, Beauty, or Art
5th ray of Concrete Science or Knowledge
6th ray of Abstract Idealism or Devotion
7th ray of Ceremonial Order, Magic, Ritual, or Organization

The Ray of Structure of Every Incarnated Human Being

Every soul extension who incarnates onto the Earth plane is made up of six rays. Everyone has a separate ray for the monad, soul, personality, mind, emotions, and physical body.

The monadic ray and soul ray are basically the same throughout all of the person's incarnations. The rest of the rays can change from lifetime to lifetime. Every incarnated personality is found upon one of these seven rays. Soul extensions with soul rays found upon the fourth, fifth, sixth, and seventh rays must blend with the first three major rays after they pass the third initiation. However, the monadic ray of every incarnated personality is one of the first three rays.

In the unevolved person, the rays of the physical, emotional, and mental bodies dominate. As the person develops a more self-actualized personality, then the personality ray becomes dominant and the three body rays become subordinated to it.

As the person continues to evolve he begins to become polarized in the soul. A battle occurs between the lower self and the higher self, or between personality ray and the soul ray. As the soul ray begins to dominate and win this battle, and the disciple begins to gain self-mastery over the personality, then the personality ray becomes subordinate to the soul ray.

The process continues until, after the third initiation, the monadic ray begins to pour in. As the disciple learns to become polarized in the monad, the soul ray becomes subordinate to the monadic ray.

Now each of the seven groups of souls is responsive to the ray of the Planetary Logos (Sanat Kumara) who is on the third ray. In truth, we are all on a subray of his ray, just as he is on a subray of the Solar Logos

(Helios) who is on the second ray. Helios is on a subray of the Galactic Logos, and the Galactic Logos is on a subray of the Universal Logos (Melchizedek). This process continues all the way back to the Godhead. All of creation is on a subray of the Godhead. Each level is stepped down in hierarchical fashion.

People who are on the same ray tend to see things in a similar fashion. This can change, however, depending on which ray and initiation they are identified with. Two people during college may both have fourth ray personalities and hence have a lot in common. This could change as they open to their soul rays if they are on different soul rays. This is not to say that people of different rays don't get along. There are a lot of factors that play into this. The rays do have a great effect and influence, however.

People who have a two, four, or six ray structure usually tend to be more introverted and spiritually focused. People with a one, three, five, or seven ray structure tend to be more extroverted and focused on form and the concrete world level. When a soul extension is two-thirds along his or her spiritual path, the soul ray begins to govern the personality. It is to the benefit of every aspirant and disciple to try to come to an understanding of the six rays that make up his spiritual constitution.

The personality ray finds its major activity in the physical body. The soul ray finds its specific influence in the astral body. The monadic ray finds its specific influence in the mental body. The personality ray causes the attitude of separateness. The soul ray facilitates the attitude of group consciousness and detachment from the form side of life. The monadic ray can be felt only after the third initiation and brings in the will aspect of the Creator.

These rays have an incredibly powerful effect on every human being's life. The physical body ray greatly determines the features of the physical body. The rays determine the quality of the emotional body and greatly affect the nature of the mind.

The rays predispose every person to certain strengths and certain weaknesses. Certain attitudes of mind are easy for one ray type and extremely difficult for another. This is why the incarnating personality changes ray structure from life to life until all qualities are developed and demonstrated.

Given these facts, a knowledge of the rays is absolutely essential to knowing thyself, and such knowledge is also essential to the entire field of psychology. What is absolutely mind-blowing is that in the field of psychology on the Earth today, there is absolutely no understanding of the rays. That is one of the many reasons psychology is not very effective at this time.

The reason the rays are not understood is that there is almost no understanding of the soul. Of all the forms of psychology taught in schools and practiced by licensed professionals, 98% are separated and cut off from soul and monadic levels of consciousness. The new wave of the future will be the study of transpersonal, or spiritual, psychology. (I would recommend reading my book on this subject called *Soul Psychology*.)

It is not only people who have rays. Countries, cities, groups, and organizations also have rays. Usually, however, these are limited to just a soul ray and a personality ray. Most of the countries on Earth, for example, are still operating out of their personality rays.

When the soul ray is able to focus fully through an individual then the disciple is ready to take the third initiation. The personality ray is then occultly extinguished. The dweller on the threshold has been subjugated and mastered. It is the soul that chooses the rays for incarnated soul extensions, or personalities, each lifetime.

Each ray works primarily through one chakra. A knowledge of ray structure provides great insight in one's character, strengths, and weaknesses, in the same way an accurate astrological horoscope can. The study of esoteric psychology and the science of the twelve rays is as important as the study of astrology. In truth, it may even be more important, given the fact that the rays, on a more cosmic level, even affect, influence, and predate the creation of stars and constellations throughout God's infinite universe.

It is important to understand that a person can utilize all the rays whether he has them in his ray structure or not. One can call forth any of the twelve rays and their qualities for personal and planetary service.

An Analysis of the Twelve Rays

The First Ray of Will or Power

The first ray is an energy of will, power, and drive. It is connected with vitality, initiative, thrust. It breaks down the old and makes way for the new. It is a very dynamic energy. The color of this ray is red. Those upon this ray have a strong personal power that can be used for good or evil.

The first ray people will always come to the front in whatever line they are working upon. They will be at the head of their professions. They are born leaders. The first ray people who are not tempered by the love/wisdom of the second ray can be extremely cruel and hard.

The literary works of first ray people would be strong and powerful, but these people often care little for style or finish in their works. Examples of this type of person would be Luther, Carlyle, Walt Whitman. The approach to the spiritual path is through sheer force of will.

The first ray people make excellent commanders and chiefs. Examples are Napoleon, Winston Churchill, General George Patton, General Douglas MacArthur, Indira Gandhi, Christopher Columbus (Saint Germain).

Many outstanding sports figures are of this type. Usually after the first ray makes its thrust, the other rays then take over. The first ray, in a sense, is connected with the energy of Aries. The first ray person begins the projects and then has other things to do.

The first ray is helpful when one is traumatized by his emotions; he can use the will energy to pull himself out of it. Wearing clothing of red can attune one to this energy. This is a very powerful ray and must be used with caution and in the appropriate amount.

Most people need a much smaller amount of first ray invocation than that of the other rays. The color red will intensify whatever condition already exists. The first ray will create an almost instant effect. All one usually needs is a little bit.

The negative manifestations of the first ray would be seen in the example of wars on the planet. The first and second rays would form a good team to counteract such negative manifestations. A person with a first ray mind would be very direct and intensely focused. A first ray emotional body would be very powerful, with intense emotional reactions.

A first ray body tends to be tall, strongly built, and large-boned. Military men and policemen are often first ray. A first ray body wills its way through anything. He would make a good football player. A first ray personality might be a little harsh.

Other famous people who were of the first ray were Hercules, Rama, Mao Tse Tung, Abraham Lincoln, and Janet McClure (founder of The Tibetan Foundation).

The special virtues of the first ray are strength, courage, steadfastness, truthfulness, fearlessness, powerful ruling, capacity to grasp great questions in a large-minded way, and ability to handle people. The vices of this ray are pride, ambition, willfulness, hardness, arrogance, desire to control others, obstinacy, and anger. The virtues to be acquired are tenderness, humility, sympathy, tolerance, and patience.

The Second Ray of Love/Wisdom

This ray embodies the Divine quality of love and desire for pure knowledge and absolute truth. The color it embodies is a deep intense blue. People on this ray are very loving, allowing, considerate, friendly, and responsible.

The second ray soul is usually a teacher or possibly an architect because of this ray's strong conceptual ability. This type of person has great tact and foresight. He would make an excellent ambassador, school teacher, or head of a college. This type of person has the ability to impress the true view of things on other people and make them see things as he does.

The second ray type would make an excellent artist as long as he would seek to teach art. This ray type is highly intuitive. He is not rash or impulsive. If anything, he might be slow to act.

The method of approach to the path would come through close and earnest study of the teachings until they become so much a part of the person that they are no longer intellectual knowledge but rather a rule of spiritual living.

A second ray mind would be very receptive. This type is not that common, however. A second ray emotional body would be very peaceful, stable, and mature. A second ray physical body is rather unusual, although more will be incarnating in the future. These types of physical bodies are usually small and delicately made. They are very refined and sensitive.

Every ray type has a higher and lower aspect. The lower type of second ray person would be trying to acquire knowledge for selfish purposes, and not for selfless service of humankind. The lower self would lead them into suspicion, coldness, and hardness. They are often over-absorbed in study and have contempt for the mental limitations of others.

Their special virtues are calmness, strength, patience, endurance, love of truth, faithfulness, intuition, clear intelligence, and serene temper. Their virtues to be acquired are love, compassion, unselfishness, and energy.

It is also to be remembered that all souls incarnated on this planet are connected with the second ray because we live in a second ray solar system. The second ray is the ray our Solar Logos, Helios, operates on. Other solar systems are on different rays. All the other rays are subrays of this great cosmic second ray.

The Lord Maitreya and the Buddha were both on the second ray, as were most of the great world teachers. Djwhal Khul is a second ray teacher as is his teacher, the Master Kuthumi.

The Third Ray of Active Intelligence

This is the ray of the abstract thinker, the philosopher and metaphysician. The people on this ray would be highly imaginative and excellent at higher mathematics. They are idealistic dreamers and theorists. They are able to see every side of a question in a very clear manner.

One of their main characteristics is their perseverance. They have an ability to hold on to something and not let go until completion, even if it should take a whole lifetime. Members of the third department are the organizers of the Hierarchy. They are the souls both in and out of incarnations who "get things done."

Their method of approach to the spiritual path is through deep philosophic and metaphysical work until realization is reached. Thomas Edison was one outstanding example of a third ray type. Others were

Eleanor Roosevelt, Paramahansa Yogananda, and Ernest Holmes.

Third ray types are very often perfectionists. They may ignore everything but their pet projects which they will do with great precision. They tend to be independent. On the negative side, they have the potential to try to make everyone partake of their own perceptions.

They are very focused, concrete, logical, clear-minded, and organized; however, they are not always aware of consequences. One of their great abilities is to be able to hold on to the thought of perfection and true divinity and not veer from this course until it is realized.

The special virtues of the third ray person are wide views on all abstract questions, sincerity of purpose, clear intellect, capacity for concentration on philosophic studies, patience, caution, and an absence of the tendency to worry over small matters. The vices of this ray are intellectual pride, coldness, isolation, inaccuracy in details, absent-mindedness, obstinacy, selfishness, and too much criticism of others. The virtues to be acquired are sympathy, tolerance, devotion, accuracy, energy, and common sense.

The Fourth Ray of Harmony through Conflict

This ray has been called the "ray of struggle." As with all the rays it has a lower and higher aspect. When this ray is governed by the lower self, then conflict and havoc ensue. When governed by the higher self, harmony occurs.

The fourth ray is connected with the emotional body and the solar plexus chakra. It is also very connected with physical existence. The fourth ray has a very reflective quality which, in a sense, forces one to look at what one hasn't finished or completed yet. In this sense it reacts rather like a mirror.

The color of this ray is emerald green. This ray is also very connected with the arts. Some of the most beautiful art, music, and sculpture on this planet has been created by people of the higher aspect of this ray. Mozart, Leonardo da Vinci, Richard Strauss, and Rubens all had a great deal of fourth ray energy. Mozart, believe it or not, had a soul, personality, mind, and emotional body that were all of the fourth ray in that incarnation.

The danger of this ray is the possibility of getting too entangled in the emotional body, which most people have tended to do. This us why the fourth ray works well with the first ray of will or with the third or fifth ray, which are more mental in nature. The fourth ray type of person needs these for balance.

Djwhal Khul has also told us that this ray seems to have an equal balance of the qualities described in the East as rajas (activity) and tamas (inertia). The average person lives in mortal combat between these two energies until soul infusion and soul merger are achieved. Examples of this type are Vincent Van Gogh and Pablo Picasso. They had great artistic ability but weren't balanced with the mental, emotional, and soul aspects, which caused greatness on one level but great torment on another.

The fourth ray person often lives on an emotional roller coaster until evenness of mind and equality can be achieved. The study of the *Bhagavad-Gita* would provide a good teaching model for the fourth ray person.

Since the fourth ray people are so connected to the Earth and aesthetics, they often have a hard time meditating and getting up into the spiritual area. Fourth ray types are often very focused on a lot of physical activities such as hiking, mountain climbing, horseback riding, driving of vehicles, and relating to animals. This is fine as long as it is balanced with the proper heavenly and spiritual integration.

One of the dangers of fourth ray people is that they can tend to be manipulative. They often like everyone to experience the same focus in life that they have. It is essential for the fourth ray types to dedicate their lives to their spiritual path. If not, they tend to be manic-depressive. The method of approach on the spiritual path will be through self-control which leads to evenness of mind and equilibrium of the warring forces of their nature.

The special virtues of the fourth ray type are strong affections, sympathy, physical courage, generosity, and quickness of intellect and perception. The vices of the fourth ray are self-centeredness, worrying, inaccuracy, lack of moral courage, strong passions, indolence, and extravagance. The virtues to be acquired are serenity, confidence, self-control, purity, unselfishness, accuracy, and mental and moral balance.

The Fifth Ray of the Concrete Mind

This is the ray of science and research. The person of this ray has a keen intellect and likes great accuracy of detail. This ray is connected with the mental body. Many people, at this time in our history, are stuck in the mental body and have not allowed themselves to open to their intuition and soul body. This is a danger of this ray type.

Being stuck in the mind prevents a person from being interested in esoteric studies. Once the fifth ray person opens to the spiritual path and begins to study in this area, he is able to understand it much better than some of the other ray types.

The fifth ray is very important on the Earth at this time. People who are more emotionally based tend to be cut off from fifth ray energy. They have not learned how to use this energy to balance their emotional bodies. On the other side of the coin, the fifth ray type must learn how to shut off the mind at times, also. For this reason meditation is extremely important for this type. The color of this ray is orange.

The fifth ray person is extremely truthful and full of knowledge and facts. The danger here is of becoming pedantic and too focused on the most trivial details. It is the ray of the great chemist, the practical electrician, the first-rate engineer, the great surgeon, or the head of some special technical department.

An artist on this ray is very rare, as the energy here is so scientific. The fifth ray approach to the spiritual path is through scientific research pushed to ultimate conclusions. This type of person can thrust to the very heart of a matter.

A fifth ray mind can probe any learning experience and dig out the very essence of it. The third ray person has a very excellent mind, but does not have the ability to pierce into the very essence and core of things as the fifth ray person can.

Wherever there is a lot of fifth ray energy there will be a lot of New Age churches. These churches are connected with the "new thought" movement which is a strength of the fifth ray. The hope of the Hierarchy is that the tremendous amount of fifth ray energy on the planet now will lead people into the core and essence of things, which is ultimately the soul and spirit. In this sense the fifth ray is helping to focus the New Age. The fifth ray puts the focus of the mind there, and the seventh ray and higher rays ground it and cause the activity.

Another one of the qualities in the pattern of the fifth ray that many people are not aware of is unconditional love. This is because the fifth ray accesses the higher mental body which is the realm of the soul. The fifth ray helps in the process of finding balance and integration within the psyche.

The special virtues of the fifth ray include the making of strictly accurate statements, justice, common sense, uprightness, independence, and keen intellect. The vices of the fifth ray are harsh criticism, narrowness, arrogance, unforgiving temper, lack of sympathy and reverence, and prejudice. The virtues to be acquired are reverence, devotion, sympathy, love, and wide-mindedness.

The Sixth Ray of Devotion

The sixth ray is the ray of devotion and idealism. The person on this ray is full of religious fervor. Everything is seen as either perfect or intolerable. It is an emotionally based ray that is also very connected with the subconscious mind. Its color is indigo. It has the ability to help individuals go beyond a mere Earth-oriented focus.

This type of person also needs to have a personal god or incarnation of a deity to adore and devote himself to. The higher type of person on this ray becomes a saint. The lower, personality-based type of person becomes the worst kind of bigot and fanatic. The fundamentalist Christians are very connected to this ray. All religious wars and crusades have originated from the misuse of this ray.

The person on this ray is often very gentle but can move into intense anger and wrathfulness quite easily. He will give up his life for his chosen ideal of devotion. This type of person, as a soldier, would hate fighting except if roused to battle over some great cause he believed in; if this is the case he will fight like a man possessed. The sixth ray type makes a great preacher and orator but a poor statesperson and businessperson.

The sixth ray person is often a poet or a writer of religious books in either poetry or prose. He enjoys beauty and aesthetics but is not always great at producing. The method of healing for this type of person would be through faith and prayer. The way of approaching God would be prayer and meditation that aim at union with God.

The sixth ray is moving out of incarnation at this time. Its highest manifestation was the life of Jesus Christ and the Lord Maitreya. The sixth ray was made available two or three thousand years ago because humanity was only at a "ten-year-old stage" of evolution. Given this fact, the sixth ray was the perfect ray to take humanity to the next step.

Humanity has matured now and this ray is no longer useful. It is really being replaced now with the seventh ray energy on a large scale. The positive side of the sixth ray in our history focused humanity on devoting itself to God and to becoming obedient to Him and His laws. It facilitated humanity's coming out of a pattern that it was stuck in. At this present period of history the sixth ray has a heavier energy because its purpose has really been completed. A lot of the work in the sixth department, which the Master Jesus heads, is about uniting the world's religions.

As the Earth moves fully into the New Age after the turn of the century, there will not be a focus of the sixth ray on Earth. It will have completed its service. Most churches in our world today are utilizing this sixth ray energy in their services.

The sixth ray was also connected to devoting oneself to a guru, teacher or Master. In the New Age and seventh ray cycle, the ideal will be more to own one's power and recognize one's inherent equality with the spiritual teachers, for all are the eternal self, in truth.

Some examples of sixth ray souls are John Calvin, Meister Eckhart, and Saint Francis (Kuthumi). Saint Francis had a sixth ray soul, a sixth ray mind, and a sixth ray personality.

The special virtues of the sixth ray person are devotion, single-mindedness, love, tenderness, intuition, loyalty, and reverence. The vices of this ray are selfishness and jealous love, over-dependence on others, partiality, self-deception, sectarianism, superstition, prejudice, over-rapid conclusions, and fiery anger. The virtues to be acquired are strength, self-sacrifice, purity, truth, tolerance, serenity, balance, and common sense.

The Seventh Ray of Ceremonial Order and Magic

The seventh ray energy is connected to the violet transmuting flame. The head of the seventh ray department is Saint Germain. This is the ray of the high priest or high priestess, the community organizer, or the court chamberlain. The motto of this type of person is "get all things done decently and in order."

It is Saint Germain who is in a sense turning the key that is unlocking the new Golden Age on this planet. He is using his violet transmuting flame to transform and transmute trouble spots around the planet.

The seventh ray helps to integrate heaven and Earth and ground spirituality into the physical material world. It is the ray of form, and hence a person on this ray makes the perfect sculptor. The combination of the fourth ray and the seventh ray would make the highest type of artist. Leonardo da Vinci had a soul ray of four, a personality ray of seven, a mind ray of seven, an emotional body of four, a physical body of seven. Here we have the ultimate example of Djwhal's teaching.

The literary work of the seventh ray person would be remarkable. The seventh ray person delights in ceremony, observances, ritual, processions and shows, reviews of troops and warships, genealogical trees, and rules of precedence.

The unevolved seventh ray person is superstitious and will be too influenced by omens, dreams, and spiritualistic phenomena. The more evolved seventh ray type is determined always to do the right thing and say the right thing at the right moment. Hence, he has great social success.

The seventh ray type of person approaches the spiritual path through the observance of rules of practice and ritual and can easily evoke the help of the elemental forces. He also very much enjoys the practice of disciplining and ordering every aspect of his life in service to and in harmony with God.

The special virtues of the seventh ray person are strength, perseverance, courage, courtesy, extreme care in details, and self-reliance. The vices of this ray type are formalism, bigotry, pride, narrowness, superficial judgments, and over-indulgence. The virtues to be acquired are realization of unity, wide-mindedness, tolerance, humility, gentleness, and love.

Another example of the seventh ray person is Nicolas Roerich, the channel for the Ascended Master El Morya, who brought forth the books on Agni Yogi. He had a seventh ray soul, a seventh ray personality, a seventh ray mind, and a seventh ray body.

The Higher Rays

In the early 1970's a divine dispensation of five higher rays were granted to this planet because of its impending movement into the fourth dimension and into the New Age. These higher rays are combinations of the first seven rays with a touch of Source Light, or white Light, which gives them a luminous quality.

Many newly incoming soul extensions now have these higher rays in their ray structures. Others are now beginning to access them in a very integrated manner. They are wonderful rays, and I highly recommend that you call them forth on a regular basis for personal and planetary healing.

All these rays come through our Planetary Logos, Sanat Kumara. There are actually rays beyond these twelve that exist in the universe; however, these are all that are planned for Earth at this time. Helios, our Solar Logos, directs them to Sanat Kumara who makes them available to us.

The Eighth Ray

Ray number eight is a cleansing ray. It helps clean out those characteristics and qualities within self that one no longer needs and wants to get rid of. This ray has a green-violet luminosity. It is composed of the fourth ray, the seventh ray, and the fifth ray with a touch of white Light, all mixed together.

Before bringing in the next ray which begins to attract on the body of Light, it is important that the four-body system be clean and pure. The eighth ray is good for cleansing the subconscious mind. It helps to raise one to a higher vibration level and frequency.

The Ninth Ray

The main quality of the ninth ray is joy. It is also the ray that attracts one's full potentials. It is the ray that begins to attract the body of Light. It also continues the cleansing process that the eighth ray started so effectively. It is composed of the first ray, the second ray, and white Light.

The color of this ray is greenish-blue luminosity. The body of Light is a beautiful, magnetic, transparent, white, luminous, electrical, life-force-filled, rainbow-like robe or body of energy that, ideally, one dons to begin each day. Over time it becomes integrated as a regular part of one's being.

It is the ninth ray that is used to attract the body of Light. It is the tenth ray that allows it to be fully anchored it into one's being. Fully integrating and anchoring the body of Light is integral to the ascension process.

The Tenth Ray

The tenth ray allows all the changes a person has been seeking to make to be locked in. Divinity is truly recognized when one meditates on this ray. It has a pearlescent-colored luminosity. It helps to facilitate the soul merge experience. It helps to code the pattern of divinity into the physical body.

The tenth ray is a combination of the first, second, and third rays mixed with white Light. It must be understood here that the Earth as a whole has a body of Light, also. As each person anchors his individual body of Light, this helps the Earth Mother to anchor hers.

The tenth ray allows the oneness of self to be experienced and allows the integration of the yin and yang aspects within self. The opportunity of the tenth ray is to fully realize the body of Light while still living in a physical body.

In the past the body of Light has not been accepted on the Earth and has lived in a higher dimension. A person has to refine and purify his being or raise his vibration to allow this integration to take place. The body of Light is not the soul itself, but it is the soul level that contains this aspect of self.

The body of Light is also connected to the monadic level. One can begin to experience this before taking the third initiation. It will not be completely locked in until after this initiation. There is a meditation at the end of this chapter to facilitate the anchoring of the body of Light.

The Eleventh Ray

This ray continues the process and is a bridge to the New Age. Its color is an orange-pink luminosity. It helps one to get in touch with Divine love/wisdom. It is a combination of the first ray, the second ray, the fifth ray, and white Source Light.

This ray is used to get to the New Age, to move up to the next level. One can call this ray in and blanket oneself or a particular area of the Earth that needs this impulse to move into the New Age. This ray has one of the most penetrating yet balanced types of energy matrix. This ray cleans up anything that was missed by the cleansing eighth ray.

The Twelfth Ray

The twelfth ray is the golden ray of the New Age. This is the ray of anchoring the Christ consciousness on Earth. It is the summit of all the higher rays. Djwhal Khul and Vywamus have predicted that the New Age will officially begin in 1996. The twelfth ray is a combination of all the rays with a sprinkling of white Light and Christ consciousness.

Even though it contains all eleven of the rays, the proportions are not all exactly the same. For example, there is less first ray than there is second ray. There is also a little less sixth ray since this ray is now going out of manifestation.

The twelfth ray also facilitates inner realizations. If there is confusion about a situation one can call this ray into consciousness and into the entire situation and it will facilitate proper understanding of it.

The twelfth ray brings in the highest invocation of the New Age. In the New Age, the main focus will be the twelfth ray. It is the highest type of energy made available to the Earth except for the energy of the Mahatma, the Avatar of Synthesis, which is an even higher frequency. It is good to call on both of them on a regular basis.

How to Determine Personal Rays

The main way a person can find out what his rays are is by careful examination of this material and by using both the rational and intuitive minds. In conjunction with this a pendulum can be used to double-check left-brain conclusions. Thirdly, it is possible to have channelings from the Ascended Masters through a qualified channel or from a qualified psychic who can give you this information. I would recommend using all three methods.

How to Use the Rays

Each of the twelve rays embodies a certain quality of energy. The idea now is to study this material and become familiar with the functioning of each ray. Then one can call forth whatever type of energy is needed at any given moment. If one wants more will and power he calls forth the first ray. If he wants more love he calls forth the second ray. If he wants more devotion he calls forth the sixth ray. If he wants the violet transmuting flame he calls forth the seventh ray. If he wants cleansing he calls forth the eighth ray. If he wants the body of Light he calls forth the grand tenth ray. If he wants Christ consciousness and the New Age he calls for the twelfth ray. All a person has to do is say, within the mind or out loud, "I now call forth the twelfth ray." A ray can be called by number, by color, or by quality of energy. For example one could say, "I now call forth the golden ray." One could say, "I now call forth the ray of love/wisdom." One can use any one of these methods or a combination of them. A combination might be, "I now call forth the golden twelfth ray." The energy and ray will flow in instantly, no matter what a person's level of evolution. All she or he has to do is ask.

One can not only call forth the rays for oneself, one can call forth these rays for world service work. It is not spiritually permissible to send a ray to another person unless one has his permission and he has asked for it. One can send rays, however, to certain areas of the world for planetary healing. For example, one might consider sending the second ray of love/wisdom into Bosnia or the Middle East. An area of the world might need the violet transmuting flame or any of the higher rays. The only two rays that are not appropriate to send for planetary healing would be the first ray and the fourth ray. These should be used only under the direction of an Ascended Master. The first ray is very explosive and has a destructive quality that could be misused. The fourth ray of harmony through conflict is one most people are not currently dealing with very effectively. It is an emotionally based ray that, when guided by the personality or negative ego, creates nothing but more conflict and havoc.

Aside from these restrictions one is really free to use his intuition and imagination in this regard. All the higher rays (rays eight through twelve) are excellent for personal and planetary service.

The next tabulation I would like to share from the Alice Bailey book on esoteric psychology deals with the higher and lower expressions of each ray. Just as each of the astrological signs under which a person is born has a higher and lower expression, so the same is true of each of the seven rays. Which one is being expressed is governed by whether a person, with his free choice, is serving his personality or his soul in terms of the ray's usage.

Ray Methods of Teaching Truth

Ray I	Higher expression:	The science of statesmanship and of government
	Lower expression:	Modern diplomacy and politics
Ray II	Higher expression:	The process of initiation as taught by the Hierarchy of Masters
	Lower expression:	Religion
Ray III	Higher expression:	Means of communication or interaction; radio, telegraph, telephone, and means of transportation
	Lower expression:	The use and spread of money and gold
Ray IV	Higher expression:	The Masonic work based on the formation of the Hierarchy and related to Ray II
	Lower expression:	Architectural construction; modern city planning
Ray V	Higher expression:	The science of the soul, esoteric psychology
	Lower expression:	Modern educational systems
Ray VI	Higher expression:	Christianity and diversified religions; note relation to Ray II
	Lower expression:	Churches and religious organizations
Ray VII	Higher expression:	All forms of white magic
	Lower expression:	Spiritualism in its lower aspects

The Rays and the Corresponding Professions

The following information shows each of the rays and the corresponding professions. It must be understood here that the type of work one is involved in may change depending on whether one is polarized in the body ray, personality ray, soul ray, or monadic ray. This is why many people move into a different profession later in life.

Ray I   Government and politics; international relations
Ray II   Education and teaching; writing, speaking, radio, TV
Ray III   Finance, trade, business and economics
Ray IV   Sociology; race and culture cooperation and conciliation;
           the arts
Ray V   Sciences; including medicine and psychology
Ray VI   Religion, ideology, philosophy
Ray VII   Structuring of society; ordering of power through ceremony,
           protocol and ritual

The Chakras Associated with Each Ray

The Crown Center	Ray I	Ray of Will or Power
The Ajna Center	Ray V	Ray of Concrete Knowledge
The Throat Center	Ray III	Ray of Active Intelligence
The Heart Center	Ray II	Ray of Love/Wisdom
The Solar Plexus	Ray VI	Ray of Devotion
The Sacral Center	Ray VII	Ray of Ceremonial Magic
The Base of the Spine	Ray IV	Ray of Harmony

The Rays Affecting Humanity

To demonstrate the enormous influence of the rays on individual lives, the following list shows all the different rays that are influencing everyone.

1. The ray of the solar system
2. The ray of the Planetary Logos of Earth
3. The ray of the human kingdom itself
4. The particular racial ray, the ray that determines the Aryan race
5. The rays that govern any particular cycle
6. The national ray, or that ray influence which is peculiarly influencing a particular nation
7. The ray of the monad
8. The ray of the soul
9. The ray of the personality
10. The rays governing:
    a. The mental body
    b. The emotional or astral body
    c. The physical body

The Rays and the Solar System

In occult thought it is understood that there are seven progressive solar systems that incarnated personalities evolve through. Personalities on Earth are evolving through the second solar system. The first solar system operated under the third ray. The current solar system operates under the second ray. The next solar system will operate under the first ray.

In regard to this solar system, the seven rays emanate and are expressions of seven great lives embodied by the seven stars in the constellation of the Great Bear. Since this solar system, governed by Helios, is a second ray system, the other six rays are really subrays of the cosmic second ray.

The rays from the seven stars of the Great Bear reach the sun by way of the twelve constellations. Each ray transmits its energy through three of the constellations and reaches the Earth through one of the seven sacred planets. There are also seven solar systems in the galactic sector of which Earth and its solar system are a part.

The Rays and the Planets

The following list shows the eight sacred planets and the rays they are associated with. Sacred status as a planet occurs when the Planetary Logos takes his third cosmic initiation.

Sacred Planets and Their Rays

Earth*	Ray IV
Vulcan	Ray I
Mercury	Ray IV
Venus	Ray V
Jupiter	Ray II
Saturn	Ray III
Neptune	Ray VI
Uranus	Ray VII

The Non-Sacred Planets and Their Rays

Mars	Ray VI
Earth*	Ray III
Pluto	Ray I
The Moon (veiling a hidden planet)	Ray IV
The Sun (veiling a hidden planet)	Ray II

*There has now been a slight adjustment in this understanding that was brought forth in the Alice Bailey material, given the fact that Earth has now become a sacred planet.

The Rays and Dimensions of Reality

The next tabulation shows the seven rays and the plane or dimension of reality each is connected with. Djwhal Khul has delineated seven dimensions of reality that humanity is working through on what is called the cosmic physical plane. There are also seven cosmic dimensions. The seven dimensions listed here are the seven subplanes of the cosmic physical, as described in the Alice Bailey book, *Esoteric Psychology*.

Ray I	Will or Power	Plane of divinity
Ray II	Love/Wisdom	Plane of the monad
Ray III	Active Intelligence	Plane of spirit, atma
Ray IV	Harmony Plane of the intuition	
Ray V	Concrete Knowledge	Mental plane
Ray VI	Devotion, Idealism	Astral plane
Ray VII	Ceremonial Order	Physical plane

The Rays that Are in and out of Manifestation

The next tabulation shows which rays are currently active in a planetary sense.

Ray I	Not in manifestation
Ray II	In manifestation since 1575 A.D.
Ray III	In manifestation since 1425 A.D.
Ray IV	To come slowly into manifestation after 2025 A.D.
Ray V	In manifestation since 1775 A.D.
Ray VI	Passing rapidly out of manifestation. It began to pass out in 1625 A.D.
Ray VII	In manifestation since 1675 A.D.

The Rays and Their Method of Development

The following chart from the Alice Bailey book on esoteric healing shows the seven rays and their methods of development. Also shown are the planets as described by Annie Besant, the former head of the Theosophical Society.

Characteristics		Methods of Development	Planet
Ray I	Will or Power	Raja Yoga	Uranus
Ray II	Wisdom Balance Intuition	Raja Yoga	Mercury
Ray III	Higher Mind	Exactitude in Thought Higher Mathematics Philosophy	Venus
Ray IV	Conflict	Intensity of Struggle	Saturn
Ray V	Lower Mind	Exactitude in Action	The Moon

Ray VI	Devotion	Bhakti Yoga	Mars
		Necessity for an Object	
Ray VII	Ceremonial	Ceremony	Jupiter
	Order	Observances	
		Control over Forces	
		of Nature	

The Seven Types of People and the Main Divisions of Humanity

What makes people so different from one another? Why does one person become an artist, another an accountant, another a businessperson, and another a priest? Djwhal Khul has elucidated five main categories that make people the way they are.

1. A person's "racial division"; in other words, is he a Lemurian type, an Atlantean type, an Aryan root race type, or a Meruvian type?

2. The twelve astrological groups which greatly affect a person's focus in life.

3. Whether one is unawakened, awakened to his individuality, awakened to the soul, and/or monadically awakened. This, of course, deals with the person's level of psychological and spiritual development and level of initiation.

4. Whether one is watched from a distance by the Hierarchy, among those awakened and attracted to the Spiritual Hierarchy, or among those being integrated into the Hierarchy, called "the New Group of World Servers."

5. The last category that determines what type of consciousness a person has is the seven main ray types. These are:

   a. The power type — full of will and governing capacity
   b. The love type — full of love and fusing power
   c. The active type — full of action and manipulating energy
   d. The artistic type — full of the sense of beauty and creative aspiration
   e. The scientific type — full of the idea of cause and results; mathematical
   f. The devotee type — full of idealism
   g. The business type — full of organizing power; given to ritualistic ceremony

The Five Groups of Souls

Djwhal Khul, in his writings through Alice Bailey, has delineated five groups of souls that humanity falls into. Some of the places the souls originated from may surprise you.

1. Lemurian egos, our true Earth humanity
2. Egos that came in with Atlantis
3. Moon chain egos from the moon
4. Egos from other planets
5. Rare and advanced egos awaiting incarnation.

Yes, some souls even developed first on the moon before coming to Earth. This is not unique to Djwhal Khul's writing. Theosophy speaks of this, as do the channelings of Earlyne Chaney. There are apparently seven races and what are termed "seven rounds." Djwhal Khul said individualization upon the moon chain took place in the third round of the fifth race.

We are now in the fourth round of the fifth root race which is the Aryan root race. Individualization in Lemuria occurred in the fourth round of the third root race. Individualization in Atlantis occurred in the fourth round of the fourth root race. The unfoldment on the moon chain occurred much earlier than our Earth's history and that is why we know very little about it.

An interesting esoteric fact is that Lord Maitreya was the first of Earth humanity to achieve ascension, whereas Buddha was the last of the moon chain humanity to do so.

On the moon chain the souls were 75% third ray and 25% first and second ray. The Lemurian souls were 75% second ray and 25% first and third ray. The Atlantean souls were 80% first ray and 20% second ray.

Short Synopsis of the Twelve Rays

Ray I	Red	Will, Dynamic Power, Singleness of Purpose, Detachment, Clear Vision
Ray II	Blue	Love/Wisdom, Radiance, Attraction, Expansion, Inclusiveness, Power to Save
Ray III	Yellow	Active Intelligence, Power to Manifest, Power to Evolve, Mental Illumination, Perseverance, Philosophical Bent, Organization, Clear-Mindedness, Perfectionism
Ray IV	Emerald Green	Harmony through Conflict, Purity, Beauty, Artistic Development
Ray V	Orange	Concrete Science, Research, Keen Intellect, Attention to Detail, Truthfulness
Ray VI	Indigo	Devotion, Idealism, Religiosity

Ray VII　Violet . . . . Ceremonial Order, Ritual, Magic, Diplomacy, Tact, the Violet Flame, Physicalness and Ground Spirit, Order, Discipline

Ray VIII Seafoam Green　The Higher Cleansing Ray

Ray IX　Blue-Green　Joy, Attraction of the Body of Light

Ray X　Pearlescent　The Anchoring of the Body of Light, Inviting of the Soul Merge

Ray XI　Pink-Orange　The Bridge to the New Age

Ray XII　Gold　The Anchoring of the New Age and Christ Consciousness

Summation

For those who want to study this material in real depth, I would recommend reading the three Alice Bailey books on this subject: *Esoteric Psychology*, Volumes One and Two, and *The Rays and the Initiations*.

11

The Reappearance of the Christ and the Externalization of the Hierarchy

Give up your unmanliness and get up and fight. This self-pity and self-indulgence are unbecoming of the great soul that you are

Krishna, speaking to Arjuna
in the *Bhagavad-Gita*

In all the major religions of the world, reference is made to the coming of a great Master at the end of the age. In the Christian religion it is referred to as the second coming of Christ, in Judaism as the coming of the Messiah. The Hindus refer to it as the coming of the Kalki Avatar and in the Moslem religion it is the Imam Mahdi. In Buddhism he is referred to as Maitreya Buddha, and his coming was predicted by Gautama Buddha over two thousand five hundred years ago.

Well, I am happy to announce that the World Teacher that all great religions have been waiting for is here on Earth. His name is Lord Maitreya. The Lord Maitreya is the head of the Spiritual Hierarchy. He is the Master of Masters and the Lord among angels and men. He holds the position of what might be called the presidency of the Great White Brotherhood, the Great White Brotherhood being those Masters of all religions who have mastered this plane and returned to spirit.

These great and noble beings have gone through the initiation process and have had to learn the same lessons that humans are currently learning. Their devotion through many lifetimes to the Fatherhood of God and the brotherhood of man and their service rendered to this ideal have gained them entrance into this most wonderful group. These Masters of most noble intent are still working from the spiritual world with humanity on Earth to help free humankind from illusion and suffering, to help them to create a heaven on Earth, and to free all men from the wheel of rebirth. It is for this purpose that the Lord Maitreya has come. He is a most glorious being. He was and still is the teacher of Jesus, Kuthumi, El Morya, Saint Germain, Djwhal Khul, and all the great Masters, saints and sages we are aware of. The fact that he is now here with us on this planet is a blessing of enormous magnitude.

The Lord Maitreya, in a previous life, was the great Master Krishna of Hinduism. Krishna was one of the greatest Eastern Masters the world has known. The Lord Maitreya then came again in the life of Jesus Christ. For it was the Lord Maitreya who, at the time of the baptism of Jesus in the river Jordan, "overshadowed" Jesus.

Overshadowing was a process of melding his consciousness from the spiritual world into the physical body and consciousness of Jesus. In a sense, they shared the same physical body during the last three years of Jesus' life. Most people do not realize this. Many of the miracles and sayings attributed to Jesus were really those of the Lord Maitreya who holds the position in the Spiritual Government known as the Christ. Jesus so perfectly embodied the Christ consciousness that it enabled the Lord Maitreya, who is the Planetary Christ, to meld his consciousness with that of Jesus.

This great sacrifice and renunciation by Jesus, along with the crucifixion experience, earned Jesus the passing of his fourth initiation which is the liberation from the wheel of rebirth. It was, in actuality, the Lord Maitreya who ascended in that lifetime and resurrected Jesus' physical body, not Jesus. The Lord Maitreya passed his sixth initiation at the crucifixion and hence the prophecy of the second coming of Christ that was given really means two things: It is the second coming of the Lord Maitreya that was predicted two thousand years ago and also the second coming of the Christ consciousness in all incarnated personalities on Earth.

The Christ consciousness is the consciousness of the soul rather than the consciousness of the fear-based, separate, and selfish negative ego. The key here is that all are meant to embody the Christ consciousness; each person is the Christ. It was not and is not just Jesus or the Lord Maitreya who is the Christ. In truth, everyone is the Christ whether she/he has realized it or not. To take it out of Christian terminology, everyone is the Buddha, the Atma, the Eternal Self. There is no choice in this because it is how God created beings. The law of the mind, however, is that thoughts create reality. So anyone who thinks he is just a physical body is mistaken, but to think this is to live in the nightmare of one's own thought creation.

Since the time Lord Maitreya overshadowed Jesus, he has been guiding humanity and the Earth from his position as head of the Spiritual Hierarchy. The Lord Maitreya was basically planning to overshadow another initiate, as he did Jesus, at the close of this last two-thousand-year cycle, which is right now. This is the end of the Piscean Age and the beginning of the Aquarian Age in planetary astrology. The great initiate he was planning to overshadow was Krishnamurti.

The Story of Krishnamurti

There have been two great dispensations of teachings that have come forth from the Great White Brotherhood at the closing of this Piscean Age. The first was the Theosophical movement started by Madam Blavatsky and carried forth by C. W. Leadbeater and Annie Besant. The second dispensation of teachings of the Great White Brotherhood was the information in the Alice Bailey books received from the Tibetan Master Djwhal Khul. The story of Krishnamurti involves the Theosophical movement.

C.W. Leadbeater was a great spiritual teacher and clairvoyant who, while in India, came across a young boy who he said was the next World Teacher. Leadbeater said that the boy had one of the most beautiful auras he had ever seen. This was very bizarre to Krishnamurti's parents and teachers because the boy was doing very poorly in school, was physically dirty, and was not a very handsome child. Leadbeater was convinced, however, and introduced the boy to Madam Blavatsky and Annie Besant. To make a long story short, Krishnamurti was trained by this Theosophical group to be the next World Teacher who would be the great initiate whom the Lord Maitreya would overshadow as he had Jesus Christ.

Krishnamurti, however, changed his mind as he moved into adulthood and decided that he did not want to be the vehicle or instrument of the Lord Maitreya. The same decision was made on the inner plane by Maitreya and the Ascended Masters. Krishnamurti decided to leave the Theosophical movement and be a teacher in his own right, separate from any spiritual movement or group.

Meanwhile, there had been a number of other initiates who were under consideration for this great honor; however, during the festival of the Christ at the full moon of June 1945, the Lord Maitreya announced that he would return to Earth again. This time he would not overshadow any initiate. This time he would come himself. The impact and implication of this great decision was enormous, as one can imagine. At this time he set a number of conditions that needed to be met before he would do this:

1. A measure of peace should be restored in the world;

2. The principle of sharing should be in the process of controlling economic affairs;

3.   The energy of goodwill should be manifesting and leading to the implementation of right human relationships;

4.   The political and religious organizations throughout the world should be releasing their followers from authoritarian supervision over their beliefs and thinking.

The Great Invocation

It was at this time in June 1945 that the Lord Maitreya released to humanity the prayer called "The Great Invocation." This prayer is one of the most powerful prayers that exists in the world today. Its power is equivalent to or even more powerful than the prayer he gave in the life overshadowing Jesus, which we all know as "The Lord's Prayer." The using of this prayer will invoke the energies that are needed to change the world and accelerate the full declaration of the Lord Maitreya. I highly recommend using it on a regular basis.

> From the point of Light within the mind of God
> Let Light stream forth into the minds of men.
> Let Light descend on Earth.
> From the point of Love within the heart of God
> Let Love stream forth into the hearts of men.
> May Christ return to Earth.
>
> From the center where the Will of God is known
> Let purpose guide the little wills of men—
> The purpose which the Masters know and serve.
>
> From the center which we call the race of men
> Let the Plan of Love and Light work out
> And may it seal the door where evil dwells.
>
> Let Light and Love and Power restore the plan on Earth.

The Lord Maitreya

The Lord Maitreya is currently living in London, England. The Lord Maitreya was not born into a baby's body; he materialized a body. In esoteric thought this has been termed the Mayavirupa body. This is done by energizing the etheric body and then just precipitating it onto the material plane.

The Lord Maitreya manifested this body and came into this world in 1977. He has made many appearances all around the world but has not fully declared his presence openly except to his closest initiates. It is planned that in the very near future he will declare his presence as the World Teacher openly to the world.

I use the term World Teacher for that is what he is. World Teacher is also a term that does not favor any religious orientation and hence alienate any group. I do want to make it very clear that he is the Master all religions are waiting for. The problem is that, just as in the time of Jesus, human-kind may not be ready to fully accept him.

Jesus Christ was, in actuality, the Messiah that the Jewish people were waiting for. He was in fact a Jewish rabbi. The problem is that the Jewish people didn't understand this. They held tightly to the old form and didn't allow the new Piscean dispensation of teachings to improve upon that which already had been taught.

The Lord Maitreya confronts the same problem today, not just with the Jewish religion, but with all the major religions, spiritual groups, mystery schools, atheists, and agnostics alike. The key question is whether the world is ready to accept that a being of his glorious spiritual magnitude is actually here. Think about it! How are the fundamentalists going to react? How are the Jewish people going to react? How are the Buddhists, the Hindus, the Moslems going to react? Maybe you can see why the Lord Maitreya has delayed the full declaration of his presence as long as he has. I am happy to say, however, that the time is near. Djwhal Khul has told me, and the Lord Maitreya has told us himself, that he will fully declare his presence before the end of this century. There is a possibility it could be as soon as 1995 or 1997. As was already mentioned, he is waiting for a measure of Christ consciousness to be established in this world before he makes this monumental step.

An Even More Extraordinary Sequence of Events

If it were not enough that the Lord Maitreya is coming himself, an even more extraordinary sequence of events is also occurring on this planet. Two cosmic entities are now adding their tremendous energies and power to the Lord Maitreya. These two cosmic entities' names are the Spirit of Peace and Equilibrium and the Avatar of Synthesis. These two cosmic beings are overshadowing the Lord Maitreya in much the same way that the Lord Maitreya overshadowed Jesus two thousand years ago. Maybe for the first time on this planet we are now dealing with cosmic Ascended Masters, not just planetary Ascended Masters. In addition, the Buddha is adding his cosmic wisdom through Maitreya. These three great cosmic beings form a triangle whose energies the Christ channels to us.

What's more, in India is living His Holiness, the Lord Sai Baba. Sai Baba is the Cosmic Christ incarnated on this planet, whereas the Lord Maitreya is the Planetary Christ. Sai Baba, as the Cosmic Christ, is the incarnation of Brahma, Vishnu, and Shiva, living in the same body. He is a totally God-realized Avatar. He has been referred to as a Spiritual Regent from out of this galaxy on a mission of service to save this planet from destruction and to help bring it into the New Age. At this time I am not going to say any more about Sathya Sai Baba because I have dedicated the next chapter to him. Read that chapter and I guarantee you that your life will never again be the same. The gloriousness of his nature and being is hard to put into words. The fact that the Lord Maitreya, the Spirit of Peace and Equilibrium, the Avatar of Synthesis, and the Lord Sai Baba are all on this planet is absolutely mind-boggling. I am happy to say, however, there is even more!

The Externalization of the Spiritual Hierarchy

If what I have mentioned so far isn't amazing enough, also on this planet now are forty senior members of the Spiritual Hierarchy who have come from spiritual planes and have externalized themselves along with the Lord Maitreya to help and support him in his work. Ten of these masters, Djwhal Khul has told us, have actually materialized physical bodies as the Lord Maitreya has. Another ten or fifteen are overshadowing their disciples and initiates as the Lord Maitreya did with Jesus. The other ten or fifteen have incarnated into babies' bodies and are growing up or have grown into adulthood already.

One of these Masters is referred to as John of Penial, although that is not his real name. He is the incarnation of John the Beloved, the disciple of Jesus who ascended in that lifetime. He is an incarnation of the Master Kuthumi; he is on the planet as one aspect of the Master Kuthumi. Djwhal has told me that Masters at that level can incarnate in more than one personality at the same time. He is the great Master that Paul Solomon, the modern-day Edgar Cayce, has said will open the halls of records in the Great Pyramid and Sphinx and release all the Atlantean records. Djwhal has also said that Saint Germain, Hilarion, and Paul the Venetian are involved in the process of externalization.

The planning for this great event has been going on for many, many centuries. The planning began as early as the 1400's. The actual externalization began as far back as 1860 with the first dispensation of the Spiritual Hierarchy's teachings through the Theosophical movement. Madam Blavatsky, C. W. Leadbeater, Annie Besant, and Colonel Olcot were all part of this initial phase of the externalization. Djwhal Khul foretold of all these events in two Alice Bailey books in the early 1900's called *The Reappearance of the Christ* and *The Externalization of the Hierarchy*. Djwhal has said that the externalization of the Spiritual Hierarchy was to take place in three phases.

1. In the early stages initiates of and under the third degree would externalize.

2. In the later stages senior members of the Spiritual Hierarchy would externalize; this is taking place now.

3. In the final stage the Christ, the Lord Maitreya, would externalize. Finally, then, at the appropriate time and moment known only to him, he will declare his identity, purpose, and mission openly to the world. At this time he will also introduce the Masters who have externalized with him.

The Progressive Evolution of Humanity

When Gautama Buddha came to this planet five hundred years before the time of Christ, he anchored the wisdom principle on this planet for humanity. When Jesus and the Lord Maitreya came to the planet five hundred years later, they anchored the wisdom of the Buddha and love which was the next dispensation, or revelation of God. In Lord Maitreya's mission now, two thousand years later, he is anchoring the wisdom of the Buddha, the love principle of his past mission, as well as anchoring the will energy and principle of Shamballa. This energy embodies the purpose and plan of God and the Planetary Logos, Sanat Kumara. (In Chapter 16 on Sanat Kumara and the Planetary Hierarchy, I have gone into great detail in explaining who he is and what this energy is about.) It is clear that in each stage of human and planetary evolution another piece of the puzzle is revealed and anchored on the Earth. Each stage brings a greater expansion of God's Divine Plan.

The Christ is Coming in Three Ways

The Lord Maitreya is coming to us in basically three ways:

1. By overshadowing all initiates and disciples with his cosmic presence;

2. By pouring out the Christ consciousness to all people;

3. By his physical appearance among men.

The Three Highest Beings on the Planet

Djwhal Khul has told us that the three highest beings on the planet are the Lord Maitreya in London, the Lord Sai Baba in India, and a third who is a Master living on the East Coast of the United States whose name will be released when Maitreya makes his declaration.

The New Group of World Servers

It is also important to understand that there are many, many other great Masters already on this planet besides the ones that I have mentioned in terms of the externalization. Djwhal has termed this group collectively the New Group of World Servers. We are, in a sense, the ground forces that are preparing the way for the Lord Maitreya and his great ashram that is in the process of fully externalizing.

It is essential to understand that the Lord Maitreya and the externalized Masters coming with him are not going to change the world for us. Their whole message is that each person is the Christ, and each is, in truth, equal to them; that the only way this world is going to change is if all people take responsibility for sharing the load, and being their brothers' keepers. Maitreya has said, "When we share, we recognize God in our brother."

The Mission of the Masters

The mission of the Masters is manyfold and multifaceted. Djwhal has elucidated some of the guidelines as follows:

1. The creating and vitalizing of a new world religion;
2. The reorganizing of the social order so it is free from oppression, prejudice, materialism, and pride;
3. The public inauguration of the system of initiation; this will include the exoteric or outer training of disciples.

Djwhal has said that in the future the first initiation will become the most sacred ceremony of the church. He also said that a third revelatory phase of the Great White Brotherhood's teaching would take place world-wide through radio and television. This would be the third revelation after the Theosophical movement and the Alice Bailey books. Part of the mission and purpose of my wife, Terri, and myself is to help Djwhal Khul in this work. This next dispensation of teachings will occur toward the end of this century.

Djwhal has also said that Jesus Christ would take over the Christian church from the spiritual plane, part of his work being to blend Eastern and Western thought, demonstrating the universality of all religions.

Djwhal has also said that there would be an initiate who would serve as a specific Messiah for the Jewish people to bring forth this particular form of religious thought. He also said that the Buddha would send two trained initiates to reform the Buddhist religion.

Groups of spirit-minded financiers who are conscious members of the Christ's ashram will take hold of the world economic situation and bring about great and needed changes. In the future each country on the planet will take stock of its resources and all excess will be put into a pool for use by those countries that are less wealthy. In essence, a revolution of the entire economic system will take place so that it will be based on sharing.

At the head of international agencies such as the United Nations, there will be a Master or at least a third-degree initiate. This will allow these agencies to be under the direct influence of an advanced member of the Hierarchy. Lord Maitreya will be very busy with the release of energies, teaching, the work of initiation, and stimulating and inspiring the formation of a new world religion. This new world religion will recognize all paths as leading back to the Creator and will stop all competition among religions.

Maitreya has said that right human relations are at the basis of everyone's lives. It is the sharing of the resources of this bountiful planet that is the first step in developing this right relationship.

Maitreya is also bringing with him great angels or devas who will work closely with humanity, teaching many aspects of the art of living.

All Aspirants are the Externalization of the Hierarchy

It is essential to understand that all those who are reading this book right now are the externalization of the Spiritual Hierarchy also; all aspirants, disciples, and initiates are taking part in this great work. One must not see these senior members of the Spiritual Hierarchy who are coming with the Lord Maitreya as being separate or different from oneself. Everyone is part of the same family, consciousness, and group purpose. They are depending on humanity as much as or more than humanity is depending on them. Unless everyone joins in and sees the oneness, the work is not going to get done. The only difference between humans and the Hierarchy is that humans are members of this great brotherhood already here on Earth. In a sense, humanity has a great advantage: in having been living on Earth for some time and therefore having adjusted to being here, humans can be of great service to the Masters who have come here more recently.

It does not matter at what level of initiation one is. All are part of one great brotherhood and sisterhood of souls whose purpose is to serve God's plan. All should recognize and fully own that they are part of this externalization of the Hierarchy and that they are, in actuality, paving the way for the Hierarchy's future work and coming declaration.

Summation

The reappearance of the Christ and the externalization of the Hierarchy is, in essence, a group incarnation that is leading to a Golden Age on this planet. We are living now in one of the most extraordinary times in the history of this planet. We are ending a two-thousand-year cycle, a six-thousand-year cycle, a twelve-thousand-year cycle, and a thirty-six-thousand-year cycle in planetary and solar astrology. We are also right at the end of the Mayan calendar which finishes in 2012. Whenever a time in history that has to do with the ending of cycles occurs it is extremely important. It is time for this planet to move to its next highest octave in the Divine Plan. It is time for the planet and all its people to move into a fourth-dimensional consciousness, which is the Christ consciousness.

The time is now, and to push through to the other side into the Golden Age will take the dedicated and devoted work of all souls on Earth. Vywamus has said that humanity is also approaching a period of mass ascension, or what he calls harvesting, because of the ending of all these cycles. Vywamus says that there is a one-hundred-year window that is open and the people of Earth are approaching the culmination of that time at the end of this century.

It has also been predicted that at the end of this cycle when Lord Maitreya leaves and moves on to his cosmic evolution, the Master Kuthumi will take his place and become the head of the Spiritual Hierarchy, filling Maitreya's place. Maitreya will return, it is prophesied, at a future cycle, as the Cosmic Christ. This is quite an exciting prospect for the future of our beloved Planet Earth.

12

The Cosmic Christ: the Advent of Sathya Sai Baba

*Hands that help are holier than
lips that pray*

Sathya Sai Baba

There is a great Master living in India at this time who is so glorious in his spiritual magnificence that words are incapable of doing him justice. This glorious and magnificent being's name is Sri Sathya Sai Baba.

The miracles that Jesus Christ performed in the last three years of his life, such as raising the dead, turning water into wine, and walking on water, Sai Baba has been doing for sixty-five years. It is hard to believe that a being of this magnitude is actually on the Earth, for Sai Baba is the Cosmic Christ.

The Lord Maitreya is the Planetary Christ. He is the head of the Spiritual Hierarchy for this planet. Sai Baba is the cosmic equivalent. So in actuality the Planetary Christ and the Cosmic Christ are on this planet at the same time. Never in the history of this planet has there ever been a better time, in a spiritual sense, to be incarnated.

Sai Baba's coming was prophesied over five thousand years ago in the *Mahabharata*. The *Mahabharata* is one of the holiest books of India. It contains the *Bhagavad-Gita* which, again, is the story of Krishna—which, interestingly enough, is the past incarnation of the Lord Maitreya. In this book Vishnu, who is part of the Hindu trinity of Brahma, Vishnu, and Shiva, foretells a future age of moral decline called the Kali Yuga. In this age, which we are now in, he said he would return as a great spiritual Avatar. An Avatar is a God-realized being at birth. Even Jesus and Buddha were not Avatars in the sense in which I am defining the term. In other words, an Avatar does not have to do any spiritual practices to attain self-realization, for he is already self-realized at birth. This was the case with Sai Baba.

The *Mahabharata* and other ancient prophecies gave detailed prophecies over five thousand years ago of the specific characteristics of this future Avatar. I would like to share some of these prophecies with you.

They said he would be short with a big crown of hair. He would be able to materialize things at will with the power of his mind. He would have all abilities at birth. He would wear a blood-red robe. He would bear the name Truth. (Sai Baba's first name is Sathya which means truth in the Hindu language.) He would have a triple Avatar incarnation. He would be born in south India. He would have the birthmark of the Avatar on the bottom of his foot. He would be born in an Indian body. His parents would be worshipers of Krishna. He would be fully Divine and fully God-realized. He would be all-knowing and the greatest living being in the world. He would have the ability to lengthen life and be in many places simultaneously. Good would accrue to anyone who saw him.

Every single one of these prophecies given over five thousand years ago perfectly describes Sai Baba. In my personal experience of all the spiritual teachers, masters, books, spiritual paths and mystery schools I have ever been involved with, I have never come across any being with the power and magnitude of Sai Baba. I have no ax to grind in saying this because most of my work is focused in the second ray ashram of Djwhal Khul and Kuthumi. I have never been to India or seen Sai Baba in the flesh. However, I have had many personal experiences and encounters with him in the dream state and in meditation. All I can say is that once one has been exposed to Sai Baba, one will never be the same, this I promise. It is my humble and joyous task now to share with you some of the stories of his life and some of his teachings.

Sai Baba Stories

There are so many incredible stories about Sai Baba it is hard to know where to begin. When he was born, musical instruments played on their own. As a small boy he was able to materialize pencils, candy, food, or whatever he needed, right out of the air. On one of the sacred Hindu holidays on which they would have a parade of all the holy men, with small floats going down the street, the people watching the parade saw Sai Baba, at five years of age, sitting on the main float in the holiest spot. They asked why this young child was sitting there. All the saints and rishis said that it was because this five-year-old child was their guru.

At thirteen years of age he was bitten by a scorpion and was unconscious for twenty-four hours. When he awoke, his family were all around and he told them that in his past life he had been the great saint, and

Avatar, Shirdi Sai Baba. His family and friends who were standing around didn't believe him. Shirdi Sai Baba was one of the greatest saints of India in the late 1800's and early 1900's. Shirdi Sai Baba was also an Avatar. During the time he lived the Moslems and Hindus hated each other; however, both groups worshiped Shirdi Sai Baba. He had many of the same powers that Sai Baba has in this lifetime.

Shirdi Sai Baba had said on his deathbed, to his devotees, that after dying he would return in eight years in a specific village in south India. Eight years later Sai Baba was born, fulfilling that prophecy. Sai Baba's family and friends didn't believe him, however, so Sai Baba picked up a vase of flowers and threw it on the ground. The flowers and vase flew all over the place and when the flowers had settled on the ground they spelled out the words "Shirdi Sai Baba."

It was shortly after this incident that he said to his family, "My devotees are waiting for me. I am leaving home for good." Sai Baba did leave home and he began his ashram.

One other childhood story before moving to his adult life: When he was a young child in school, all the other children called him Guru and he would lead them all in devotional songs and in the creation of spiritual plays. One day, however, he was in class and one of the substitute teachers wrongly accused him of some misbehavior that was not his fault. The substitute teacher made him stand on a chair in the back of the classroom as a punishment and wouldn't let him leave until permission had been granted. Meanwhile, the bell to dismiss class rang and all the kids left. Sai Baba still had to stand on the chair.

The teacher, meanwhile, was sitting on his chair in the front of the classroom, inexplicably glued to his chair. He was trying to leave to go to his next class but he couldn't. The next teacher came into the classroom and asked why the teacher hadn't left yet. The substitute teacher explained his strange predicament and then the new teacher saw Sai Baba standing on the chair in the corner and knew what had happened, for all the teachers knew of his remarkable powers. He told Sai Baba to come down from the chair. As he came down, the substitute teacher was also released from his chair.

Sai Baba has said that his coming is a triple Avatar incarnation. In his last life he was Shirdi Sai Baba. In this life he is Sathya Sai Baba. He has said he will incarnate one more time in the future as Prema Sai Baba. Sai Baba is sixty-five years old now (1992) and has said he will live until he is ninety-six. At the age of ninety-six he will pass on to the spirit world and then two years later he will incarnate again as Prema Sai Baba. He has even materialized a ring for a devotee that shows the picture of himself in his future incarnation as Prema Sai Baba.

As Sai Baba has grown older his fame has increased throughout India and the entire world. It is estimated that he may have over seventy-five million devotees. At his last birthday over two million people were at his ashram to celebrate. Sai Baba said that in his incarnation as Shirdi Sai Baba he was the incarnation of the Shiva, or father energy. In his present incarnation as Sathya Sai Baba he is the incarnation of the Shiva and the Shakti, or mother energy. In his next life as Prema Sai Baba he will be the incarnation of just the Shakti energy.

Sai Baba is able to materialize whatever he wants instantly with just the swirl of his hand, and he does this on a regular basis. There is a video which you can get from the Bodhi Tree Bookstore in Los Angeles called "Aura of Divinity" which actually shows him materializing things. They also have seven other videos you can rent or buy. I would highly recommend renting or buying them, especially this one.

Sai Baba's Adult Life

In Sai Baba's early adult life he often would leave his body when a devotee on the other side of the world would call for his help. The devotees with him at the time were in charge of taking care of his physical body when this would happen. One evening he left his body and the devotees laid his body on the bed. All of a sudden his body began to levitate in the air and float around the room. Sacred ash began to pour out of his feet in great abundance. The devotees heard him mumbling, "Maharshi is at my lotus feet." He floated downward after a while and landed on the bed. The next day the ashram received a message that Ramana Maharshi, the God-realized saint from India, had died the previous night at 9:00 p.m., just the time that Sai Baba had been levitating.

In another instance, Sai Baba was known to be lecturing at the ashram even though he was staying at a house in another part of India. In other words, he bilocated for two days. Another time his car ran out of gas. He told the driver to go to the river and fill up the bucket with water. The driver did what he was told to do and gave the bucket of water to Sai Baba. Sai Baba put his finger in it and turned the water into gasoline. He poured it into the tank and they continued driving.

Another time he was driving with a couple of people and they stopped for lunch. Sai Baba asked, "What kind of fruit do you want?" Each person named an exotic fruit, some of which didn't even grow in India. Sai Baba said to them, "Go get it from the tree over there." They looked up at the tree and it had grown the fruit that each of them wanted.

One of the most remarkable stories tells of how one day Sai Baba was walking with his senior devotee from the West, Jack Hislop. Sai Baba bent down, picked up a twig and for about ten seconds moved his hand in the motion that usually indicated he was about to materialize something. All of a sudden a beautiful wooden crucifix appeared, with a metal statue of Jesus Christ attached to it. Sai Baba said that this crucifix was exactly how Jesus had looked on the cross when he was crucified. Then Sai Baba said something that was even more remarkable. He said that the wood of this crucifix was actually the wood from the cross that Jesus Christ had been crucified upon. He also said that it was no easy task materializing this wood because it had decomposed into the Earth; that is why it had taken him a little bit of extra time to materialize it. He gave this crucifix to Jack Hislop as a gift. Jack was deeply touched. He returned to America and had the crucifix carbon-dated. The scientist told him that it was two thousand years old.

An elderly couple from the United States by the name of Mr. and Mrs. Walter Cowan had long been Sai Baba devotees. They were traveling in India when one morning Walter Cowan had a heart attack and died in a city far from Sai Baba's ashram. The wife tried to send a telegram to Sai Baba but couldn't get hold of him.

Six or eight hours later Sai Baba appeared at the hospital, having received the telegram. Walter Cowan's family and friends had already left. Sai Baba told the hospital administrators that he would like to see Walter Cowan's dead body. He was escorted into the room and the administrator left. Five minutes later, out walked Sai Baba with a *totally alive* Walter Cowan. The hospital officials and doctors were floored, to say the least. Walter Cowan then went to see his wife and family and they almost had heart attacks, too.

He proceeded to tell them that when he had died Sai Baba had been there with him in the spiritual world. He had been taken with Sai Baba up through the dimensions of reality to a council chamber filled with people surrounding a council chairman. The chairman proceeded to pull scrolls from behind him that were Walter Cowan's past lives and for two hours he read these different scrolls of past lives out loud. Walter Cowan was amazed at all of his past lives of service and helping people. At the end of the two hours Sai Baba said to the chairman that Walter Cowan had not yet completed his mission on Earth and that he wanted to take him back to his physical body so he could complete his mission. The chairman said okay, and Sai Baba then took Walter back to his physical body where he woke up next to Sai Baba!

Another, even more remarkable story is about an Indian couple who were devotees of Baba. The husband was diagnosed with a super-severe illness and all the doctors said he would die any day. The wife telegrammed Sai Baba for help. He responded by saying he would come. The man became sicker and sicker and finally died. His wife wired Sai Baba again, and again he said he would come. One day went by, two days went by.

Rigor mortis was starting to settle into the body. A third day went by and the family had given up on Sai Baba. After three full days, all of a sudden Sai Baba arrived.

The family were all still grieving their loss. Sai Baba said he wanted to be alone with the dead body. He shut the door and, as the story goes, gave one of his fiats, much like Jesus did when he said, "Lazarus, arise!" The man woke up after being dead for three days! Sai Baba gave him some hot tea which the man drank. Then Sai Baba told him that his family was worried about him and that he should go out and comfort them.

Another time Sai Baba was walking with a very conservative geologist who was not very open to spiritual things. As they were walking together through a forested area Sai Baba picked up a rock and said to the geologist, "What's this?" The geologist said, "It's a rock, Baba." Sai Baba said, "No, no, deeper, deeper." The scientist said, "It's atoms and molecules vibrating at a certain rate of speed." Said Baba, "No, no, deeper, deeper." The geologist got flustered and said, "I don't know, Baba, what is it?" Sai Baba, holding the rock in his hand, blew on it and immediately, right in front of his eyes, the rock transformed into a statue of the Lord Krishna. The geologist was in a state of shock. Then Sai Baba said, "Eat it." The geologist said, "What?" Sai Baba repeated, "Eat it." The statue was made of rock candy.

Another time Sai Baba was lecturing a group of students at a school he had started. One particular day he was telling them a story about an emerald necklace that Krishna had worn in his life seven thousand years before. All of a sudden Sai Baba said, "Would you like to see this emerald necklace?" With a wave of his hand he materialized Krishna's necklace and passed it around the room for the students to see and touch. After everyone had had a chance to see and touch it he dematerialized it and sent it back to where it had come from.

A friend of mine told me a story of something that happened to a friend of his. The person had been a devotee of Baba's but was then living in California. He was apparently going through a very rough time emotionally and was seriously considering killing himself. One night he finally decided he was going to do it. He got out his rifle, loaded it with bullets, and was about to pull the trigger when the doorbell rang. He hid the gun under a blanket in his bedroom, closed the door, and opened the front door. There was a friend of his from junior high school, whom he had not seen for something like twenty years.

This friend barged in and they talked for a couple of hours, which kind of cheered him up a bit. Then all of a sudden the friend said he had to leave. The friend had not left his sight the entire time he had been there, but when the man went to the bedroom to get the gun, it had disappeared.

He had a vague feeling that Sai Baba was involved. He couldn't kill himself then because he no longer had a gun, so he ended up going back to India on another pilgrimage. One of the first days he was at the ashram he was picked out of the crowd by Sai Baba for a private interview with a group of about twenty-five other people. When Sai Baba came out to greet the people he singled out this man and told him to follow him. They went into one of Sai Baba's back rooms and as the man walked into the room he saw a rifle on the table. As he looked closer he realized that it was his rifle. Sai Baba politely smiled and said to him, "Will you still be needing this?"

When a person wants to take a picture of Sai Baba, it never turns out unless Sai Baba has given permission. A woman from the United States requested a photo of Baba. Sai Baba agreed, but he said to the woman, "I will allow you to take this picture; however, in this picture I will show you my true form." When the woman got home and had the picture developed it turned out that the picture was not of Sai Baba's physical body at all, but was a picture of the Lord Datatreya. The Lord Datatreya, in Hinduism, is the incarnation of Brahma, Shiva, and Vishnu in the same body.

Sri Aurobindo, the great spiritual Master from India, was meditating one day. When he came out of meditation he said to his disciples that Krishna had descended into the physical world as of the previous day, November 23, 1926. This was the day Sai Baba was born.

Mohammed, the founder of the Moslem faith, prophesied the coming of what he called "the Golden One." Three specific prophecies were that the Golden One would be short in stature, would have a mole on his face and would live until he was ninety-six years old. This describes Sai Baba perfectly. The Hopi Indian prophecies spoke of a great future Avatar who would come from the East and would be clothed in red. Sai Baba always wears red and orange robes. These prophecies were very specific and Sai Baba fits every one of them.

Sai Baba has said that an Avatar can be known by sixteen signs: control of the five functions of the body, control of the five senses of the body, control of the five elements of nature. These first fifteen are attainable through spiritual practice and spiritual disciplines. The sixteenth quality, Sai Baba says, is attainable only by the descent of a Divine Incarnation and Avatar who is God-realized at birth—absolute omniscience, omnipresence, and omnipotence.

When Sai Baba was asked how often he sleeps, he said never. When asked why he performs miracles, he said that he does so to get people's attention in order to turn them on to God. One remarkable miracle that is occurring all over India and the world is his creation of Virbutti Ash. This sacred ash is something that Sai Baba creates with a wave of his hand and it is used for healing purposes and as a blessing. There are people all over the planet who have jars and urns that are constantly being filled, no matter how much of the sacred ash they use or give away. It literally grows by itself limitlessly in jars, containers, and on pictures of Sai Baba all over the world.

Once I was chatting with a woman who was leading a channeling class I was attending. We got to talking about Paramahansa Yogananda because she had a picture of him, and then I innocently asked if she had heard of Sai Baba. She proceeded to tell me that she had never heard of him until a couple of years before. She had been meditating and doing astral traveling. She had been gone for about an hour or two and when she came back, for some strange reason she couldn't get back into her body. She got frightened after about half an hour when all of a sudden a great many dark, lower-astral entities started coming toward her with evil intent. She told me that she had started screaming in absolute terror in her astral body for God to help her. All of a sudden, she said, a man in an orange robe with bushy black hair had appeared and shouted, "SILENCE!" She said every molecule in the universe just stood still after that command. Sai Baba proceeded to tell her that when she had left her physical body to astral travel, she had somersaulted out of her body and to return to it she had to somersault in the reverse way. Sai Baba had picked her up, flipped her over, and somersaulted her back into her physical body. She was very grateful to this being for his help; however, she still did not know who he was.

A couple of weeks later she went to the house of a friend who was a devotee of Baba's and had his picture on the wall. She exclaimed, upon seeing the picture, "That's the man who helped me! Who is he?" Her friend responded, "That is His Holiness, the Lord Sai Baba."

One last incident I will mention happened to an elderly Indian devotee who was on some very strong pain medication. In the middle of the night he got up to go to the well to get a drink of water and fell down to the bottom of the well. As he was falling he yelled Sai Baba's name. Instantly, Sai Baba was at the bottom of the well holding him up to prevent him from drowning. A couple of hours later his family realized what had happened and pulled him out of the well. When Sai Baba later saw the elderly man at the ashram, before the man had a chance to thank him, Sai Baba said to him, "My arm sure got tired holding you up in that well for so long!"

At the end of this chapter I will give you his address so you can write him letters. Sai Baba says he reads all letters. All he has to do is touch the letter and he instantly knows what is in it. Sai Baba has also said that no one ever dreams about him without his willing it, so if you do have a dream about him it is because you have made personal contact with him. One of the nice things about Sai Baba is the fact that he is physically incarnated and is very accessible in both a physical and a spiritual sense.

Sai Baba's Teachings

When Sai Baba was asked how he is able to perform all these miracles he said that the reason is that he is God. The only difference between him and other people is that he knows it and the rest of humanity hasn't realized it yet. In essence, he creates all these things with the power of his mind. These miracles are all very wonderful, but the most beautiful thing about Sai Baba is his unconditional love and absolute selflessness. He never charges for his miracles or creates a miracle for a selfish purpose. He is here only to love and serve.

He says he is not here to create a new religion but rather to repair the ancient highways to God. His recommendation is that a person keep whatever religion he or she is affiliated with. He will come to any sincere request for God, regardless of the form, for he says all forms are in reality one. He most eloquently states that

"There is only one religion, the religion of love.

There is only one language, the language of the heart.

There is only one race, the race of humanity.

There is only one God and He is omnipresent."

His basic message is that everyone is God, the Christ, the Buddha, the Atma, the Eternal Self; that all should see themselves this way and see each person they meet this way, for how one treats each person one meets is how one treats Him.

His definition of God is this: "God equals man minus ego." Ego is the illusionary belief in separation, fear, and selfishness. He says that it is "our minds that create bondage, and our minds that create liberation." Another pearl of Sai Baba's is, "Hands that help are holier than lips that pray."

Two of the most important spiritual practices that Sai Baba recommends are the repeating of the name of God and singing of devotional songs. It does not matter what name of God is chanted or what is visualized. This is a very common practice in the Eastern religions, although much less so in the Western cultures. Mahatma Gandhi said that it was one of the keys to his success. He would chant the name Rama all the time. When he was assassinated, as he was dying he was saying the name Rama.

It is said in the *Bhagavad-Gita* that where one goes after death has to do with the last thought in one's mind as one dies. I cannot recommend highly enough the practice of repeating the name of God and visualizing the form of God. Whenever a person gets off center or is being taken over by a negative emotion, it will work to clear negativity and reattune him to God. The singing of devotional songs is a similar practice, but it involves the emotional body a little more, which is quite wonderful.

Of gurus, Sai Baba said, "A guru is the Light to show one the road, but the destination is God. One is grateful to one's guru but it is God that one worships. Nowadays one worships the guru, which is quite wrong."

Sai Baba is also a strong proponent of the transcendence of duality. This is the ability to remain even-minded and in a state of equanimity regardless of what is going on. The idea is to remain in equanimity whether one has profit or loss, pleasure or pain, sickness or health, victory or defeat, criticism or praise. The transcendence of duality is part of the process of disengaging from one's ego. It has a lot to do with the Buddhist teaching of how to stop being attached to things.

The meditation practice that Sai Baba teaches is the exact same one that Paramahansa Yogananda and Baba Muktananda taught. It is basically the Om mantra and the So Ham mantra. The idea of the So Ham mantra is to say the word "So" on the in-breath, and the word "Ham" on the out-breath. The idea is to let the breath guide the cadence of the mantra. If the breath is slow then the cadence of the mantra will be slow. If the breath is fast then the cadence of the mantra will be fast. The words "So Ham" basically mean "I Am God" or "I Am the Self." These words, Sai Baba says, are actually not even Indian or Sanskrit words; "So Ham" is actually the sound of the breath as God is listening to it. When one goes to sleep at night the So Ham merges into the sound of the Om.

There is one other mantra that Sai Baba has recommended which is also a name he goes by as well as Sai Baba, and that is the term "Sai Ram." Sai Ram is, in essence, Sai Baba's calling card. Devotees of Sai Baba often greet each other and say good-bye by saying Sai Ram. The repetition of this name or the chanting of this name as a mantra attracts Sai Baba, as does his real name, also. One can also say his name and visualize his form throughout the day or call his name when his help is needed.

In respect to love, Baba says, "Start the day with love. Fill the day with love. Spend the day with love. And end the day with love, for this is the way to God." Baba also teaches that one should get rid of all desire except the desire for liberation and God-realization.

Sai Baba says that most people are like light bulbs with different wattages. "We are all light bulbs, except my wattage is one thousand whereas most people's wattage is from twenty to one hundred." He also says that God is hidden by the mountain range of ego, that one who is able to control his anger, his ego, and his attachment is a great yogi.

Sai Baba says the physical body is a house rented to one by God. One lives there as long as He wills it and pays Him rent of faith, devotion, and spiritual practice. Baba also speaks a great deal about the importance of developing a flawless character. He says, "Do your best and God will take care of the rest." He says that whatever the Lord hands out, one must welcome with equal calmness. He says the removal of immorality is the only way to immortality.

I have attempted here to give you a little flavor of Sai Baba's teachings which are very much in accord with those of Djwhal Khul, Jesus, Saint Germain, Buddha, and everyone else. There are literally hundreds of books about Sai Baba and some that he has written. If you have never been exposed to Sai Baba before and would like two introductory books, I would recommend Howard Murphet's two books. The first one is called *Sai Baba, Man of Miracles*. The second one is called *Sai Baba, Avatar*. There are also Sai Baba meetings in most cities. Devotional songs are sung and more information can be attained. If one is so inclined one might consider a trip to India. It is not often that the Cosmic Christ is incarnated on the planet and accessible to be visited in the physical. There are tours available that include other people from the Sai Baba meetings; very often they are able to get personal interviews with him. However, I can't make any promises. Whatever path one is on, Sai Baba will fit into that path quite nicely.

Sai Baba's mailing address:
    Sri Sathya Sai Baba
    Ashram Prashanti Nilayam
    Anantapur District
    Andhra Pradesh 515134
    South India

Sai Baba's main bookstore:
    305 West First Street
    Tustin, CA 92680
    (714) 669-0522

Sai Ram!

13

Babaji, the Yogi Christ

*Kriya Yoga is the airplane
method to God*

Paramahansa Yogananda

There is another ascended being who is physically incarnated on Planet Earth and who is of extraordinary proportions. I would be remiss if I didn't mention him. He, of course, is the deathless Avatar, Babaji.

The Babaji I refer to is the great and noble being who started the spiritual lineage of Lahiri Mahasaya, Sri Yukteswar, and Paramahansa Yogananda, of Self-Realization Fellowship renown.

Babaji has also been called MahaAvatar Babaji, Shiva Babaji, Mahamuni Babaji, and Kriya Babaji Nagaraj. His physical body remains at the deathless age of sixteen years. (It is interesting that those who have personal contact with our Planetary Logos, Sanat Kumara, see him as very youthful, as well.)

Babaji has lived for centuries in the Himalaya Mountains, appearing only to a small group of disciples. He is able to materialize and dematerialize his body at will and does so frequently. Babaji was born on November 30, 203 A.D., in India. His name as a child was Nagaraj which means king of the serpents and which honors the primordial force of the kundalini Shakti. He was apparently born under a star configuration similar to that under which the Lord Krishna (the Lord Maitreya) was born.

In Babaji's early quest for self-realization he finally found his guru, the great Siddha Yoga Master Boganathar and became his disciple. After intensive yoga practice, Boganathar inspired Babaji to seek Kriya Kundalini Pranayama from the legendary Siddha Master Agastyar. Agastyar was hard to find and extremely selective about the disciples he would take on. Babaji traveled to southern India and made a solemn vow to the Divine

Mother that he would not leave the spot where he was sitting to meditate until Agastyar would initiate him into the secrets of yoga.

Babaji began to pray and meditate unceasingly. It would rain, then it would get hot, insects would attack him, but he would not move. As doubts assaulted him, he would pray even harder. His physical body became emaciated and pilgrims, recognizing the nobility of his quest, would occasionally feed him. Babaji was prepared to die to his physical body, if necessary, for he felt his life was over anyway if he didn't get initiated by Agastyar.

After forty-eight days of unceasing prayer and meditation, being close to death, he repeated the name Agastyar over and over again. Suddenly Agastyar appeared out of the forest, gave Babaji food and drink, and initiated him in the secrets of Kriya Kundalini Pranayama Yoga. After intensive training, Agastyar directed Babaji to go into the upper ranges of the Himalaya Mountains and become the greatest Siddha (Perfect Master) the world had ever known.

Babaji spent eighteen months practicing the Kriya Yoga techniques by himself. After eighteen months he entered a state of Soruba Samadhi, or ascension and physical immortality. Since that time over seventeen hundred years ago it has been Babaji's mission to assist humanity in its quest for God-realization.

It was Babaji who initiated Shankaracharya, Kabir, and Lahiri Mahasaya, which started the Self-Realization Fellowship lineage. Babaji has rekindled the science of Kriya Yoga and brought it back to the world after it had died out. Babaji has said that Krishna taught Kriya Yoga to Arjuna and that Patanjali and Jesus Christ knew of it. It was taught to St. John, St. Paul, and other disciples. His great disciple, Paramahansa Yogananda, in my opinion, is one of the greatest God-realized beings of our century. He trained over one hundred thousand people in Kriya Yoga, including Mahatma Gandhi, Luther Burbank, and many others.

Babaji began other spiritual lineages in India with which we of the West are less familiar. Babaji also started another organization in the West called the Teachings of the Inner Christ with which I have been involved. It is a wonderful organization that was organized by a woman by the name of Ann Meyer. Babaji materialized himself in a business suit rather than appearing with his normal Indian-looking appearance. He became her spiritual teacher, and her life totally transformed.

This organization, the Teachings of the Inner Christ, is a combination of Science of Mind-type training along with inner sensitivity training to channel the Masters and the I Am Presence directly. It is a different kind of training from the Eastern Kriya Yoga path, but it is one of the most profound I have ever studied. I have also been initiated by Self-Realization

Fellowship into the advanced Kriya techniques so I have great familiarity with Babaji's teachings which I will share with you at the end of this chapter.

Babaji has had a dynamic influence on this planet and its inhabitants, far beyond the little bit that has been written about him. His mission has been to assist the prophets, saints, and spiritual Masters in carrying out their special missions. Babaji has also been very interested in spreading his teachings to the East and West.

It was Babaji who told Paramahansa Yogananda to leave India and teach Kriya Yoga in the West. The interesting thing about Babaji is that his mission is different from that of someone like Sai Baba, for he has never appeared openly in any century. He works behind the scenes with a small number of selected disciples in humble obscurity. Even though this is the case, his effect on this planet has been incredibly profound. Many of the great spiritual Masters and teachers of our time have come from his teachings and guidance.

Lahiri Mahasaya, the great spiritual Master and self-realized being, said that any devotee who utters, with reverence, Babaji's name will attract an instant blessing. Paramahansa Yogananda said that when Babaji appeared to him, he appeared no older than twenty-five, with no mark of age on his body. His immortal body requires no food.

An interesting story was told by one of his disciples by the name of Swami Kebalananda. One evening Babaji and his disciples were sitting around a huge campfire for a sacred Vedic ceremony. Babaji suddenly seized a burning piece of wood and lightly struck the bare shoulder of a fellow disciple. Lahiri Mahasaya was horrified. Babaji explained to his disciples that this disciple was about to incur some serious past-life karma and would have been burnt to a cinder had Babaji not intervened. Babaji instantly placed his hand on the wound and miraculously healed the disciple, explaining to him that he had saved him from death.

On another occasion their sacred circle was interrupted by a man who had been searching the Himalayans for Babaji. Upon finding him he begged to become his disciple. Babaji didn't respond and the man threatened to jump off a cliff, for life had no further meaning for him without his perceived guru. Babaji said to jump for he couldn't accept him in his present state of development. The man threw himself off the cliff. Babaji told his disciples to get the dead and mangled body. Babaji then resurrected him from death and as the man's eyes opened, he told him that he was "now ready for discipleship." The whole group then dematerialized from the mountain.

Another interesting story has to do with Babaji's God-realized sister, Mataji. One night Lahiri Mahasaya, a disciple by the name of Ram Gopal, Mataji, and Babaji were all sitting in a particular cave in India. Babaji proceeded to tell his sister, Mataji, that he was intending to shed his

physical body. I share with you Mataji's response from the great Paramahansa Yogananda's book, *Autobiography of a Yogi.*

> Mataji replied with a quaint flash of wit, "Deathless guru, if it makes
> no difference, then please do not ever relinquish your form."
>
> "Be it so," Babaji said solemnly. "I shall never leave my physical
> body. It will always remain visible to at least a small number of
> people on Earth. The Lord has spoken his own wish through your
> lips."
>
> "Fear not, Ram Gopal," he said. "You are blessed to be a witness at
> the scene of this immortal promise."

To my way of thinking, this is incredibly profound. I am not sure there
is another being on Planet Earth who has made this commitment other
than Sanat Kumara, who is incarnated into the physical body of the entire
Earth itself. We are greatly blessed to have such a great one as Babaji still
here with us on Planet Earth. What a great and noble sacrifice he has made
out of his great love for humankind. Lahiri Mahasya later explained that
Babaji will be here for the entire manvantara, or world cycle; in other
words, for the completion of the evolution of the seven root races and for
the completion of the inbreath and outbreath of Brahma for Planet Earth.

One more fascinating story has to do with Lahiri Mahasaya's initiation,
on his thirty-third birthday, into Kriya Yoga by Babaji. Lahiri Mahasaya had
been Babaji's disciple in a previous life. Upon finding his deathless guru
again, it was planned that the following night he would be reinitiated. At
midnight he was being guided through a forest area in the Himalayans,
when all of a sudden there before him was a magnificent golden palace that
had been materialized by Babaji for his beloved disciple. Babaji told him
that in a past life he had once expressed a desire to enjoy the beauties of a
palace such as this and Babaji was fulfilling that desire which was Lahiri
Mahasaya's last bond of karma that needed to be cleared before his
initiation. Upon receiving his initiation from Babaji, the palace instantly
disappeared right before his eyes.

Babaji appeared to Sri Yukteswar, Paramahansa Yogananda's guru, on
a number of occasions. On one occasion Babaji appeared and told Sri
Yukteswar that at an early stage of his life, he would be sending him a
disciple whom he wanted him to train, and who would hence bring forth the
science of Kriya Yoga to the West. Paramahansa Yogananda was that
disciple. Two of the best books I have ever read are Paramahansa's *Autobiography of a Yogi* and *Man's Eternal Quest.*

Kriya Yoga

There are actually some varied traditions of Kriya Yoga, depending on
the lineage of teachers with whom one studies. Paramahansa Yogananda

refers to Kriya Yoga as "the airplane method to God."

Kriya Yoga is an ancient science that was lost in the dark ages and revived and clarified by Babaji. Krishna twice referred to it in the *Bhagavad-Gita*. It was also mentioned twice in the writings of Patanjali. Kriya Yoga is an instrument through which human evolution can be quickened. Kriya Yoga is a vast science of physical, emotional, mental, and spiritual mastery, leading to self-realization.

Patanjali referred to it as body discipline, mental control, and meditating on the Aum. It also has to do with the science of breath mastery, meditation, yogic postures, the awakening of the chakras, the awakening of the kundalini, mantras, devotional practices, devotional songs, chanting, service, sexual transmutation, spiritual retreats, spiritual fellowship, vegetarian diet, yogic rest, mental, emotional, and physical purity, total surrender to God, mind control, mudras, bandhas, pranayama, purification of the nadis (etheric nerve channels), clearing of the subconscious mind, transcendence of ego, union with God, physical healing, and pilgrimages to sacred places—to name just a few.

Two of the many meditation techniques have to do with meditating on the sound of the Aum and learning to listen and hear the Aum without saying it ourselves. The second meditation is the Hong Sau or So Ham meditation. This is the meditation of Babaji, Paramahansa Yogananda, Sai Baba, and Baba Muktananda. As I have mentioned in previous chapters, it is actually the sound of the breath as God listens to humans breathe. The Aum is the sound of our breath when we sleep. The words mean, "I am God" or "I am the Self."

There is, however, an actual Kriya technique that the Self-Realization Fellowship and qualified Kriya Yoga instructors give out that is for advanced students who have been initiated. It is a breathing technique which I am not allowed to share in detail; however, it has to do with directing life force and energy to move up and down the spine in a special way. The half minute it takes to do one of the Kriya techniques, according to Paramahansa Yogananda, is equal to one year of natural spiritual unfoldment. Paramahansa Yogananda states in his book, *The Autobiography of a Yogi*, "One thousand Kriyas, practiced in eight and a half hours gives the yogi, in one day, the equivalent of one thousand years of natural evolution—three hundred sixty-five thousand years of evolution in one year. In three years, a Kriya Yogi can thus accomplish, by intelligent self-effort, the same result that nature brings to pass in a million years." This is why it is referred to as the jet plane method to self-realization. The beginning student uses this technique only fourteen to twenty-four times a day.

According to Paramahansa Yogananda, a number of yogis achieved liberation in six or twelve or twenty-four or forty-eight years. The doing of the Kriya builds the wattage of the light bulb each of us is. Day by day, our four bodies and consciousnesses become transformed.

Babaji has recommended the reading and study of the *Bhagavad-Gita* before becoming initiated. He teaches an ideal of being pure in all spheres of life—that is, disciplined, honest, and sincere. Meditation and Kriya practices help in the dissolution of the mind so one may have a direct experience of the Eternal Self.

He advocates a life of renunciation of the ego and attachment. When the mind is turned inward it becomes the self; when it is turned outward it becomes ego. He teaches to destroy the ego and be happy forever. (Of course, he is talking about the negative ego.) He has said the first problem is ego. Solve that and all other problems will be solved thereafter.

He has also said that if we want to be free, we must learn to love and forgive under all circumstances. We must not hold a grudge against anybody. When realized, we see everyone else as realized and as a manifestation of God. He, like Paramahansa Yogananda, teaches that work and meditation go hand in hand. We should strive for balance physically, psychologically, and spiritually.

My Personal Experience

My personal spiritual path is very universal and eclectic, as I am sure is true for many of the readers of this book. Given this, I never recommend only one path, as I find that to be very limiting.

I have been initiated into the path of Kriya Yoga by the Self-Realization Fellowship. I have the supremely highest respect for Babaji and Paramahansa Yogananda. I have no doubt that everything they say and teach is true. I, personally, am not now doing the actual Kriya techniques of breathing up and down the spine in that special manner only because for reasons of physical health I have been guided not to do them. I once had hepatitis which has made my electrical system a little too sensitive for this particular type of spiritual practice, and Paramahansa Yogananda came to me himself and told me to stop.

I do, however, practice the basic principles and many of the other practices of the Kriya Yoga path. This is not hard since all the other spiritual paths with which I am involved have similar practices. In reality, I practice a mixture of everything I have ever been involved in.

The advanced Kriya technique given by Yogananda is said to be the "equivalent of a year's worth of spiritual evolution in thirty seconds." This is quite a statement. I have such enormous respect for Paramahansa Yogananda that I very much doubt that he could be mistaken. I feel guided to bring this information to you even though I am not practicing it at the present time. If you feel drawn to follow it, I recommend that you check it out. It is not necessary to follow or learn this particular path, however, as this is only one of many paths up the mountain.

These types of breathing exercises can be very dangerous if not learned correctly and guided by a qualified teacher. I consider the Self-Realization Fellowship to be a valid and safe path. The problem is that to become initiated you must receive the lessons for a full year, then practice the Hong Sau meditation for six months and the energizing exercises for six months. Then you have to write out your experiences on special forms and apply. The whole process can end up taking two years, plus you are accepting Yogananda as a type of teacher or guru. When I applied, I knew I had other teachers so this was not a problem for me; I loved Yogananda, but he was not my only guru or teacher.

To be perfectly honest, without meaning this as any criticism, I, personally, do not resonate with staying confined within the Self-Realization Fellowship. It is a wonderful organization, but it is too confined for my more universal and eclectic nature and purpose in this lifetime. The techniques are wonderful and they may be the "airplane method" to self-realization, but it is kind of a long, strenuous, and arduous process even to receive them.

There are alternatives and also other teachers of Kriya Yoga. Marshall Govindan wrote a fantastic book about Babaji called *Babaji and the Eighteen Siddha Yogis*, which I highly recommend reading if you are interested in the techniques of this particular path. In this book he gives an address you can write to in order to receive more information and get training. Intuitively, I have a really good feeling about Govindan, but I am not sure that he teaches the Kriya methods in the exact same way that Yogananda was trained, for he came from a different lineage. Both groups, however, consider Babaji the Master and Teacher. Babaji has appeared and physically taught both lineages.

The address for this group is:

Babaji's Kriya Yoga Satsang
165 de la Gauchetière West, #3608
Montreal, Quebec, Canada H2Z 1X6
(514) 284-3551

The Self-Realization Fellowship address is:

Self-Realization Fellowship
3880 San Rafael Avenue
Los Angeles, CA 90065
(213) 225-2471

The Self-Realization Fellowship lessons that come every other week are quite good, and Paramahansa Yogananda's books are some of the best on the market today, in my personal opinion.

There is an interesting third alternative, which has to do with the mystery school called Astara, started by Earlyne and Robert Chaney. Earlyne is a channel for the Master Kuthumi, among other Ascended Masters. To reiterate, Kuthumi is the Chohan of the Second Ray and in line to become the head of the Spiritual Hierarchy and/or Great White Brotherhood when the Lord Maitreya completes his term and moves on to higher levels of spiritual evolution.

Earlyne has written a series of seventy-seven lessons that come in pamphlet form. In these lesson booklets, all kinds of teachings are represented, many of which are very similar to the teachings of Djwhal Khul for which I, personally, have the greatest affinity of all the teachings I have studied.

In a portion of these lessons, Earlyne has channeled advanced lessons in what she has called Lama Yoga. I have all the lessons and have studied them intensively and what interests me is that many of the advanced techniques of Kriya Yoga taught by Babaji and Paramahansa Yogananda are exactly the same as those channeled by the Master Kuthumi. So another alternative would be to skip the Self-Realization path and just order the lessons from Astara.

The nice thing about Astara is that the lessons can be ordered right away and there is no long waiting or initiation process that you have to go through in order to become a member. The only problem is that the lessons can be a little expensive and the exact techniques are not in the beginning of the lessons.

I have read all of Earlyne Chaney's books and I think her material is excellent. Some of the lessons are not so interesting but others are extremely interesting. I, personally, feel that these Kriya techniques are really "hot," and if what Paramahansa Yogananda says about them is true, then who wouldn't want to take the airplane method to God? The only qualification I will make is that when you are dealing with Kriya techniques involving pranayama, you are dealing with the kundalini energy and you must be extraordinarily careful about what you are doing or you can seriously damage yourself. These are advanced techniques that must be used with *extreme caution* and only as directed, preferably with guidance from a qualified spiritual teacher.

I trust the Self-Realizations Fellowship, and I trust Earlyne Chaney's material, but it is not necessary to work with these specific techniques, for there are many paths to God; these are not techniques that, for example, Sai Baba, Djwhal Khul, Jesus, or Saint Germain taught. Except for these Kriya techniques, I find the other teachings and techniques quite similar among all these groups. I leave you this information for your further consideration and contemplation.

I would recommend that you read Yogananda's books and Earlyne

Chaney's books before making your decision. My personal philosophy is to use whatever works, and to access tools and techniques from all religions, all spiritual paths, and all mystery schools.

The address of Astara, should you be interested, is:

Astara
P.O. Box 5003
800 West Arrow Highway
Upland, CA 91785
(909) 981-4941

You can order the lessons one at a time or a large chunk at a time, and you can use a credit card. I do first recommend reading some of her books before making any big financial expenditure. This goes for Paramahansa Yogananda, also. After reading some of their books I am sure you will get an intuitive sense of whether or not it is a path you wish to pursue. Do call and get on their mailing lists, and ask for a catalogue of books and tapes. The bookstores don't always have Earlyne's books in stock. If you resonate with Djwhal Khul's teachings, I think you will resonate with a lot of her material also. All of her books are well worth reading.

14

The Untold Story of Jesus the Christ

Nothing real can be threatened.
Nothing unreal exists.
Herein lies the Peace of God.

A Course in Miracles

The purpose of this chapter is to share with you some of the absolutely fascinating information that the average person does not know about the life of Jesus the Christ. I did not make up the information I am about to bring you. I have received this information from in-depth research into the Edgar Cayce files, the Alice Bailey books, the Aquarian Gospel of Jesus the Christ, lost manuscripts recently found in Tibet, India, and the Himalaya Mountains, and the channeling of Djwhal Khul. It is with great pleasure, then, that I bring you the untold story of Jesus the Christ.

The story begins long before his life as Jesus. Edgar Cayce and Djwhal Khul have listed his past lives. According to Edgar Cayce, Jesus' past lives were as Amilius, Adam, Melchizedek, Enoch, Zend, Ur, Asapha, Jeshua, Joseph, and Joshua. Djwhal Khul added two more that occurred after his life as Jesus: Appolonius of Tyanna and an incarnation in a Syrian body in which he ascended during this century.

Djwhal Khul has confirmed Cayce's listing of past lives. Amilius was the first-begotten of the Father, who came into the Atlantean land and allowed himself to be led into the ways of selfishness. He then came as Adam, as in the story of Adam and Eve. He then came as Melchizedek, the Priest of Salem. He then came as Zend who was the father of Zoroaster, the great Avatar of the Persian religion. In my research I found out that Zoroaster was one of the incarnations of the Buddha. He then came as

Enoch, the "man who walked with God." He then came as Asapha.

He was Jehoshua, who reasoned with those who returned from captivity in those days when Nehemiah, Ezra, and Zerubbabel were factors in the attempts to reestablish the worship of God. Jehoshua was the scribe who translated the books written up until that time. Jesus was also the Joseph in the Old Testament who wore the coat of many colors, was thrown into a ditch by his jealous brothers and later became the dream interpreter of the Pharaoh. He then came as Joshua, who was the mouthpiece for Moses and who led the Jewish people to the promised land.

In his life as Jesus the Christ, he took his fourth initiation at the time of the crucifixion. During the last three years of his life he was overshadowed by the Christ. The Christ was none other than the Lord Maitreya who was and is the head of the Spiritual Hierarchy and the Great White Brotherhood. The Lord Maitreya holds the position of the Christ, which is an office or title in the spiritual government. The Lord Maitreya was Jesus' guru and teacher. During the last three years of Jesus' life, they shared the same physical body. The Lord Maitreya was the one who ascended at the crucifixion, not Jesus. Jesus took his fourth initiation which made him a Master and which was also the breaking of the wheel of reincarnation and the need for rebirth.

Jesus reincarnated nine years later, according to Djwhal Khul in the Alice Bailey books, as Appollonius of Tyanna and took his fifth initiation. Appollonius was a great, great soul, and many people actually confused him and Jesus because they were so similar in what they taught and because they lived so close together chronologically.

In Jesus's last incarnation in the Syrian body, he ascended. He came into this body approximately three hundred fifty years ago and ascended into the spirit world in this century, according to Djwhal Khul.

Djwhal Khul also said another fascinating thing about Jesus. While on the cross, at one point Jesus said, "Father, why hast thou forsaken me?" I, personally, have always been confused by that statement. It didn't sound like the statement of a Master. Djwhal said, in the Alice Bailey books, that he said this because he was passing through the fourth initiation which has to do with the soul body or causal body burning up, and the soul returning back to the monad or spirit. What Jesus was experiencing was his soul or higher self leaving, which was a strange experience for him because his soul had been his teacher for all his incarnations. He didn't realize in that moment that his teacher from then on was to be the monad, or mighty I Am Presence. For that brief moment he was experiencing the loss of his soul until he reconnected with the spirit. He did so very shortly thereafter when he said, "Father, forgive them for they know not what they do." The Father is the monad or spirit.

One interesting sidenote is that Jesus was born of the immaculate conception, according to Djwhal and Cayce, and so was the Virgin Mary. Edgar Cayce says that the Virgin Mary and Jesus were from the same soul, or were what Cayce called twin souls. According to Djwhal Khul, Jesus came into his incarnation as Jesus as a third-degree initiate.

In reviewing Jesus' past lives it is fascinating to see how they indicate the interrelationship of two of the major religions of this planet. Very often Christians and Jews have competed with each other, each trying to say his own religion is "right." The absurdity of this can be seen in the fact that it was the same souls who were involved with both of them. Jesus was a Jewish rabbi. He was Joshua who led the Jewish people to the promised land. He was Joseph in the Old Testament. He was the guide and teacher of Abraham, who started the Jewish religion as Melchizedek.

A further fascinating connection between the Jewish and Christian religions is the fact that John the Baptist had been Elijah in a past life, Elijah, of course, being one of the great Jewish prophets.

What makes this even more interesting is the fact that Joseph, the husband of the Virgin Mary, was none other than Saint Germain. The three wise men who came to visit the Christ child were none other than Djwhal Khul, Kuthumi, and El Morya. The only disciple to ascend, according to Djwhal Khul, was John the Beloved (Kuthumi). One other interesting sidenote is that Abraham was the Ascended Master El Morya who is the Chohan or Lord of the first ray.

The Essenes

The next fascinating entry in this story is the importance the Essene community played in the life of Jesus. That community was very important in the coming of the Messiah, according to Cayce. Strangely enough, the Essenes were not mentioned in the Bible. It was only with the discovery of the Dead Sea Scrolls in 1947, in the ruins at Qumran, that widespread interest in and excitement about the Essenes began to flourish.

The scrolls were the religious literature of the Essenes. There were, according to Cayce, a number of groups or communities of Essenes. The group that played the most significant role in the life of Jesus was the group on Mount Carmel, the place where the original school of prophets had been established during Elijah's time. The Essenes were students of astrology, numerology, phrenology, and reincarnation. These beliefs were in direct conflict with the beliefs of the Sadducees and they brought about persecution of the Essenes.

One of the chief characteristics of the Essenes, which distinguished them from other sects, was their "expectancy" of the coming Messiah. It was the chief reason for the group's existence. According to Edgar Cayce, the name Essene actually means expectancy.

It was the belief of the Essenes that through a strict observance of spiritual law they could purify themselves so the Messiah might enter the Earth plane and take on a physical body. (Jesus Christ, of course, was that Messiah whom they sought. However, the traditional Jewish people didn't understand this.)

Jesus was bringing the next dispensation of spirit for the Piscean Age. The Jewish people, to a great extent, held on to the dispensation brought forth by Moses, which had to do with the law. Jesus came to bring forth the knowledge that love was even greater than the law.

The preparations of the Essenes went into a new phase when they chose twelve girls to come to the temple at Mount Carmel to prepare themselves to become the mother of the Messiah. Mary was one of these children. They were trained in physical and mental exercises as related to chastity, purity, love, patience, and endurance. Special diets were given the children along with overall training in the spiritual life.

The head of the Essenes at this time, according to Cayce, was a woman by the name of "Judy." It was quite unusual for a woman to be the head of this sect in such patriarchal times. Judy was a prophet, psychic, and spiritual teacher. She had been trained not only in Jewish mysticism, but also in the teachings of India, Egypt, and the Persian lands. She was also a healer and the recorder of the teachings. It was Judy who recommended to Jesus later in his life that he travel to Egypt, India, and Persia for further training and study.

Mary was only four years old when she entered the temple. According to Cayce she was chosen by the Archangel Gabriel when she was twelve or thirteen. Mary was then separated from the other children for further preparation and training. That period in Mary's life lasted four years. A husband had been chosen for Mary, according to Cayce, even before the announcement by the angel that she was the chosen mother of the Messiah.

Cayce said that the actual marriage did not take place until some time after her conception of the holy child. Joseph, her husband (Saint Germain), was much disturbed at finding Mary already with child at the time of the wedding. The choice of Mary as his bride had not been his own; at that time Jewish families arranged marriages. The choice for this marriage had actually been made by the priests, and although Joseph didn't like the choice of Mary as his wife (he was thirty-six and Mary was only sixteen), he changed his mind when he was informed in a dream and then by direct voice channeling that it was Divine will. It was the Archangel Gabriel who came to Joseph and convinced him.

The birth of Jesus and his early training are well documented in the Bible so I do not need to focus on them. The area I would like to focus on, however, is the time when Jesus was between the ages of twelve and thirty, which is not depicted in the Bible.

The Unknown Years of Jesus' Life

According to Cayce, Jesus had become a master of Jewish law previous to his twelfth year. From his twelfth to his fifteenth or sixteenth year he was taught the prophecies by Judy in her home at Mount Carmel. He was then sent into Egypt, then to India for three years, and then to Persia for further training. From Persia he was called back at the death of Joseph. He then went back to Egypt for the completion of his preparation as a teacher.

The teachings he received in India were of "those cleansings of the body as related to preparation for strength in the physical as well as the mental man. In the travels and in Persia, the union of forces as related to those teachings of Zu and Ra in Egypt."

According to Cayce, Jesus was registered under the name Jeshua, "Jesus" actually being the Greek form of the name. Both of these names are contractions of Jehoshua, meaning Help of Jehovah, or Savior. John the Baptist was apparently with Jesus during portions of the period spent in Egypt. They were in Heliopolis, Egypt, to attain priesthood, take examinations, and pass tests there. *The Aquarian Gospel of Jesus the Christ*, by Levi, actually gives an account of the seven levels of initiation Jesus took. The Great Pyramid was built as a Temple of Initiation for the Great White Brotherhood. Jesus took his final initiations in this pyramid. In the Bible it was referred to as three days and three nights in the tomb. According to *The Aquarian Gospel of Jesus the Christ*, Jesus studied the Brahmic religion and the Vedas in India. He also spent time in Nepal, Tibet, Syria, and Greece. In India, Cayce said, he studied under a spiritual teacher by the name Kahjian. In Persia he studied under Junner. In Egypt he studied under Zar.

The channelings of Cayce, Levi, and Djwhal Khul all document Jesus' eighteen-year journey in the East. What is fascinating, however, is that in this century ancient documents have been discovered in India and Tibet proving that Jesus traveled there. In the late 1800's Nicholas Notovitch, a Russian journalist who was traveling in Tibet was told by a lama at the archives of Lhasa, capital of Tibet, that there were several thousand ancient scrolls discussing the life of the prophet Jesus. (In the East they called him the prophet Issa.) Notovitch traveled to a great convent at Himis, which is the largest and most celebrated monastery in Ladakh, where he found these documents. In 1894 he published the verses as allegedly read to him in translation by an interpreter. In these documents are to be found descriptions of the life of the Buddha Issa, who preached the holy doctrine in India and among the children of Israel.

These transcripts speak of how Jesus became a disciple of Brahmins, lived for three years with Buddhist monks, and studied Buddhist scriptures. It tells of how he toured Nepal and the Himalayas and then proceeded to Persia where he studied the doctrines of Zarathustra, or Zoroaster.

In 1922, Swami Abhedananda also went to Himis, Tibet, and confirmed Notovitch's story. Swami Abhedananda, with the help of a lama, translated the same verses which he later published along with Notovitch's English rendition of the text.

In 1925 Nicholas Roerich visited Himis. He published writings he discovered at the monastery and elsewhere which paralleled Notovitch's and Swami Abhedananda's accounts. He also reported finding throughout his journey many other accounts, both oral and written, of Jesus' journey throughout the East. He published them in a book called *Altai-Himalaya, Heart of Asia and Himalaya*.

In 1939, with no prior knowledge of the legends of Issa, Elisabeth Caspari was shown three books by the librarian at Himis who told her, "These books say your Jesus was here."

The channeled and actual proof that Jesus traveled to the East to train and study and teach is overwhelming. It is also interesting that Jesus' activities between the ages of twelve and thirty are pretty much left out of the Bible.

It is important to understand that the Bible was not written by God, as some may try to tell you. The Bible was written by people; a great deal of the material in it is man's interpretation of God, not direct revelation by God. There most definitely is much inspired writing; however, it must be read with discernment.

A second key point in this respect is historical fact: in 553 A.D. at the Second Council of Constantinople, a decree was made that all references to reincarnation be removed from the Bible. They didn't like the concept.

The meaning of this is quite obvious. Not only is the Bible man's interpretation of God, but what man does not like in it, he removes. It is my personal belief that this is also what happened to records of the lost eighteen years of Jesus' life that are not included in the Bible. I don't think the church higher-ups were too pleased with the idea of having the common people know that Jesus had studied Buddhism, Hinduism, Zoroastrianism, and the Egyptian Mysteries.

There are some further pieces of information I have come up with from the Cayce files. Jesus had three siblings. This is what the Universal Mind said through Edgar Cayce. Jesus was born of the immaculate conception, but after Mary and Joseph were actually married, they went on to have three more children, according to Cayce—two boys and one girl. The boys' names were James and Jude, but I have not been able to find out the daughter's name.

After being chosen to be one of the twelve maidens, Mary was allowed no wine or fermented drink and was placed on a strict diet. When she was chosen by Archangel Gabriel while on the steps leading up to the temple, there was thunder and lightning in the sky, according to Edgar Cayce. The Essene temple I speak of here was also a school and one of the main things they taught was the ability to channel. Judy, the head of the Essenes, taught Jesus the prophecies, astrology, and how to soul travel, at which Judy was quite proficient.

Cayce said that the three wise men symbolized the three phases of man's experience in materiality. Gold represented the material, frankincense represented the ethereal, and myrrh, the healing force—thus body, mind, and soul. The three wise men also served as needed encouragement for Mary and Joseph.

According to Edgar Cayce's readings from the Universal Mind, Jesus was born at the midnight hour. The Essenes, because of their gifts in channeling and prophecy, had total foreknowledge of Jesus' coming and that was a major reason for their joining together in the first place. One last interesting point that Djwhal Khul told me is that Mary did ascend at the end of her life on Earth.

More Fascinating Information

In my continuing research some more absolutely fascinating information has come to me. One point is that Enoch was one of Jesus' past lives, according to Djwhal Khul. Enoch achieved his ascension and in that lifetime was overshadowed by a being who currently sits on the Galactic Council, named Melchizedek. It is interesting that in a later life Jesus took the name of Melchizedek.

The second fascinating piece of information is from Brian Grattan and it has been confirmed by Vywamus. After Lord Maitreya resurrected the body of Jesus, he lived on Planet Earth for thirty-one more years. During this time he went to India and also teleported to America.

One other interesting piece of information is that in a past life Mohammed, the founder of the Islamic faith, was the disciple of Bartholomew. During his life as Mohammed, Archangel Gabriel and Jesus were two of his main teachers on the inner plane. In a later lifetime he took his fifth initiation as a yogi in India. He came back one more time as Patrick Henry, one of the great patriots of the American Revolution. I don't think the fundamentalist Arab world would be too happy to learn this most fascinating piece of occult information.

Lord Maitreya, the Planetary Christ, is the most highly evolved being of our Earth's chain. According to Paramahansa Yogananda, Mary Magdalene was the Catholic stigmatist, Therese Neuman. Krishna, the past life of the Lord Maitreya, came to teach humanity the second initiation. If I am not mistaken, I think he attained his fifth initiation in that lifetime.

Jesus does use the name Sananda on the inner plane, as many of the extraterrestrial channelings of the Ashtar Command and others indicate. I got a confirmation of this from Vywamus.

St. Peter was a past life of Brian Grattan, author of *The Rider on the White Horse* and *Mahatma I & II*. Brian Grattan is currently alive and well on this planet and doing some incredible work.

15

Sanat Kumara's Training

*The Lord of the World, the One Initiator, he
who is called in the Bible "The Ancient of
Days" and in the Hindu scriptures the First
Kumara. He, Sanat Kumara, it is, from his
throne at Shamballa in the Gobi Desert,
who presides over the Lodge of Masters and
holds in his hands all reins of government in
all the three departments.*

Djwhal Khul

Each of us as incarnated personalities on Earth must make a choice at
the time of our ascension of which of the seven paths of higher
evolution we will choose in continuing our cosmic journey on our return to
the Godhead. These seven paths are kind of like specialized professions.
God is so infinite that there is no way we can learn everything, so we must
focus our development and service along specific lines.
1. The Path of Earth Service
2. The Path of Magnetic Work
3. The Path of Training for Planetary Logos
4. The Path to Sirius
5. The Ray Path
6. The Path the Logos Himself Is On
7. The Path of Absolute Sonship
I have given a more detailed understanding of these seven paths in the
chapter on the initiations. I would also suggest the Alice Bailey book called
The Rays and the Initiations, which gives an even deeper understanding of
these seven paths.

This chapter deals with our beloved Planetary Logos, Sanat Kumara, who, with the help of Vywamus, Sanat Kumara's higher self, shares with us his life and training to become a Planetary Logos. This would correspond to path number three on the list above. I have researched this information from a book that was channeled by Vywamus and put out by The Tibetan Foundation. It is honestly one of the most interesting books I have ever read. Much of the information in this book had never been allowed to be released until this planet had passed through the Harmonic Convergence, which allowed the fourth-dimension energies to come to this planet in a new and more profound way. Sanat Kumara tells of his actual training which took him well beyond the ninth initiation and on into the cosmic levels of consciousness. The book is *The Story of Sanat Kumara—Training a Planetary Logos* by Vywamus. I cannot recommend highly enough that you try to find it at your favorite metaphysical bookstore. It is one of the most inspiring books I have ever read, and it will give you a good sense of whether or not this particular path is one you might consider taking.

Before beginning this story I would like to describe Vywamus more clearly. He is a cosmic being who evolved to his present position in the Hierarchy through physical incarnations on a planet similar to Earth. In his incarnations on that planet he was a channel for higher sources of knowledge, as was Janet McClure, who channeled the above-mentioned book. He achieved his ascension after only thirty-seven incarnations on that particular planet. He might be considered the soul or monad of Sanat Kumara.

Sanat Kumara

Sanat Kumara also evolved to his present position through a series of Earth lives on a small planet in our Milky Way Galaxy. It is a planet that is very similar to Earth in size and density. Over a period of many years he had sixty-nine lives on that particular planet, upon which he achieved his ascension.

After his ascension he studied music on the higher planes with the angels for a time. He attended classes on the theory of music dealing with all the instruments in the known universe. Music serves as an excellent medium through which to better understand vibration and energy. This might be called the study of the music of the spheres.

After this short interim period on deeper spiritual levels he made the decision to follow the path of becoming a Planetary Logos. The job of a Planetary Logos is to ensoul an entire planet, much as we on Earth now inhabit a physical body. The difference is that he has a much larger body and he has responsibility for the evolution of all souls and life forms on that planet.

A Planetary Logos is like the president or king of the planet. Every being and every thing lives within his aura. He does not ascend or leave his new physical body (the Earth) until all life forms ascend. As you can see, this is quite a job and responsibility. A Planetary Logos is not responsible to any one individual but rather to all life forms simultaneously. The training to become a Planetary Logos is extremely strenuous, as you can imagine.

The first and most amazing part of Sanat Kumara's training was that he had to divide his consciousness into nine hundred thousand pieces or fragments, and each piece had to incarnate onto a different planet in the galaxy. The idea of this training was to bring each soul extension back into the oneness and to gain an understanding as to how each part fit gently into the other parts to support the larger Divine form.

In one great burst of creativity this occurred and after a long period of time, eventually all nine hundred thousand came back into the oneness. All nine hundred thousand parts had now become equal partners. A great sense of cosmic unconditional love had been achieved. Sanat Kumara was now ready for the next step in his training to become a Planetary Logos.

This next step entailed the creating of a physical body and going to the planet Venus in physical form. Venus is a very highly evolved planet of a more fourth-dimensional nature. It is a planet that is able to blend both its inner and outer beauty. It was far more advanced than any other planet Sanat Kumara had ever been on.

It was on this planet that Sanat Kumara was privileged to meet one of the greatest Planetary Logos experts in all of existence. His name is Adonis. He is a cosmic being of vast proportions who chose to set up and organize this great school and training ground long ago. The true name of the planet Venus is really Eysmnje, which is pronounced "Ice-mon-ya." Venus, or Eysmnje, is a part of the third eye chakra of the Manifesting Creator.

On Venus seven temples and twelve training facilities were built. Each facility had a specific function which Sanat Kumara would have to learn to master in order to complete his training. When this training facility was first set up eons ago, the plan was for it to train six billion souls. Twelve thousand souls initially came and became the original teachers for this training program. A cosmic call for students went out in the cosmic newspaper, and millions of souls replied. Eons of time later, souls are still arriving from this original cosmic call. Part of Adonis' theory was that if you can make your life work on the physical level, it will work anywhere in the cosmos. I think all who read this chapter would agree with this.

In Sanat Kumara's training group of students planning to become Planetary Logoi, there were two thousand. Adonis, being the cosmic being he is, could teach all two thousand simultaneously and individually. At this cosmic level of evolution a Master can split his consciousness into as many parts as he needs to and still retain total comprehension of all parts simultaneously.

Part of Sanat Kumara's training was to learn how to put together a loving and supportive system of consciousness for an entire planet, one that would his be his personally.

In one particular phase of Sanat Kumara's training, a very interesting thing happened. He didn't do well on a particular exercise and when Adonis and fellow students tried to correct him his buttons got pushed and he became very angry. I think that Sanat Kumara has most graciously shared this information to show us that even a Master being who has ascended, had had nine hundred thousand pieces of himself returned back into the oneness, and has passed on into cosmic levels of evolution can still have a small fragment of negative ego left over in his subconscious mind. He, himself, had thought that he was beyond such responses.

Part of the training was to learn to undo these old remnants. At each stage of evolution he was told that he had to release old points of view which allowed, then, for more expanded states of consciousness. We go through this same process on our level. We die to the physical body and then get used to the astral plane. We then must die to the astral plane and get used to the mental body. We then die to the mental body and rise and expand to the Buddhic plane. We die to the Buddhic plane and rise to the atmic plane. We die to the atmic plane and rise to the monadic plane. We get used to each level and in a sense think of it as our home, but then we must let go of it to expand and rise in consciousness. This is a never-ending process as we rise toward the Godhead and what Vywamus has termed the Cocreator level.

Sanat Kumara became aware of other remnants or patterns having to do with not liking to train his negative ego so part of his training was to clear out this final 3% to 4% of his negative ego. He was told that a person can ascend and still have this amount of resistance left.

As time went on in their training Sanat Kumara's group was able to comprehend 30% of the lessons that were needed to become a Planetary Logos. This took two thousand years of Earth time to achieve.

In the next part of Sanat Kumara's training he was assigned to work with the Venusian Planetary Logos. Part of this training had to do with the greater letting go of an individual perspective so he could pull into view all beings and life forms from every point of view at once.

The job of the Planetary Logos is to set up a framework on the physical level for all evolving life forms which allows them all to evolve and grow. The Planetary Logos could be symbolically likened to a mountain and the paths on the mountain which the life forms travel to evolve. The Planetary Logos is also at the top of the mountain so he can guide all life forms toward the top. This is why it is essential to remove all resistances or patterns that might interfere with the climbing by any particular life form.

Other students were releasing other patterns that Sanat Kumara had resolved, such as fears, betrayal, and so on. The training of a Planetary Logos can be likened to our evolution as personalities on Earth. We, as incarnated soul extensions or personalities, live within physical, emotional, mental, and spiritual bodies. We are in charge of unifying, integrating, and balancing our thoughts, feelings, instincts, vital forces, intuition, and all the cells and organs in our physical bodies. We are simultaneously trying to evolve all aspects of ourselves in a balanced manner. If we neglect one aspect we end up getting sick and having suffering of some kind. We have to make sure that all cells in our bodies evolve in a unified manner. We can't favor one over another. The same can be true of a Planetary Logos but on a much larger scale. He or she must evolve all life forms (cells) in his or her greater body.

In one particularly fascinating training exercise done with a type of cosmic computer, Sanat Kumara concentrated too deeply on one particular entity on the planet and forced him into his point of view. This took away the free choice of the entity involved, and if the situation had been real, it would have killed the entity and forced Sanat Kumara to take on his karma. This is the delicate balance a Planetary Logos must tread, of guiding, yet letting all evolving life forms retain their free choice even if that means they are going to create suffering for themselves. To go too far in either direction would throw off the guidance system for the entire planet.

As Sanat Kumara's training progressed he was shown that the planet he was meant to be in charge of was Planet Earth. Now we must remember that Sanat Kumara came to this planet to start this job over eighteen and one half million years ago. He has been on the job for a long time already. In the initial stages, before he fully began this process, he first connected his energy and life force with the planet. This was done, of course, with the help of his teacher. He basically placed the planet within his heart chakra. The next phase of his training was to explore every level and part of the planet to prepare it for the next step. This process alone took two thousand years.

Because Sanat Kumara was a new Planetary Logos and this was his first job, he was told that three brother Kumaras would go with him from Venus to assist him in creating certain needed spiritual links with the planet. These three assistants were very experienced and would serve as a triangular configuration. Sanat Kumara's teacher, Adonis, was also connected, as were the Solar, Galactic and Universal Logoi.

Sanat Kumara was then told by his teacher to take a fifty-year vacation before the full incarnation into the planet would occur. After fifty years he returned to the training center and all the Planetary Logos trainees had a party to celebrate the completion of their training and the new opportunities that were about to begin for each of them in their service. Even though they would all be going on separate missions they would all continue to network together in the cosmos. Sanat Kumara had some final sessions with his teacher to clear out any last lingering remnants or patterns, and a special link was created between Sanat Kumara and the angelic kingdom. This was done to allow the angels to work more closely with the Earth.

The Final Transfer to Earth

On the day of the transfer, Sanat Kumara was placed in some kind of powerful device. A very powerful energy connection was built up and Sanat Kumara was brought to Earth. The three Kumaras held their triangular formation to stabilize the transfer process. The complete incarnation into the Earth took place. This process of totally linking with all parts of the Earth took another thousand years. Many electrical storms occurred on the planet during the adjustment period. They occurred because of the readjustment of the energy grid system that was then taking place. It was also during this pre-Lemurian period that the electrical wars took place. They were the wars between the Electrical Ones and the people of Earth for control of the planet. They lasted for about five hundred years. Sanat Kumara's guidance helped to end this conflict.

Sanat Kumara landed and headquartered himself and his group in Shamballa, located near the Himalaya Mountains. Upon his arrival he met with the existing spiritual government and received a full briefing. Many then left for new assignments and some stayed to help Sanat Kumara in his mission.

Sanat Kumara also began to guide more closely certain individuals existing on Earth whom he saw as future members of the spiritual government. The plan was to eventually have as many souls as possible in the spiritual government who were already part of the Earth chain.

Since Sanat Kumara has been in charge of this planet for the past eighteen and one half million years, it is hard to think of him as a young Planetary Logos. It is amazing to think that one day each one of us could go through a similar training program and take on similar responsibilities if we choose to do so.

Some Final Thoughts

I would like to thank The Tibetan Foundation (although it is no longer in operation) for putting out a book that gives such an extraordinary insight into the evolution and training of a Planetary Logos. Sanat Kumara and Vywamus can be contacted in your meditations for the asking and I highly recommend you do so.

For advanced students, I am ending this chapter by including a diagram from the Theosophical literature which goes one step further by depicting the evolution of a Solar Logos. This diagram actually shows the seven subplanes of the cosmic physical plane and the seven cosmic planes. One gets a sense of the Planetary Logos as compared to the Cosmic Logoi. It also compares the Planetary Monads to the Cosmic Monads. I don't claim to understand this diagram completely myself; however, it does give a glimpse of the infinitude and limitlessness of God.

EVOLUTION OF A SOLAR LOGOS

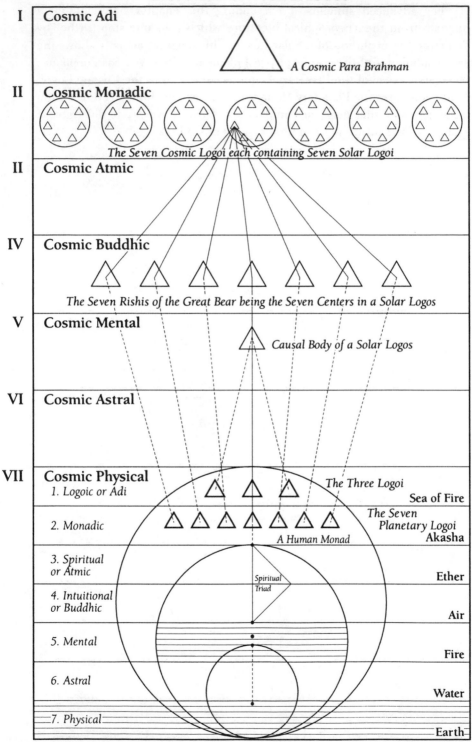

The Seven Cosmic Logoi each containing Seven Solar Logoi

The Seven Rishis of the Great Bear being the Seven Centers in a Solar Logos

Causal Body of a Solar Logos

The Three Logoi

A Human Monad

The Seven Planetary Logoi

Spiritual Triad

16

Sanat Kumara and the Planetary Hierarchy

*In my Father's house there are
many mansions*

The Master Jesus

In this chapter I would like to focus on Sanat Kumara and this Planetary Hierarchy in a more in-depth fashion. I would like to begin with the Lord of the World, the Ancient of Days, the One Initiator, the highest being in our entire planetary system, our Spiritual King and Divine Director, Sanat Kumara.

Sanat Kumara

Eighteen and one half million years ago the Planetary Logos of our Earth system, who is one of the seven spirits before the throne, took physical incarnation under the name of Sanat Kumara. It was Sanat Kumara who started the Spiritual Hierarchy for this planet.

Sanat Kumara came from Venus with three other glorious beings. Before they came here the Earth was a very dark planet with a very heavy atmosphere and no possibility of raising its energies, spiritually speaking. Sanat Kumara and his brother Kumaras incarnated into etheric bodies, not physical bodies, and have been here with the Earth ever since.

Sanat Kumara is the greatest of all the Avatars. Sanat Kumara and his three Kumaras, also known as the three Buddhas, reside in Shamballa. Shamballa is not on the physical plane. Shamballa could be likened to the White House in the United States, as it is the seat of the planetary government. Shamballa is both a location and a state of consciousness. Shamballa is where the council meetings are held, which include all members of the Spiritual Hierarchy who have passed the fifth initiation. The Spiritual Hierarchy is headed by the Lord Maitreya and is a separate department in the spiritual government. Sanat Kumara is not a member of the Hierarchy.

Shamballa embodies the will aspect of the Creator. The Spiritual Hierarchy embodies the love/wisdom center of the Creator. Sanat Kumara receives the Creator's energies mainly from the Solar Logos, Helios, as I have explained.

In Sanat Kumara's charge is the evolution not only of humanity, but also of all beings on Earth—mineral, plant, and animal alike. Sanat Kumara's physical body is actually Planet Earth itself. We all, in a sense, live within his glorious aura. In his mind he holds the plan of evolution for this planet. His appearance is said to be that of a handsome youth. The geographic location on Earth that is connected to Shamballa is the Gobi Desert.

The three Kumaras who help Sanat Kumara have also been called the Pratyeka Buddhas. They assist Sanat Kumara in his work of guiding the evolution of this planet. The Spiritual Hierarchy, who report to Sanat Kumara, often report to these three Buddhas. When council meetings are held at Shamballa, members of the Spiritual Hierarchy either attend in their etheric bodies or attune to it in consciousness.

Masters at this level can split their consciousnesses into more than one place at the same time. I asked Djwhal Khul about this once. I knew that he was channeling through many people on this planet. I asked him what would happen if all the channels on the Earth that he was in contact with wanted to speak with him at ten o'clock on Sunday morning. How many ways could he split his consciousness and still give clear and coherent guidance? Djwhal told me he could do fifty channelings simultaneously and remain clear. He also told me that Sanat Kumara and Vywamus could split their consciousnesses into one thousand parts simultaneously and give readings in the same moment. What is even more remarkable is that in one of these projectiles, Sanat Kumara can encompass an entire state and know everything that is going on. This is the magnificence of the being that we have guiding the evolution of the Earth.

It is also Sanat Kumara who performs the third, fourth, fifth, and sixth initiations. Sanat Kumara is in actuality a young Planetary Logos, compared to the Planetary Logoi on other planets; however, he is very old in experience.

Sanat Kumara, in his omnipotence, omnipresence, and omniscience, passes down directives to members of Shamballa and the Hierarchy. Humans, then, as his representatives, carry out these directives and pass them down to those whom we are in charge of.

One interesting story of how this can work is something Djwhal Khul told me. Djwhal, upon his ascension, had chosen the Path to Sirius, in terms of choosing one of the seven paths of higher evolution. Sanat Kumara asked Djwhal if he would forgo his movement to Sirius and help him with a certain line of service work that was needed on the Earth plane, which he was currently doing. Djwhal most graciously agreed to Sanat Kumara's request and we are all very lucky to have him here still working with us and helping us.

So Sanat Kumara might be termed the "mastermind" of Earth's evolution. He is literally God for this planet, just as Helios is the mastermind and God for the solar system. I also want to make it clear here that he is in charge of the Planetary Hierarchy. It is important to understand, however, that there is a distinct and separate Solar Hierarchy, Galactic Hierarchy, and Universal Hierarchy. Each planet has its own Planetary Logos and Planetary Hierarchy. Isn't it amazing to think that each one who is reading this book might some day be in charge of a planet's evolution? And in the future beyond that, one could be in charge of a solar system or galaxy, if that is the cosmic path of evolution one chooses to follow.

For Sanat Kumara it is the totality of evolution upon the Earth that concerns him; his is not just an individualistic approach. However, he does pay attention to the development of his initiates. It is also important to understand that Sanat Kumara is in a state of evolution just as humans are. As he goes through his cosmic initiations, it helps humanity and as humanity goes through its planetary initiations, it aids him.

Sanat Kumara and the Planetary Hierarchy receive energies from the Solar Logos and Solar Hierarchy just as they, in turn, receive their energies from the Galactic Logos and Galactic Hierarchy. This process continues all the way back to God Himself. At each level the energies are stepped downward, in a ladder-like fashion. If the energies were not stepped down at each level, people on Earth would just burn up because the frequencies would be so high.

One of the three Kumaras, one of the Buddhas, has recently left the Planetary Hierarchy and moved on to his cosmic evolution. His name is Sanaka Kumara. He has been replaced by the one who was the former Manu in our government. As these higher beings move on in their cosmic evolution, it is those in the Hierarchy and eventually those on Earth who will fill these vacated positions. They cannot leave until there is someone spiritually developed enough to take their place. So, again, they are as dependent on humans as humans are on them. It is one gigantic cosmic chain of command with God being our ultimate commander and chief.

Sanat Kumara and his three Kumaras achieved, in an earlier solar system, that which those on Earth and in this solar system are attempting to perfect now. Standing around Sanat Kumara, but more withdrawn and esoteric, are three more Kumaras whom I have not yet mentioned. These added three make a total of seven Kumaras of our planetary manifestation.

The three esoteric Kumaras embody a type of energy which is not yet in full manifestation on this planet. Each of the six Kumaras is a distributing agent for the energy and force of the six other Planetary Logoi. (The word logoi is the plural of logos.) Sanat Kumara is one of the Planetary Logoi. Through each of the Kumaras passes the life force of one of the six rays. Sanat Kumara is the synthesizer and embodiment of the seventh type. Each is distinguished by one of the six colors. Within Sanat Kumara is the full planetary color spectrum.

They are also involved with helping souls from other planetary systems to incarnate on Earth. Each one of them is in direct communication with one of the sacred planets. (Certain planets within our system have achieved sacred status, and others are not yet at that state of evolution.)

Lastly, according to solar and planetary astrology, certain of the Kumaras will be more active than others. The three Buddhas of activity who are more exoteric change from time to time and then become more esoteric, or hidden. Only Sanat Kumara remains consistent.

The seven Kumaras are the seven highest self-conscious beings in our solar system. They manifest through the medium of a planet in the same way as a human being manifests through a physical body. Sanat Kumara is, in essence, the personal god of this planet. Because of Sanat Kumara's great efforts on behalf of Planet Earth, he is receiving aid and energy from a member of Universal Hierarchy. This is an extremely high source flowing through him to aid the Earth.

Now, I also need to add here that above Sanat Kumara is Vywamus, Vywamus, again, being the higher self or monadic level of Sanat Kumara. Sanat Kumara receives guidance from Vywamus as those on Earth receive guidance from their souls and monads. Vywamus is very available to channel through people on this plane and does so frequently. He is a master psychologist, and he brings through a great deal of cosmic information that is just not available to the average guide and teacher. He has many books and transcripts that are available through Light Technology Publishing and local bookstores.

Another set of beings that many readers of this book have heard of but that have not been mentioned so far are the Lords of Karma. These Masters are focused specifically on the evolution of the human kingdom. Their purpose is the distribution of karma as it affects individuals. They also take care of the Akashic Records. In Christian terminology they are known as the recording angels and they participate in Solar Councils.

Cooperating with the Lords of Karma are the large groups of initiates and angels who occupy themselves with the right adjustment of karma on all levels. They also help to bring the souls into incarnation at the correct times and seasons according to their ray types.

Emanating from the Creator are seven great rays of energy which are discussed in extensive detail in Chapter 10. For the purposes of this chapter it is important to understand that these seven rays are stepped down through the Universal, Galactic, and Solar Hierarchies in a graded fashion so they will be usable on Earth's level of development. The remaining personnel of the hierarchies are divided into three main departments and four subsidiary groups.

The Manu: The First Ray

The first ray deals with the will aspect of the Creator. This department in the spiritual government is headed by a being in a position called the Manu, which is a title much like the titles of president or senator. The Master who currently holds this position, we have been told, is Allah Gobi. This is a recent appointment. The one who was the Manu previously has replaced one of the Buddhas of Activity, or Kumaras. This has allowed Sanaka Kumara to move on to his cosmic evolution.

The Manu and his work are not readily available to humanity. If too much is known about the Manu and his work, more people attune to him, which distracts from the important work he is doing. His work is largely connected with government, planetary politics, and the founding and dissolution of the root races. The Manu is the one who is responsible for the will and purpose of the Planetary Logos. He also works in close cooperation with the building angels. He is also involved with changes in the Earth's crust. It is he and his coworkers in this department who try to direct the minds of the statesmen and politicians all over the planet.

One of the assistants of the Manu is the Master El Morya, who has been called the Chohan, or the Lord of the First Ray. We have been told that in the future El Morya is in line to become the Manu when Allah Gobi moves on. El Morya holds an even more responsible position than he did before, although he is still maintaining his previous responsibilities. It is for this reason he is not currently doing any teaching. Many of his students have been delegated to the Master Djwhal Khul, who serves this function for many of the Masters.

Ray one is very active now and soon a young initiate will be training to take over some of El Morya's former responsibilities. One other Master that has been very involved with the first ray is the Master Jupiter. To be perfectly honest, I do not know a lot about him other than the fact that he is one of the older Masters and has been around for a very long time. He is a very great being and I would be amiss not to mention him.

The first ray is a very catalytic ray. It serves as a cleanser and a changer. It serves the function of breaking down old conditions and moving them forward to a more productive and practical means of expression. Those working with this ray are dealing with a very intense energy. They are specifically chosen for their adeptness at working with energy.

The World Teacher, the Christ: the Second Ray

The second ray deals with the love/wisdom aspect of God. This department of the spiritual government is headed by a position called the Christ, the World Teacher, the Bodhisattva. The great Master who heads this department is, of course, the Lord Maitreya. I have spoken of him a great deal in the chapter on the reappearance of the Christ and the externalization of the Hierarchy (Chapter 11) since he is currently physically incarnated on this planet. For this reason I will not repeat too much of what I have said already. What I will say is that he is the great Lord of Love and Compassion. He has presided over the destinies of humankind since 600 B.C. His predecessor was Gautama Buddha.

Through the Lord Maitreya flows the energy of the second department from the Planetary Logos, Sanat Kumara. To Lord Maitreya is committed the guidance of spiritual destinies of men. It is his job to help all soul extensions on Earth realize God and achieve liberation. He works closely with the Manu and the Mahachohan (third department). The second department is involved with the teaching and education aspect of humanity.

Helping the Lord Maitreya as his main assistant is the Master Kuthumi. He is, again, in line to take over for the Lord Maitreya when he moves on to his cosmic evolution. Djwhal Khul is Kuthumi's senior assistant. Master Kuthumi is very well known and has a large ashram with many students studying under him. Djwhal Khul has taken over the charge of many of his students as Kuthumi has taken on more and more responsibility. Master Kuthumi is one of the great Masters who is also involved with the externalization process of many of the Masters on Earth right now.

Many of the great changes on the Earth are a direct result of the combined energies of Sanat Kumara, the Buddha, Lord Maitreya, and the Master Kuthumi. The Master El Morya is also in constant contact with the Lord Maitreya and Master Kuthumi. The Master Djwhal Khul has also assumed a much greater responsibility than he previously had. He has two young masters helping him in his work. The Master Kuthumi has also been termed the Chohan or Lord of the Second Ray. This is a position under the Lord Maitreya, although at this time he is functioning almost as an equal. The second ray is the ray of the great teachers of the world.

The Mahachohan, the Lord of Civilization: the Third Ray

The third ray deals with the quality of active intelligence. This department in the spiritual government is headed by a position termed the Mahachohan. The name of the Master who holds this position currently has not been released. What we do know is that the present Mahachohan is not the original one who headed the office at the founding of the Hierarchy eighteen and one half million years ago. At that time it was held by one of the six Kumaras who came into etheric incarnation with Sanat Kumara. He took hold of his position during the second subrace of the Atlantean root race (see Chapter 1).

The work of the Mahachohan concerns itself with the flowering forth of the principle of intelligence on Planet Earth. The Mahachohan is the embodiment of the intelligence aspect of Divinity. He has also been called the Lord of Civilization. The Mahachohan gives the world its thrust forward on its path of evolution.

The Mahachohan works with energy in a very concrete way. His work involves making things happen in a grounded sense. He manifests on the earthly plane with the will of the Creator. The first two departments do this but not in a concrete way. The Mahachohan manipulates the forces of nature and is largely the source of electrical energy as humans know it. Energy flows to him from the throat center of the Planetary Logos.

These three great departments represent the will, love, and intelligence aspects of the Planetary Logos. They could also be termed government, religion, and civilization. A third way to look at this would be to say that we have the physical manifestation of the root races, the love aspect, and the mind of the Planetary Logos working out into physical manifestation.

The work and responsibilities of the Mahachohan and the third department have greatly increased to the extent that Sanat Kumara and his coworkers have realigned this department recently. The Mahachohan has been raised closer to Sanat Kumara, and everyone else in this department has been raised to fill the vacant positions.

The Master Serapis Bey has hence moved up to take on much added responsibility, although Serapis Bey still carries out some of his former work as previous head of the fourth department. In the Masters who are engaged in this third ray work there is a very strong characteristic of adaptability. This quality helps them to work well with people and be "all things to all men," as St. Paul said. These Masters have great tact and a rare faculty for doing the right thing at the right time. Astrology is very connected with this ray. The Master Serapis Bey still works extensively with the devic or angelic evolution. He is a very able Master who carries out the work of the Mahachohan very well.

The Mahachohan receives directives from the Christ, the Buddhas of Activity (Kumaras), and, of course, from Sanat Kumara. The Mahachohan also receives a direct input of energy from the Solar Logos and his third ray Mahachohan on the Solar Hierarchy level. From the Mahachohan this energy then flows to Serapis Bey. It also flows to the Christ and the Manu and out in every direction.

The department of the Mahachohan is divided into five sections. Besides the third ray department itself, the rays four, five, six, and seven and their corresponding departments are all under the leadership of the Mahachohan and the third department. The Master Serapis Bey previously headed the fourth ray and department, and this is now being taken over by the Master Paul, as Serapis Bey has moved to the third department. The fifth ray and department are headed by the Master Hilarion. The sixth ray and department are headed by the Master Jesus. The seventh ray and department are headed by Saint Germain.

Again, I emphasize that these rays and departments are subsidiary rays and departments all working under the authority of the Mahachohan. One can see that the Mahachohan is one very busy Master who holds an incredibly important job. The great Master who is in line to take over this position when the present Mahachohan leaves to continue his cosmic evolution is Saint Germain.

Saint Germain will be moving from the head of the seventh ray to take on this most important position. Saint Germain has been offered many positions within other spiritual governments of other planetary systems. It may be surprising that this can happen. Other solar systems can make spiritual offers of prime assignments to Masters they hear about and work with. This is much like businesses on the Earth that make offers of jobs to executives in other companies.

Saint Germain, being the extraordinarily competent Master that he is, has decided not to take the many prime spiritual assignments he has been offered and instead has decided to remain working with the Earth's evolution. Earth is very lucky to have him.

Saint Germain's extraordinary past lives have had an incredible impact on the evolution of this planet. He is now very busy with the seventh ray energies that are pouring onto this planet. The four subsidiary departments of the third department receive energy from the Mahachohan. However, they also receive energy from the second and first departments. The Mahachohan's job intensifies whenever a civilization reaches a critical point, as Planet Earth's is now. The rays that are most emphasized on this planet now are the first, second, and seventh, the seventh ray being the responsibility of the third department.

The Mahachohan has great responsibilities and is not available for personal or personality contact on Earth. Serapis Bey is kind of like an administrator of the energy that he receives from the Mahachohan. After receiving it he distributes it wherever it is needed. The third ray is very practical in its form and method, much more so than the other departments. Serapis Bey is very involved with helping the Mahachohan oversee the fourth, fifth, sixth, and seventh rays and the Masters who head them.

The Fourth Ray and Fourth Department

The fourth ray and fourth department are, again, under the auspices of the Mahachohan and the third department. This ray deals with harmony through conflict. The Chohan of this ray is the Master Paul the Venetian, who used to be the head of the third department and has switched to the fourth. The most important area being worked on at this time is the field of the arts.

A whole new approach is being focalized on the Earth. For example, in the field of music it will soon be possible to experience exactly what the composer meant to portray. This is very different from just listening to music. People will be able actually to become almost a part of the music. People, for the most part, have been separate from it in the past. In the future they will be able to experience it completely.

The same will be true for visual art. People will be able to fully experience what the artist meant to portray. Untold artists have been frustrated in the past by not being able to get across the complete message and meaning of their art.

The fourth ray in its lower aspect creates conflict and in its higher aspect creates harmony. There is another Master apparently working under Paul the Venetian who has recently taken his ascension. His name is Paul. He is very connected to working with the angelic or devic kingdom. The Archangel Gabriel is apparently like a brother to the Master Paul. Archangel Gabriel is also connected to the arts, but from the angelic kingdom's perspective.

Paul the Venetian reports to the Lord Maitreya in a very direct sense and also to the Master Serapis Bey. At the level of the Ascended Masters this ray is always harmonious. It is only when it reaches the Earth and personalities become involved with it that it can become conflicted. The fourth department also deals with the giving out of certain types of information about the Hierarchy through the senses. People who are very connected to this fourth ray are not happy unless they can introduce beauty into their environments.

The Fifth Ray and the Fifth Department

The fifth ray and the fifth department deal with concrete knowledge and science. The Chohan of this ray is the Master Hilarion. Many of you may know of him from the occult book he channeled called *Light on the Path*. This department is also under the auspices of the Mahachohan and the third department. This department is involved with bringing into being the New Age. This is done by learning to use the mental area in an ever more forceful and productive manner. Hilarion shares this focus with a Master many may have not heard of before by the name of the Master Marko. The mental capacity in this department is emphasized. Masters in this department are able to split their consciousnesses in many directions simultaneously, even more than in the other departments, because of this mental focus.

Master Hilarion no longer takes many students because he is busy working to bring in the New Age. He does this by holding higher mentally focused energy patterns. There is a special triangular pattern that runs from the three Buddhas to the Manu to the fifth department and then to the Master Hilarion and back again. The Master Marko has taken over many of Hilarion's formerly assigned duties. The Masters in this area are very creative in using the higher mental energies.

Among Master Marko's responsibilities are all the scientific pursuits going on in the world at this time. Many of the scientific inventions on the Earth are first created on the inner plane and then channeled through scientists in some manner, sometimes even without the scientists' conscious awareness that this process is going on.

Master Marko has agreed to help strengthen the mental and higher mental abilities within if one calls upon him by name. He can be called upon in meditation using the color orange to aid in attunement to this department. Part of this work also deals with helping humanity attune to the intuitive as well as the concrete scientific mind. The Master Hilarion is also the Master stimulating all the psychical research and it was through him and his work that the spiritualistic movement began. He has under observation all those who are psychics of the higher order, and he assists in helping them to develop their powers for service to humankind.

The Sixth Ray and the Sixth Department

The sixth ray and department deal with abstract idealism and devotion. The Chohan of this department is the Master Jesus. His pupils are frequently distinguished by their fanaticism and devotion to ideals as were the Christian martyrs of the past.

Djwhal Khul has described Jesus as a martial figure with much strength, will, and purpose, a strict disciplinarian, yet in service of love. This department has been directing the Christian religion since its inception. A lot of his focus now is to integrate and blend the Eastern and Western schools of thought and religion. He is particularly suited for this job in that during his life in Palestine, he studied extensively in the East during the eighteen "lost" years that the Bible doesn't account for. The sixth department is in a transitional phase because the sixth ray is on its way out in a planetary sense and is being replaced by the incoming seventh ray. The sixth department is finishing up the work of this ray in a very focused manner as we move into the Aquarian Age.

They have a tricky job in this department for they must finish up what they are doing on the sixth ray, yet allow the new work to come in. Besides the integrating of the religions of the world, the sixth department is also very involved with the devic or angelic kingdom.

The Master Jesus does not work with too many students now because the Lord Maitreya depends on him for so many other projects on Earth. Some still receive instructions, but most have been passed into the great seventh department as it is now assuming much more responsibility.

Jesus works especially with the masses and is doing a lot of work in preparing the masses for the coming declaration of the Lord Maitreya. He has also been working diligently at neutralizing as much as possible the mistakes and errors of church theologians in the interpretations of his teachings.

The sixth ray is that of devotional saints and mystics of all religions. Jesus and the sixth department work under the Mahachohan and the third department. One of the goals of this department is the creation of one world religion that incorporates all paths as valid in the journey to the kingdom of God. He is also working to raise humanity out of the morass of fear and self-doubt so as to awaken the Christ consciousness in all beings. He is also striving to achieve a union between science and religion, which he hopes will counteract the extremely materialistic attitude of so many people in this world.

The Seventh Ray and the Seventh Department

The seventh ray and department are also under the auspices of the Mahachohan and the third department. They deal with ceremonial magic and order and they are headed by the Master Saint Germain. He has also been known to be called the Master Rakoszi. This department has become extremely important because of the approaching Aquarian Age. As the New Age comes into full manifestation, Saint Germain's responsibilities will increase tenfold.

The seventh ray is also involved with bringing forth the five higher rays that just came into manifestation in the 1970's. These are the rays eight, nine, ten, eleven, and twelve. (See Chapter 10.) These energies come to the Earth from Sanat Kumara through Shamballa, from where it is then channeled to the seventh department. Saint Germain works to a large extent with ceremonial magic, and he employs the services of great angels. He is the executive officer of the lodge of Masters as far as the work in

Europe and America is concerned, where he executes the plans devised by the inner council of the Christ.

He is especially concerned with Europe's racial affairs and the mental unfoldment of the American and Australian people. It is his job to help materialize the new civilization of the New Age. Saint Germain is, in actuality, a much greater being than just the Saint Germain phase of his development that most people are familiar with. His competence has earned him the right to go wherever he wants to go and even to leave the Hierarchy of the Earth if he so chooses. As already mentioned, he has been offered jobs in much more vast networks of government.

Currently two unknown Masters are being trained to take over many of the responsibilities of Saint Germain. Many of the students of Saint Germain are now being trained by these two unknown Masters. They are unknown in the sense that the Hierarchy has deemed it inappropriate at this time to release their names.

17

God and the Cosmic Hierarchy

*Only as a man understands himself can he
arrive at an understanding of that which is
the sum total that we call God*

Djwhal Khul
as channeled by
Alice A. Bailey

In metaphysical esoteric thought it is understood that there are seven great
dimensions of reality. The seven dimensions we are working through as
incarnated soul extensions on Earth are:

1. The physical plane
2. The astral plane
3. The mental plane
4. The Buddhic plane
5. The atmic plane
6. The monadic plane
7. The logoic plane

The Planetary Hierarchy

Each initiation of the seven major initiations we pass through takes us
one step higher in terms of our level of attunement to that plane and the
stabilization of that attunement. The first initiation deals with physical
mastery; the second, astral mastery; the third, mental mastery. The fourth
initiation takes us to the Buddhic plane, the fifth to the atmic plane, the
sixth to the monadic plane and ascension, and the seventh to merger with
the Planetary Logos on the logoic plane.

The Masters we are so familiar with such as Jesus, Djwhal Khul, Saint
Germain, Kuthumi, El Morya, Hilarion, Serapis Bey, Paul the Venetian,

Buddha, and the Lord Maitreya, are all Masters of these planes and deserve our highest respect and admiration.

It is important to understand, however, that these great Masters are only Masters of what is referred to as the cosmic physical plane. The above-mentioned dimensions of reality are only the seven subplanes of the cosmic physical plane and thus are only a small fraction of the seven cosmic planes.

The seven cosmic planes are:
    1.   The cosmic physical plane
    2.   The cosmic astral plane
    3.   The cosmic mental plane
    4.   The cosmic Buddhic plane
    5.   The cosmic atmic plane
    6.   The cosmic monadic plane
    7.   The cosmic logoic plane

There are, in actuality, nine levels of initiation within the seven subplanes of the cosmic physical plane. Liberation from the wheel of rebirth is the fourth initiation. Ascension is the sixth initiation. The seventh initiation is the highest initiation that can be taken on this earthly plane. In the ascended state we will be able to take two more initiations which will bring us to the ninth initiation. Upon passing the ninth initiation we leave the seven subplanes of the cosmic physical plane. We will then begin our spiritual evolution up through the six remaining cosmic planes.

Vywamus, the higher aspect of our Planetary Logos, Sanat Kumara, has compared the passing of the first nine initiations to a ten-inch ruler. If this ten-inch ruler is the full expanse of the seven cosmic dimensions of reality leading all the way back to God, or the Godhead, then nine-tenths of our evolution as soul extension lie beyond the dimensions we are currently working through. In other words, the great Masters for whom we have such respect and admiration are themselves only one inch up this ten-inch ruler. They are planetary Masters but not cosmic Masters. They are just beginning their cosmic evolution. This indicates the incredible vastness and limitlessness of God and His creation.

A Brief Cosmology from the Bottom to the Top

I will now attempt to provide a very brief and simplified cosmology of human evolution from the beginning stages all the way back to God who created everything and whence all things fan out. (See the Godhead diagram on the next page.)

GODHEAD

Hyos Ha Koidesh

(The Seven Mighty Elohim)	**The Cocreator Council of Twelve**	(The Seven Mighty Archangels)
	24 Elders before the Throne	
	(Paradise Sons) — Cocreator Level — (Cocreator Gods)	
	Metatron	
Seven Cosmic Planes	Universal Logos	Seven Cosmic Planes
	Galactic Logos	
The Elohim	Melchior	**The Archangels**
1. Hercules		1. Michael
Amazonia	(Seven Great Beings who ensoul	Faith
2. Apollo	the Seven Stars of the Great Bear)	2. Jophiel
Lumina	Logos of the Great Bear	Christine
3. Heros		3. Chamuel
Amora	Logos of Sirius	Charity
4. Purity		4. Gabriel
Astrea	Solar Logos — Helios	Hope
5. Cyclopia		5. Raphael
Virginia	Vywamus	Mother Mary
6. Peace	Seven Planetary Logoi	6. Uriel
Aloha	Three Planetary Spirits	Aurora
7. Arcturus		7. Zadekiel
Victoria	Planetary Logos	Amethyst

The Lords of Karma	**The Lord of the World**	**The Lords of Karma**
Quan Yin, Pallas Athena	Sanat Kumara	Portia, Vista, Lady Nada
Goddess of Liberty		Overseer, the Great
	The Six Kumaras	Divine Director
	(Buddhas of Activity)	

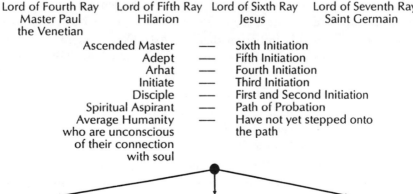

1. Manu	**2. Office of the Christ**	③ **Mahachohan**
Allah Gobi	Lord Maitreya	St. Germain, soon to hold office
Chohan — El Morya	Chohan — Kuthumi	Chohan — Serapis Bey
Lord of Fourth Ray	Lord of Fifth Ray Lord of Sixth Ray	Lord of Seventh Ray
Master Paul	Hilarion Jesus	Saint Germain
the Venetian		

Ascended Master	—	Sixth Initiation
Adept	—	Fifth Initiation
Arhat	—	Fourth Initiation
Initiate	—	Third Initiation
Disciple	—	First and Second Initiation
Spiritual Aspirant	—	Path of Probation
Average Humanity	—	Have not yet stepped onto
who are unconscious		the path
of their connection		
with soul		

Mineral Kingdom   Vegetable Kingdom   Animal Kingdom

At the very lowest of human evolution on the cosmic physical plane is the soul extension who is totally over-identified with matter to the point of being completely disconnected in consciousness from his soul. This state of consciousness can go on for many, many lifetimes, until the soul extension begins to awaken, steps onto the path of probation and becomes what may be termed a spiritual aspirant. This process continues until the soul extension begins to gain mastery over his physical body and vehicle in service of the soul's purpose and passes the first initiation. The soul extension can then be termed a disciple.

The soul extension begins to gain mastery over his feelings, emotions, and desires in service of the soul and passes the second initiation. The soul begins to gain mastery over the mental body and hence over the threefold personality in service of the soul and passes the third initiation. He has achieved merger with his soul and has become an initiate.

The soul extension continues to evolve and passes the fourth initiation, which completes the building of the causal or soul body, and achieves liberation from the wheel of rebirth. The causal body (or soul body) burns up and the soul, which has been the soul extension's teacher and guide throughout all the soul extension's incarnations merges back into the monad. The monad, the spirit, the I Am, the Father in heaven now becomes the guide and teacher. The soul extension is now considered a Master of Wisdom and Lord of Compassion. The soul extension is now called an arhat.

The arhat continues to evolve and passes the fifth initiation which has to do with merging with the monad, the spirit, the I Am, the Father in heaven. The person is now called an adept, a full-fledged Master.

The adept continues to evolve and passes the sixth initiation which leads to resurrection or ascension. His bodies and vehicles are totally transformed into Light as the monad descends completely into the four-body system. The Ascended Master now has a choice whether to stay on the physical plane and continue his or her service or return to the spiritual world. It is also at this initiation that the Ascended Master must decide which of the seven paths to higher evolution he will choose for his cosmic destiny.

The Ascended Master continues to evolve and passes the seventh initiation which has to do with a merger with the will of the Planetary Logos and the logoic plane. The highest level of initiation has then been reached in terms of initiations that can be taken on the earthly plane.

Above the Ascended Masters are now three positions or posts in the spiritual government having to do with the seven great rays that emanate from the Creator. Heading the first ray within our Planetary Hierarchy is a position called the Manu. The Manu is not a person, but rather a title like president. The being who currently holds that position is a great Master by the name of Allah Gobi. Under him is the Chohan or Lord of the first ray who is currently El Morya.

Heading the second ray is the position in the Planetary Hierarchy called the Office of the Christ. The being who holds this position in the government is the Lord Maitreya. The Chohan or Lord of the ray working under Lord Maitreya is the Master Kuthumi.

Heading the third ray and third department is the position called the Mahachohan. I do not know the name of the person holding this position currently. However, the Master who will be taking over this position very soon is Saint Germain. The Chohan or Lord of this third ray working under the Mahachohan is the Master Serapis Bey.

Then stemming out from the third department are four more rays of energy and positions in the spiritual government. Heading the fourth ray is the Master Paul the Venetian. Heading the fifth ray is the Master Hilarion. Heading the sixth ray is the Master Jesus and heading the seventh ray is the Master St. Germain. The heads of the rays are often called the Lords of the rays or Chohans of the rays. In the next chapter I will go into greater depth about the inner workings of the Planetary Hierarchy, but for present purposes I just want to give a broad overview.

Above these departments in Shamballa is the position of Planetary Logos, which is held by Sanat Kumara. He is the Lord of the World and the highest being of all within our entire planetary system. It is he who is in charge of all aspects of evolution in all kingdoms on this planet.

Below him are what have been termed the Three Kumaras or Buddhas of Activity who help Sanat Kumara in his work. There are also three esoteric or Hidden Kumaras or Buddhas. These seven beings are the seven highest self-conscious beings in our planetary system. In the next chapter I will give more detailed information about the nature of their work.

Just below them are four beings referred to in esoteric thought as the Lords of Karma. They are in charge of the dispensing of karma for the human race. (I am continuing to move upward now, and I must emphasize that this cosmology is very simplified.)

Next are the three Planetary Spirits, the trinity of the Logos, the Christ, and the Hierarchy in their higher aspects. Just as the personality is subservient to the soul, and the soul is subservient to the monad, the monads in operation within our planetary system are subservient to the Three Planetary Spirits.

Above them are the seven Planetary Logoi. These seven beings are in charge of the Earth's evolution, and Sanat Kumara is the only physically incarnate one. The seven Planetary Logoi serve as seven beings within a greater being who is the Solar Logos.

Above them is Vywamus. Vywamus is the higher self or higher monadic level of Sanat Kumara. It is Vywamus who started The Tibetan Foundation with Djwhal Khul. This is a glorious being of cosmic intelligence. Humanity is very lucky to have his guidance so readily available on Earth.

Above Vywamus is the Solar Logos whose name is Helios. Helios is the being who embodies the entire solar system, just as Sanat Kumara is the being who embodies the entire Planet Earth. Sanat Kumara and the planet Earth would be like a chakra within the body of Helios. Helios is anchored in the sun and is in charge of the evolution of the entire solar system.

Between the Solar Logos and the Galactic Logos is a very interesting process and organization of cosmic beings. Above the Solar Logos is the Logos of the star system of Sirius. Above the Logos of Sirius is the Logos of the Great Bear star system.

The relationship of these three beings could be likened to the relationship of the monad, soul, and personality. Just as the soul guides the personality on Earth, and the monad guides the soul, so the Logos of Sirius guides the Solar Logos and the Logos of the Great Bear guides the Logos of Sirius. Again we have the Hermetic law operating: "As within, so without; as above, so below." Above the Logos of the Great Bear we have the Seven Great Beings who ensoul the seven stars in the Great Bear star system.

The seven rays that are experienced on Earth are in part an expression of the Seven Great Beings who ensoul these seven stars.

Moving higher, expanding still further, one comes to the Galactic Logos. The name of the Galactic Logos has not been given; however, the name of the head of our galactic quadrant is Melchior. This being is in charge of the Milky Way Galaxy of which the Earth is a part.

Above him is the Universal Logos. Again, no name is given but this glorious being embodies and is in charge of the entire universe.

At the very pinnacle of creation is the cocreator level, those Masters who have returned all the way back to Source, or the Godhead. They might be called Cosmic Ascended Masters, not just Planetary Ascended Masters. They have returned back to the cosmic logoic plane of existence.

Apparently at the supreme highest level exists what Vywamus has referred to as the Cocreator Council of Twelve. At our level of evolution I don't think it is even possible to imagine all of what they do and are in charge of; however, I do know that this council exists.

On the right hand of the Godhead are what have been termed the Elohim, or Creator Gods. When God created the infinite universe, He created the Elohim, or Creator Gods, to help Him. These beings are referred to as the thought attributes of God. The Bible makes reference to the Elohim over two thousand five hundred times. They are a kingdom of beings different from the human kingdom. In the I Am teachings of Saint Germain the names of the seven mighty Elohim that are connected with the seven great rays of God are given. Some of them are quite interesting. Each ray has a male and female counterpart.

First Ray Elohim:	Hercules and Amazonia
Second Ray Elohim:	Apollo and Lumina
Third Ray Elohim:	Heros and Amora
Fourth Ray Elohim:	Purity and Astrea
Fifth Ray Elohim:	Cyclopia and Virginia
Sixth Ray Elohim:	Peace and Aloha
Seventh Ray Elohim:	Arcturus and Victoria

Metatron

Above the Universal Logos is Metatron. Metatron is an Archangel who is also at the crown of the tree of life in Kabbalistic teachings. He is referred to in *The Keys of Enoch* as "The Garment of Shaddai" and is the visible manifestation of the deity of the Father. He is the Almighty Eternal Lord and Divine Voice of the Father, Creator of the outer worlds, teacher and guide to Enoch and Creator of the Keys of Enoch. Metatron is the creator of the electron. He is the representative of the Source. He helped in building the Great Pyramid of Giza and placed within it the purity that goes with that high-vibrational area. He teaches classes on inner planes, especially in the use of Light within physical manifestation to raise consciousness.

Above this level are the Paradise Sons. They are defined in *The Keys of Enoch* as the Sons of God who exercise spiritual teaching authority over the Councils of the Elohim and govern several Son Universes collectively. The Cocreator Gods are those Sons and Daughters of God who have returned back to God at the highest cosmic level. These Cocreator Gods have either never left or have evolved back to the Godhead. The twenty-four Elders before the Throne sit in the presence of God at the highest level, exchanging their commission and glory periodically with other Masters. They control twenty-four thrones and dominions which administer the law of central control through Councils of Light to all universes that recognize God.

The Hyos Ha Koidesh are the highest servants of God. These Lords serve the Father's infinite plan of creation by working with His trinitized forms of appearance. They are nonevolving Hierarchy according to *The Keys of Enoch*. When I asked Djwhal Khul about the Hyos Ha Koidesh, he said that they could be likened to the Cocreator Gods.

On the left hand of God are what have been termed the archangels. The archangels are direct extensions of the Creator and are of a kingdom different from that of humans. It is understood that they do not have free choice in the same manner that humans have it. When humans pray to God, God does not come Himself, he sends His angels. Just as with the Elohim, there are Seven Great Archangels of the Seven Great Rays of God. Each archangel has a female counterpart.

First Ray Archangel: Michael and Faith
Second Ray Archangel: Jophiel and Christine
Third Ray Archangel: Chamuel and Charity
Fourth Ray Archangel: Gabriel and Hope
Fifth Ray Archangel: Raphael and the Mother Mary
Sixth Ray Archangel: Uriel and Aurora
Seventh Ray Archangel: Zadekiel and Amethyst

Angels are most wonderful beings. They will be much more involved with evolution on Planet Earth in the future. They already are now, but in the future it will be much more open and people in general will be much more aware of it.

The ultimate pinnacle of creation itself, at the very highest level of all, is the First Cause, the heavenly Father-Mother God Himself, the Beloved Presence. It is from God that all things have been created and to which all things will return, for this is the Divine Plan. All the beings I have spoken of in this chapter and all the ones I haven't mentioned are extensions of this one vast Infinite Being who embodies everything in all creation, in all dimensions. All live and breathe and move in Him. He is the ultimate Divine Director of all creation.

When we return we will be "conscious" and we will surely appreciate that to which we have returned. This is the destiny that we all have in store for us. It is just a matter of time and, in truth, time does not really exist. So I end this chapter with the challenge to "be about the Father's business," for how can the small, petty pleasures of earthly life fulfill and satisfy us like the supreme fulfillment of full union with God? Did not Jesus say, "Knock and the door shall be opened" and "Seek and ye shall find"?

18

The Galactic Core
and the Cosmic Masters

*"A master can, at any time, find out anything
on any possible subject without the slightest
difficulty"*

Djwhal Khul
as channeled by
Alice A. Bailey

The accelerated evolution of humanity and our recent movement as a
planet into the fourth dimension have made it possible, for the first
time, for us to become more aware of the Spiritual Hierarchy governing
our galaxy. Previous to this we were limited in our spiritual awareness to
the Planetary Hierarchy or at most the Solar Hierarchy. Planet Earth's
recent movement into sacred status as a planet has changed all this.

Sacred status could be likened to our taking the third initiation, except
in this instance it is Sanat Kumara, our Planetary Logos, who has taken his
third cosmic initiation.

The Milky Way Galaxy, to which the Planet Earth and its solar system
belong, is governed from a place called the Galactic Center or the Galactic
Core. The center of our galaxy is located in the constellation of Sagittarius.

The galaxy itself is divided into four quadrants. Each of these quadrants is divided into three sectors. This means there are twelve sectors
within this galaxy. There is a governing point for each quadrant, each
sector, and for the galaxy as a whole. The sector that the Earth is in is
guided from the Great Bear constellation.

The spiritual government of this planet receives guidance from the
center of this sector and from the center of the galaxy itself. The chief

administrator of this sector, one-twelfth of the galaxy, is a cosmic being whose name is Melchior.

Melchior and his associates have worked for eons through our Solar Logos, Helios, who works through our Planetary Logos, Sanat Kumara. Because of the spiritual acceleration of Planet Earth, the entire galactic sector of Melchior has been mobilized to help Earth in its evolution. Melchior is a cosmic being who can be attuned to, and he is happy to give his aid and assistance.

It is only since Planet Earth has moved into the fourth dimension that the Galactic Core has been so easily accessible. Previous to this, the highest level of attunement that was readily available on a collective level was the Solar Center and Core. Our attunement to the Galactic Masters and Galactic Core helps us to heal the separation from our Galactic Center that has been in existence in the mass consciousness.

Our attunement to Melchizedek and the Universal Masters helps us to heal the separation on a universal level. Our attunement to the Mahatma, the Avatar of Synthesis, helps us to heal the separation from God Himself. The monumental leap in consciousness that the Earth has taken in recent times by becoming a sacred planet and moving into the fourth dimension can clearly be seen in our ability to now access the Galactic Core in a direct manner.

One of the other things that the attuning to the Galactic Masters and Galactic Core does is help us use our bodies of Light on the physical level. The power of these Galactic Masters is much higher in frequency than even the Planetary or Solar Masters. In the past we received only stepped-down energies from these Masters. Now we on Earth have the opportunity to access them directly.

Some of these beings may actually begin to manifest on the Earth plane soon. One of them already has. His name is His Holiness, the Lord Sai Baba. Many of the Masters from these levels are beginning to over-shadow initiates and Masters.

According to the channelings of Vywamus through The Tibetan Foundation, there were five beings from the Galactic Core who initially made the approach to Earth. They sent down "rods of power" into India, Germany, Brazil, Greenland, and South Africa. The changes that have occurred in India, Germany and South Africa on a mass scale are evidence of the influence of this energy.

Soon, if it hasn't already happened, three of these rods of power will be placed in China to stimulate the raising of consciousness there. There will also be one in the United States. Vywamus has said there will be a total of twelve of these direct links with the Galactic Core.

As we learn to accept the body of Light even into the physical level, we will be able to learn to instantly teleport ourselves anywhere on Earth. As our consciousnesses develop in this regard we will also be accessing the language of Light. This will lead to the ability to precipitate out of the ethers anything we want to manifest. The attunement with the Galactic Core is a great accelerating force and factor in this development. In essence, it is an accelerator of the ascension process.

Vywamus

Vywamus, again, is the cosmic being who might be considered the higher self of Sanat Kumara, our Planetary Logos. If Vywamus is Sanat Kumara's higher self, then up above him on the monadic level is Lenduce. Here we have the personality (Sanat Kumara), the soul (Vywamus), and the monad (Lenduce) on a cosmic scale.

Vywamus no longer has a physical body but exists as Light. He is considered to be a master psychologist. It was Vywamus, along with Djwhal Khul, who started The Tibetan Foundation. One of Vywamus' main jobs is to help humanity clear the subconscious mind of misconceptions and faulty beliefs and patterns.

Vywamus had thirty-two lifetimes on a physical planet in a universe other than ours. He had lives as a soldier, teacher, mother, father, sea captain, and owner of a chain of restaurants. The planet he ascended on, however, didn't have oceans as vast as Planet Earth has. In his life as a restaurant owner, he owned a chain that existed around his entire planet. In his work now, he is still dealing with food of sorts. It might be called spiritual food, the energy of Light. Do call on him for help.

Melchizedek

Melchizedek is another cosmic and galactic Master who is very available for people to contact and channel. There are many beings with the name Melchizedek because the Order of Melchizedek is a cosmic order and priesthood throughout our universe. In the ancient writings the term Melchizedek was given to any initiate who passed the seven levels of initiation in the Order of Melchizedek.

Jesus had an incarnation under the name Melchizedek, and the Universal Logos' name is Melchizedek. The particular Melchizedek to whom I refer in this section is a cosmic being who is a member of the governing council of this galactic sector. He is a new member of this council. In the initial focus of his work, he served as a liaison between the Earth and other planets and the Galactic Center. He has recently replaced another cosmic Master who has moved on to a position on the universal level.

Melchizedek has also had some lifetimes on Earth, besides working with the Earth on an inner plane level. His last life on Earth was as a king named Melchizedek. He has overshadowed many beings on Earth, one of whom was Enoch, "the man who walked with God."

Through Enoch's work with Melchizedek, he ascended in that lifetime. He is currently working through a number of people to bring forth information about how to use Light. He is readily available to be contacted and channeled.

Adonis

Adonis is a great and glorious being. He has been Vywamus' teacher as well as Sanat Kumara's teacher. It was Adonis who ran the school on Venus to train Planetary Logoi. He is considered the best in the universe at what he does.

He embodies the heart focus of the universe. He is the keeper of the Christ Light within each soul in the universe. He has been holding this position since the Earth came into existence, which is at least eighteen and one half million years ago and in reality, much longer.

At one time he had a great many lives on the physical level in other universes. He spent two thousand six hundred lifetimes on one planet. In one stage of his evolution he became a leader of a large group that was spiritually supporting the evolution of a particular planet. With his help every being on that planet learned to align with the spiritual idea. It was from that planet that Adonis came to our universe and galaxy and took the exalted position of the heart focus of the universe.

He has been working with the Lord Maitreya for many eons in helping to bring forth the love/wisdom ideal on Earth. By tuning in to Adonis, we on Earth are being offered a galactic perspective rather than just an earthly perspective.

As average unevolved people we can't see beyond the selfishness of our negative egos. As we evolve we begin to see one humanity or one Earth. Then we realize that even this is limiting for we are part of a solar system that is a whole. Then as we continue to evolve we recognize that our group consciousness is really that of a galaxy. As we evolve further we see that we are part of a universe that is a whole. This is the expanded perspective that Adonis can begin to give us.

We are not just working for the Earth, we are working, in reality, for the galaxy. To work just for the Earth would be selfish. In truth, we are creators working for a universal goal, not just an Earth-centered or personality-centered goal. Call on Adonis for help, for we are very blessed to have him so available at this time.

Atlanto

Atlanto is another vast cosmic being who is available to be contacted. I first learned about him through The Tibetan Foundation. He is one of twelve beings who focus the energy or thought that sustains the Cosmic Day. The Cosmic Day has also been called a Day of Brahma. It lasts 4.3 billion years and we are three-quarters of the way through ours. We needn't be concerned about this, as we still have at least 1.1 billion years left. The history of Earth since Sanat Kumara's arrival is only 18.5 million years. Physical bodies have been on the Earth, according to Edgar Cayce, for 10.5 million years. The fact that Atlanto is one of the twelve beings who sustain this Cosmic Day is quite an extraordinary concept.

There are eleven beings who hold this cosmic consciousness focus. The twelfth includes all those who are directly involved with the experience. These are the beings who are cocreators or are learning to be cocreators as we are. This combined effort helps us to focus the will of the Divine Source.

Atlanto had lifetimes on a physical planet many cosmic days ago. If we think of how long one cosmic day is (4.5 billion years) and he says "many cosmic days ago," we begin to see how infinite the nature of God is.

Atlanto is not directly involved in focusing specific energies on the earth to accelerate the New Age. His focus is much more on a cosmic level rather than a planetary level. Even though this is the case he still is very open to being contacted and is available to be channeled.

In a channeling he gave in a book called *Reach for Us, Your Cosmic Teachers and Friends* by Dorothy Roeder, he said that he cannot direct his energies directly to us on Earth or it would burn us up in a spiritual sense because the frequency is so high. What he does instead is focus his energies through two lakes on Earth. One of these lakes is in Kansas and one is in Tibet. He can also focus his energy through a person's soul and monadic structure. We can call on him for help and are very likely to receive guidance that is quite out of the ordinary because of his cosmic perspective.

Averran

The last cosmic being is named Averran. He is a cosmic Master who resides within the cosmic center of our galaxy. His job is to oversee the evolution and progress of Planet Earth. His specific task is to organize the Light of the creation of this galaxy into a form that can utilize the plan and bring it into creation.

Averran had many lifetimes on a physical planet much like Earth in a universe that existed before this one. (Just think about this: a universe that existed before this one. When we are dealing with cosmic Masters, we are dealing with sequences of time that are so vast it is hard for the mind even to fathom them.)

The planet Averran lived on struggled with the exact same lessons that we on Earth have been dealing with. His planet eventually moved back to the Light and away from the pull of matter. This is the same point in evolution the Earth is at right now. The tide is beginning to turn back to spirit after many, many millions of years of Earth's being enmeshed in the pull of matter. Because of Averran's past experience, he is very available to be called on and communicated with and would very much appreciate anyone who would consider doing so.

Summation

The cosmic Masters of the galactic sector and Galactic Core are now available to be contacted. The Masters I have mentioned here are awesome spiritual beings and we are incredibly blessed to have such galactic and universal beings so readily available to us. It must be understood that it is a very recent occurrence for beings of such a vast magnitude to be so readily available. We must feel especially honored when we consider how many millions and even billions of planets and stars in our galaxy and in our universe these beings are responsible for. Please do call them in, for they are not allowed to enter unless they are asked to do so.

19

Teachings of Vywamus on the Avatar of Synthesis, the Mahatma

I, Vywamus think that the Mahatma, or Avatar of Synthesis, is the most important thing that's happened on your Earth and for humanity

Vywamus, in Brian Grattan's
book, *Mahatma I & II*

What I have to share in this chapter is some of the most awesome information I have ever come across and it will literally accelerate a person's path of ascension and the building of his Lightbody one-thousand-fold. This information has to do with the cosmic being I spoke of briefly in Chapter 11, the Avatar of Synthesis that is overshadowing the Lord Maitreya on Earth, along with the Spirit of Peace and Equilibrium and the Buddha. This chapter deals with the glorious nature of the Avatar of Synthesis and the fact that his or its energy is available to every person on Planet Earth.

This being has been referred to by Vywamus in the following manner: "I, Vywamus, think that the Mahatma, or Avatar of Synthesis, is the most important thing that's happened on your Earth and for humanity." This is a pretty amazing statement, given the fact that a lot of pretty amazing things have gone on on this planet in the past eighteen and one half million years.

Most people on the spiritual path are focusing their attention on their higher selves or souls, and that is appropriate and good. As one evolves to the third initiation and achieves the soul merge, one begins accessing the monad or spirit. Eventually the initiation process leads one to the fifth and sixth initiations which have to do with complete merger with the monad and, hence, ascension.

Most people on the spiritual path are in the process of building the antakarana, or bridge of Light, to the soul (higher self) and to the monad or spirit. The Mahatma, or Avatar of Synthesis, is the cosmic being who has been made available to Earth since the Harmonic Convergence in August of 1987. He is the connecting link between us, as incarnated personalities, and the Godhead Himself or Source of all creation. Just as the soul is the intermediary between the incarnated personality and the monad, the Mahatma is the intermediary between incarnated personalities and the Godhead.

In past chapters I have spoken of the seven levels of initiation that can be taken on this earthly plane. There are two more initiations after this that take one out of the cosmic physical plane all together. Vywamus has said that there are, in actuality, three hundred fifty-two initiations from Earth to the Godhead. The Mahatma is the cosmic being that embodies all these levels for us. The Mahatma (which means the Father or Great Soul) also embodies the energy of Melchior (the Galactic Logos) and Adonis (Vywamus' teacher and the heart focus of the universe). It is obvious that this is an awesome being who is really a group consciousness.

At the occurrence of the Harmonic Convergence, Planet Earth moved from a third-dimensional consciousness to a fourth-dimensional consciousness. This was a momentous occurrence for the Earth and few people realized what a momentous occasion it actually was. Because we are now functioning at this fourth-dimensional level, for the first time in the history of the Earth the Mahatma can anchor itself "physically" on the Earth. This occurred one year after the Harmonic Convergence, in 1988. Lord Maitreya and other beings were accessing this energy; however, it was on mental and causal levels, not on the level of physicality.

The Mahatma allows us, in a sense, to build the antakarana all the way to the Source itself. Vywamus has told me that there is no energy in the infinite universe of a higher frequency than the Mahatma's that is available to Earth at this time. It is available to everyone and all one has to do is ask for it. This Mahatma energy can accelerate one's ascension process and the building of one's Lightbody by one-thousandfold, literally. These are not idle words I speak now.

Vywamus has told me that the Mahatma energy is even beyond the twelve rays. This energy comes to our planet through the Galactic Core, through the Solar Logos, through the Planetary Logos and to Earth. There is no danger of burning out one's body with such a high-frequency energy because it is also channeled through each person's monad and soul, if necessary, to make it usable for the incarnate personality on Earth. I will repeat one more time that there is no energy one can call on that is of a higher frequency and vibration, and it is available to everyone, not just certain special people. I cannot recommend highly enough calling forth this energy. It can help with ascension, with building the Lightbody, or any other issue or lesson one is dealing with.

I asked Vywamus if it is possible to channel this energy through the voice and he said it was a little difficult because it embodies all three hundred fifty-two levels back to the Source, so it might be a little confusing at first because of its group-consciousness nature. However, it can be done. One singular consciousness will speak for the group entity.

I was first turned on to the Mahatma, the Avatar of Synthesis, through the Alice Bailey books and Djwhal Khul's writings. More recently, information has come through Vywamus and through a book called *Mahatma I & II* by Brian Grattan.

The idea is to fill the physical, emotional, mental, and spiritual bodies with this energy. It is the desire of the Avatar of Synthesis, Mahatma, to anchor as much of its energy as possible on Earth. This is facilitating a merger and integration of the Creator (the highest) and the cocreator levels. Ascension and cosmic ascension are nothing more than the integration and blending of matter, soul, monad, Mahatma and God. It is the goal of the Divine Plan to merge all these levels back together in consciousness. The anchoring of this cosmic Mahatma energy into Earth helps to facilitate this and supremely accelerates one's personal ascension process.

Many people have been tapping into this energy without referencing its specific name. The specific awareness of what it is and how it can be called can accelerate this process greatly, however. When one wants to speak to a specific Ascended Master, one must call that Master's name to make the contact. If I want to speak to Vywamus on the inner plane I must call to him by that name. The same is true of the Mahatma energy. We can just call to the Mahatma by that name, ask it for help and ask to receive and anchor its energy. I asked Vywamus how Earth was doing in anchoring the Mahatma energy and he said Earth was doing really well.

The Mahatma is a combination of all the twelve rays and much more. The calling forth of this energy can help to break up the crystallized and fixed patterns that are locked in our physical, emotional, and mental bodies. The ultimate goal is to raise these bodies into the frequency of Light, which is what occurs at one's ascension. The calling forth of the Mahatma energy, because it is of such a high frequency, can greatly facilitate the movement in this direction. All one has to do to invoke this energy is to call the Mahatma and make the request.

When I am in attunement I can feel my whole body start to heat up as the energy pours in. Sometimes I feel it more strongly than at other times, but know that it wants to come in and will come in. However, you must ask for it. This is cosmic law. No consciousness or energy comes forth from these levels unless they are requested, for we have been given free choice. I would recommend calling for this energy at least three times a day, if not more often, especially when meditating.

Another interesting thing that Vywamus has said deals with the under-standing of what is called the Cosmic Day and Cosmic Night. Just as we on Earth have day and night, God on a cosmic scale has some kind of equivalent. What I have learned from Vywamus is that the Cosmic Day of our source actually lasts 4.3 billion years. We have already gone through 3.1 billion years, so there are 1.2 billion left in our Cosmic Day.

I asked Vywamus what happens at the end of a Cosmic Day. He told me that everything is breathed in or brought back to Source; at least that is what has happened in the past. A Cosmic Day is very long compared to Earth's history. Sanat Kumara came to the Earth from Venus 18.5 million years ago and, according to Edgar Cayce, physical man has been on the Earth for only 10.5 million years. A Cosmic Day is 4.3 billion years.

The graduation of Earth at the time of the Harmonic Convergence to the fourth dimension has allowed the source of this planetary system to consult with a higher-level source. Each level source has a higher level, vision and consciousness, like a microscope or telescope that can be turned up one thousand times. This is what has allowed the Mahatma to come forth and anchor its energy on the Earth for the first time.

In his book, Brian Grattan has also called this energy the I Am Presence. I discussed this with Vywamus and he suggested using the name Mahatma instead, since the I Am Presence, in most spiritual systems, has referred to the monad. Another function of the Mahatma energy is to show us that suffering does not exist. It is a creation of our own negative egos, and does not exist in God's reality.

The reason the Mahatma has come is because of an invocation on the soul level. Enough souls, higher selves, or soul-merged individuals called out for help which then invoked the Mahatma consciousness and energy. The Mahatma energy has the ability to create a vehicle, or base of support, as we rapidly expand our consciousnesses so we don't get overwhelmed. The Mahatma energy takes us beyond individuality. Once the connection or bridge of Light is established with the Mahatma it will flow very naturally without a lot of effort. Vywamus has also referred to this con-sciousness as the cosmic walk-in.

The Avatar of Synthesis first made contact with the Earth In Atlantean times and prophesied that he would come in the future when there was enough of an invocative response on the soul level. The Lord Maitreya, the Planetary Christ, is now physically incarnated; the Avatar of Synthesis has anchored with him. If we add to this Sai Baba, the Cosmic Christ in India, the externalization of the Hierarchy, the angels, the Ashtar Command, the positive extraterrestrials, the completing of cycles of two thousand, six thousand, twelve thousand, thirty-six thousand and ten million years, we begin to see what an extraordinary time we are currently living in. There is no better time in the history of the planet to be incarnated if one is interested in spiritual growth.

We are here now to integrate the Mahatma energy and become living embodiments of its energy. This will astronomically raise our overall cellular vibration. We are, in a sense, allowing the Mahatma energy to "walk in" to our consciousnesses and become a part of his great army of cosmic Lightworkers. The color of this energy, for those who are somewhat clairvoyant or would like to visualize it, is golden-white. As it comes in we can let it fill our bodies and flow down into our feet and down our grounding cords into the Earth and into the center of the Earth. This energy may also be used for healing on a psychic or physical level for oneself or for others.

Because our planet has now moved into the fourth dimension, everything is new. The blueprint we are operating with now is completely different from the third-dimensional blueprint. Isn't it interesting that all the prophecies we are all so familiar with—Cayce's prophecies, the biblical prophecies, and so on—end right now. This is because we have ended third-dimensional consciousness and have entered the fourth. The star system of Arcturus is a fifth-dimensional consciousness, a picture of our future selves.

The Avatar of Synthesis reports to the Council of Twelve on the Creator level. The Mahatma reports to this council about the nature of physical existence. The Lightworkers who are dealing with this energy are really on the cutting edge because, as I said, this energy has been available on the physical level only since 1988, although it had been available on the causal and mental levels before that.

The Mahatma is here, in essence, to integrate the separation between God and His creation. What is amazing about this is that for the first time we have the opportunity to heal the separation from God directly, and not just to heal the separation from the soul and monad (spirit).

In Djwhal Khul's terminology, the Mahatma allows us to heal the separation on the seven cosmic dimensions, not just the seven subplanes of the cosmic physical plane. If all of creation is a ten-inch ruler, we have been focusing only on the first inch. The Mahatma is the other nine inches we haven't even been dealing with. Merger with the monad at ascension is really only two-thirds of the first inch. The calling of the Mahatma is accessing the energy and consciousness of the other three hundred forty-six levels and initiations. I think the profundity of this information about the Mahatma and its incredible importance and magnitude is clear. Again, Vywamus said that the Mahatma is the most important thing that has ever happened to humanity.

The more the energy and consciousness of the Mahatma are grounded into the Earth plane, the greater will be the transformation of consciousness of this planet. Humans are the bridge between the Mahatma and the Earth plane. The Mahatma is also overshadowing the entire externalization of the Hierarchy as well as Lord Maitreya and Sanat Kumara. This energy is equally available to every person on Earth. The idea is to let the Mahatma become the auric field and let it permeate the entire four-body system. The idea is also to fully integrate with this energy so the separation between God and the sons and daughters of God on Earth may be healed.

The Mahatma can provide tremendous support for us emotionally as we continue to expand our realization of God. Brian Grattan gives an example in his book that likens this support metaphorically to a glass of water. The glass is taken away to get a clearer glass. While this process is happening, the water in the glass can remain and not spill because of the support of the Mahatma energy. This is what the Mahatma can do for us in an emotional and spiritual sense.

The Harmonic Convergence on August 15-17, 1987, moved humankind and Mother Earth into spiritual adulthood for the first time. The Mahatma would like to have one hundred thousand cosmic walk-ins that it shares its body with. This would have a tremendous healing and cleansing effect on all of Planet Earth. Cosmic walk-ins are those incarnated personalities who have integrated the Mahatma energy. They would be the living embodiment of the Mahatma on Earth.

I would like to share with you an affirmation/prayer Vywamus gave me that you might say every day:

"I choose to accept and invoke a deep penetration of the Mahatma energy into my entire energy matrix, thereby allowing a full open radiation of my Divine self in service to All That Is, now."

According to Brian, the invocation of the Mahatma allows for the building of the Lightbody in a way that has never been done before in the history of the Earth. The Mahatma's energy is of such a high frequency and cosmic nature that it creates a Lightbody that has a likeness to the spiritual or monadic body.

Since the Harmonic Convergence and the coming of the Mahatma energy, it is now conceivable that an incarnated personality could evolve from a second-degree initiate to a Galactic Avatar in one lifetime. This possibility was not open before the Harmonic Convergence. The coming of the Mahatma is a special dispensation from God. Even Djwhal Khul, in his writings through Alice Bailey, never conceived of its being possible to anchor this energy beyond the causal plane, or level of the higher mind.

Planet Earth has benefited exponentially from the Mahatma's anchoring itself on Earth. It is the first time in the history of Planet Earth that there has been a complete circuit from the Godhead to Earth. The Mahatma has come directly into this quadrant of the galaxy and has become anchored on Earth. Brian Grattan may have been the first person to be consciously aware of anchoring the Mahatma energy into the physical. At the end of his book, he speaks of having achieved his ascension (sixth initiation) on May 9, 1990, and having chosen to remain on Earth for the time being.

The actual anchoring of the Mahatma energy on the Earth on June 14, 1988, was done with the assistance of the Council of Twelve for this quadrant of this galaxy and with the help of the thousands of Christs and Planetary Logoi of other planets in our galactic quadrant. The idea is for us, as incarnated personalities, to become partners with the Mahatma on Earth. It is also suggested that we ask the Mahatma to help each of us to complete our circuitry to our soul, monad, Mahatma and the Source itself. The Mahatma takes its orders from the Cocreator Council of Twelve at the Source level.

Another interesting piece of information about the Mahatma is that the greater our invocation of this energy, the better our likelihood of remaining in physical existence through the raised vibrational movement to the fourth dimension we have just experienced. The combination of the Harmonic Convergence along with the anchoring of Mahatma has raised the evolutionary circuitry of this quadrant of this galaxy one-thousandfold.

Even though Brian was apparently the first incarnated soul to consciously anchor the Mahatma energy, that didn't mean he had fully integrated this energy. The process of integrating the Mahatma takes some time, patience, prayer, affirmation, meditation, and spiritual work. If there is anyone who would like some help in anchoring the energy more fully into the Earth itself, I would suggest calling upon Archangel Sandalphon to help in this process. Archangel Sandalphon is especially adept at dealing with Earth energies.

Another fascinating piece of information in Brian's book is that in past lives he was St. Peter and Zarathustra (Zoroaster) who were physical probes from the Council of Twelve for this quadrant of our galaxy and senior members of the White Lodge. He also says that the energy that is St. Peter has a monadic connection with Sai Baba. I asked Vywamus about this since I have such a special connection with Sai Baba, and he said that it was something like being soul extensions from the same monad.

Janet McClure (founder of The Tibetan Foundation and my wife's spiritual teacher) channeled much of the information in Brian's book. She ascended in Egypt but chose to release her physical body at the time of her ascension.

20

The Inbreath and Outbreath of Brahma

One Cosmic Day equals 4.3 billion years.
Earth's evolution has currently used up
3.1 billion years of the present Cosmic Day
in which we are involved. The Planet Earth
will evolve more in the next forty-year cycle
(1988 to 2028) than it has in the last
3.1 billion years.

Vywamus

There is a cosmic event that is about to happen to Planet Earth and the cosmos as a whole that almost defies description. We are very, very close to the middle of a cosmic cycle, soon to reach the exact midpoint between the outbreath and inbreath of God.

Many people might not realize that just as humans on Earth breathe, so does God. Djwhal Khul has said that the process of breathing occurs even after the Ascended Master state of consciousness is reached. God breathes out creation and then breathes it back in again.

The outbreath and inbreath of God could be likened to the swing of a pendulum. As the pendulum swing reaches its uppermost apex, there is a moment of complete rest before it continues its movement in the opposite direction. This moment of rest and lack of movement in God's breathing is a moment of non-time, of eternity. Since the microcosm is like the macrocosm, this same process occurs many times each second as atoms of the physical world vibrate back and forth.

In the meditations of Sai Baba, Paramahansa Yogananda, and Baba

Muktananda, the mantra So Hum or So Ham or Hong Sau are used. These mantras mean I Am God or I Am the Self and are actually the sound of humans breathing as God listens. The idea of this meditation is to say the mantra in accordance with the breath. The main idea of the meditation is to listen to the stillpoint, or point of eternity, between the inbreath and outbreath as we say the mantra. This point of null time is a doorway into the presence of God.

Just as we have the opportunity to experience this at any time if we choose to tune in to it at the moment between our own breaths, we also have the most unbelievably profound opportunity to listen to this stillpoint between God's inbreath and outbreath which occurs, according to to Vywamus, only every ten million years in Earth's time. The exact moment between the expanding and contracting of the entire cosmos coincides, by no accident, with the second coming of Christ and the end of the Mayan calendar.

This exact midpoint between the inbreath and outbreath of God (Brahma) will occur in 2012. It will provide an opening for the emergence of something incomprehensible. In this moment God will have the opportunity to slip into His creation. All materializing processes will become suspended.

This event will not be experienced simultaneously in all parts of the universe but will travel as a wave across the sea of creation. Existing within this moment of non-time will be the focused conscious attention of the Creator. The Archangel Raphael, in *The Starseed Transmissions* by Ken Carey, has predicted the year 2012 as its most exact point of focus for Planet Earth. Archangel Raphael has said that no single conceptual structure is capable of conveying the enormity of what is soon to take place.

In that moment we will experience ourselves as the Christ, the Atma, the Buddha, the Eternal Self. We will recognize the unified collective consciousness of all humankind as our own true identity. We will fully realize our identity as God defines us, rather than as matter and the negative ego define us. We will recognize ourselves as one conscious being expressing itself through a multitude of separate forms. This will initiate the second period of planetary awakening that has been called the millennium or the one-thousand-year cycle.

In this future state we will be able to live in two realities simultaneously, half the time in form and half the time in the totality of All That Is. We will truly see ourselves as the bridge between spirit and matter and as the means through which the Creator relates to His creation. It is in this period that the fictitious identity of ego, with its sense of separation, fear, and selfishness, will be transcended.

Djwhal Khul has referred to this shift from the outbreath to the inbreath of God as the completion of a Cosmic Day. The profundity of this can be seen in the fact that ten million years is the total amount of time humankind has been on Earth. In this shift we will release our identification with the past, with the future, and with our material bodies and begin to live more in the present moment. We will see our true mission to be expressing God on Earth. In the future we will no longer be a random note in the symphony of God, but rather totally unified with the music of the spheres. None of us will consider ourselves better or worse than anyone else, for everyone will share the same identity as the Christ, as God. Christ is the single unified being whose consciousness we all share.

As we begin to play our individual note in attunement with the great conductor, God, we will play in rhythm and in harmony with the planetary symphony. We will play our note in harmony with all other humans, animals, plants and minerals on Earth.

What has been happening is that we have each been playing our own negatively egotistical, selfish note that has made the symphony sound very discordant. This is about to change. None of us will ever again have to act superior out of imagined importance and put others down, because the truth of our real identity as the Christ is far beyond anything the negative ego could dream up. The spirit and soul recognize that all are of supreme importance equally.

In the new millennium we will all communicate in the universal language of Light. This form of communication is far more specific and inclusive than words or even telepathic communication. The living language of Light is the true universal language of God. The new millennium will bring back the pre-fall state of awareness that in truth never left. We just think it did. We have been rethinking this illusion that is programmed into us by our society every morning when we wake up from our dreams and get out of bed. It can be changed any moment we choose to change it.

As we move through this final twenty-year cycle of the Mayan calendar, slowly but surely a critical mass of awakened and enlightened people will emerge. This will cause a hundredth-monkey effect and instantaneously transform humanity as a whole. This is a transformation from self-centeredness to God-centeredness.

This process, in truth, is as simple as where we put our attention. If we put our attention on our imagined negative ego identity, then that is where we will live. If we put our attention on our God-self identity then we have awakened to the truth of our being. So many of us do not control the focus of our attention and operate on automatic pilot. That is our downfall. So in truth, we live in two states of consciousness simultaneously. We are large enough to encompass all of creation and yet, with our attention, can make ourselves small enough to climb inside of creation into a physical body.

The problem is that the negative ego tells us that all we are is the body. In the God-realized state we oscillate between the two as circumstance and our mission require. There is an appropriate movement from the totality of being to form and back again. In the God-realized state, even though our attention has moved back to our form identity, we still retain our awareness of our oneness with and identity in God. The God-realized state allows both states of consciousness, whereas the negative ego tells us that all that exists is our form identity.

In the new millennium there will be a return to ecological balance and international cooperation, including an end to war. We will all seek to realize God's Divine plan instead of our own. We will become the means through which God will implement His will in the realm of form.

Awakening from the Spell of Matter

In this new millennium humanity as a whole will wake up from the spell of matter. This planet is a seven-dimensional planet; however, in the past we have been perceiving it as a three-dimensional planet. From the perspective of spirit and the angels we have had some strange, debilitating perceptual disorder. We have identified with form rather than with essence. We have identified ourselves with temporal time rather than with eternity. We have identified ourselves with the visible rather than with the invisible. We have been living in a negative hypnosis.

The challenge of the New Age is to retain our human forms and yet awaken from this hypnosis. According to Archangel Raphael in *The Starseed Transmissions* by Ken Carey, the angels have been programmed to awaken us at a certain point in history. This point was reached at the birth of Jesus Christ. He has described himself as the way we were, are now, and will be after the spell of matter is broken. It has taken the angels two thousand years to prepare us on mass levels for the profound transformation that is about to take place—fully moving into the New Age.

The Ego and the Spirit

In coming to a proper understanding of this whole process I would like to discuss an understanding of the ego different from the one I have previously given. In other chapters I have defined ego as the attitude system that is opposite of the Christ consciousness, the attitude system that is based on the premise that we are physical bodies rather than spirit living in physical bodies. This illusion leads to the illusionary belief in separation, fear, selfishness, and so on.

I am purposely putting into this chapter a semantically different understanding of the term ego because it is a dilemma that all disciples on the path are running into in their studies. Half the schools of thought use the term ego as Sai Baba does when he says that God equals man minus ego. The other half of the schools of thought use it in another way which I would like to explain now, for it is probably a better understanding of the process.

The ego, in this new understanding, is the valid and most important part of self that gives us a sense of identity and individuality. It helps us to function in this world and to complete our missions here. Having an ego goes along with having a physical body.

The ego's true function is to be a retriever of information and to remind the soul extension who is living in the body to take care of its physical body. The ego prevents the soul extension from doing something that would prove damaging to the physical vehicle. The ego is the material-plane expert. If we didn't have an ego we might forget that we are even incarnated. So the ego reminds us that we need water, food, and sleep.

Now the problem arises because the ego was never meant to interpret the rest of our lives for us. The rest of our lives were meant to be defined and interpreted by the soul and spirit. We have let the ego interpret our reality, which interpretation is based on the faulty belief that we are bodies (because that is all it knows about), and we have let the ego override intuitive ways of processing information of the spirit. The spirit's right-brained method of processing information using intuition, higher mind, spiritual will, and other faculties can process information instantaneously. In interpreting our realities, the ego has misused the conscious, reasoning mind and created an illusionary belief system based on fear, separation, selfishness, and death.

It has also overridden and blocked out the superior computer-like circuitry of the spirit's primary information system. The ego at best can use only 10% of the brain. It is only when the spirit's information processing system is used that the potential of using 100% of the brain can be tapped.

When the fall occurred, humankind as a whole shifted to the ego's cumbersome and illusionary manner of interpreting. The ideal would have been to balance the ego's and the spirit's functions in the proper manner. I emphasize that the ego was never meant to interpret our reality, only to be a retriever of information and to be the resident expert on the physical body. To interpret reality through the ego is to interpret reality through the physical eyes only. We have not allowed the ego to become spiritualized; it has become a negative ego. When Sai Baba and other teachers say we should die to our egos, what they are really saying is we must die to the negative ego, or spiritualize the ego. Both schools of thought are totally valid. It is just a semantics issue.

In the ideal state the spirit and ego work in perfect balance, and we live in two worlds simultaneously. This will be the prototype individual in the new millennium.

The New Millennium

The next twenty years will see the most rapid period of change human civilization has ever known. We have already seen this happening in the fall of Communism in the Soviet Union and East Germany. There have been many predictions by many psychics and prophets of both ancient and modern times of a coming shifting of the axis of the Earth.

There will be no physical shifting of the poles, based on the information I have received. It is not that this information was wrong when it was prophesied, but rather that humankind has changed enough that the shift doesn't need to happen in this way. The true axis shift will occur in consciousness. It will be a shift from negative-ego thinking to spiritual or Christ-thinking, on a mass scale. It will not need to happen in the physical because it is beginning to happen in consciousness.

If things seem to be moving fast now, we can only imagine how fast things will seem to move when the soul and spirit are allowed to interpret our reality in proper relationship to the ego function, as God would have it. When this happens we will be using the other 90% of our brains to process information. In truth, we are still living in the dark ages, or like cave men, compared to what it will be like when we are utilizing the lightning-like ways of the spirit to process information. All new technologies will no longer be based on limited egotistical and materialistic thinking. The technologies of the future will all be environmentally helpful, not hurtful. They will also be based on the ability to transcend time, space, and gravity. The Earth Mother is about to give birth to a New Age and we are just leaving our adolescence. In truth, our egos are relieved to be able to give up culturally induced responsibilities that they were never meant to take on. They can release this burden at any moment and not wait until 2012. It is as simple as letting go of a faulty belief and replacing it with a balanced one.

Each of us has a type of etheric antenna that connects us to the guidance of soul and spirit. The etheric antenna becomes disconnected from this higher guidance when we indulge in anger, hatred, and fear. It is not endangered by outside emotions, only by our own emotions. As long as we don't take on the negative vibrations and emotions of others, letting them slide off the golden bubble that is our shield, we are fine. It is also essential to learn to remain calm, peaceful, even-minded, and, most of all, loving and forgiving.

By learning to transcend the negative ego in this way, we remain connected to the etheric antenna and superior spiritual guidance. When we lose this attunement, we should just stop, forgive ourselves, try to learn the lesson, attitudinally heal ourselves, and ask ourselves whether we want God or our negative ego in that situation. By constantly choosing God rather than negative ego over and over again, a habit will develop over time of not losing our etheric antenna's full sensitivities and attunement.

The Year 2012: A Quantum Leap in Consciousness

At the exact moment between the inbreath and outbreath of God there will be a massive change in the world that has no historical precedent on Planet Earth. Everything in Earth's gravitational field will be affected. There will be a mass awakening to the interconnectedness of all life. More energy will be released in those few moments than is normally released in many years. We will experience heightened perception and an emotional connection to God.

Each of us will experience these moments of non-time between the outbreath and inbreath of God differently. Some will experience them as minutes, some as hours, some as a lifetime, some as many lifetimes. Some of us may have a revelation of God while others will react in fear, depending on our state of consciousness. Some may choose to leave the physical body in that moment and return to the spiritual world. There will be a shift on a mass scale from fear to love, from outer-directedness to inner-directedness. We all will feel a surge of power. How this is interpreted, again, depends on our state of consciousness.

Archangel Raphael, in Ken Carey's *The Starseed Transmissions, The Third Millennium*, has said that there could be Earth changes, but not on the scale once predicted. The media may react in fear, and it is important that we not buy into their glamour, illusion, and maya, for this is not a fearful event, but a glorious, joyous, and wonderful event. In truth, it is something that we can experience at any moment if we listen to the null time, the eternity between our own breaths, for the microcosm is like the macrocosm, and we are made in God's image. However, this event will be occurring on a mass level, not just on an individual level. It could be said that we will be having a global meditation on God.

It is time for us to realize that as humanity, we are the oak tree and no longer the acorn. In the future the ego and spirit will work in harmony much like the specific parts of a cell work in harmony. Just as we normally don't analyze the parts of a cell to see if it is functioning properly, so will ego and spirit function as a whole. Each of us is a cell in the body of God. When ego and spirit are integrated, then each of us will be a healthy cell in God's body.

We are living in an astonishing period of history. After ten million years, humanity is about to fully awaken. It is a great blessing to be incarnated at this time in Earth's history, for there has never been anything like it in terms of spiritual growth. Our work over the coming years is to prepare ourselves and others for the reappearance of the Christ, the externalization of the Hierarchy, and this coming quantum leap in consciousness.

The ideal would be to get all soul extensions to this Christ consciousness before these events even occur so we may move into the new Golden Age in total grace and love with no fear or karma. We have our work cut out for us during this last twenty-year cycle of the Mayan calendar. Lord Maitreya has said that he will not declare himself and the full manifestation of the externalized Spiritual Hierarchy will not occur until humankind is ready. The more work we can do on ourselves to realize the Christ and God within ourselves and within others, the sooner we will be catapulted into the New Age.

We on Earth at this time who are aware of these things are in a sense like God's infantry, an army of Lightworkers laying the groundwork for our leader, the Christ, the Lord Maitreya. The only way he can succeed is if we help him, for his work and ours is to reawaken the Christ, the Buddha, the Atma, the Eternal Self, in all soul extensions on Earth.

The more awakened humanity is by the year 2012, the more powerful will be this moment of mass enlightenment. The combination of Lord Maitreya's coming, the externalization of the Hierarchy, the presence of Sai Baba, the Cosmic Christ, the work of the angels, the work of the positive extraterrestrial groups, and last but not least, the work of all the Masters and the New Group of World Servers already on Earth cannot fail.

Our challenge is to become steadfast and focused in our personal work and in our service work as we never before have been. We are each and every one cells in the body of God, and God will not be healthy until each and everyone of us has realized our oneness and potential in Him. It is time to be born again to our true identity as the Christ and as one unified being. It is time to see all people as equals, regardless of their state of spiritual development or lack thereof. It is time to be about the Father's business, for His identity is, in truth, our identity. His purpose is our purpose. There is only one being in the infinite universe and that is God. He is incarnated in every mineral, plant, animal, human, planet, star, and galaxy.

In the future all kingdoms will be looked at as equals. We are not superior to a flower, a cat, a dog, a crystal, or a rock. Each is a specific incarnation of God, with a specific purpose, mission, and attribute of God's infinite nature to express. As we transcend our negative egos, we will realize our proper place in the scheme of all life that is God.

21

The Melchizedek Priesthood

Melchizedek, the Eternal Lord of Light
The Keys of Enoch

The Melchizedek priesthood has always held great interest for me. I feel an incredible attunement and affinity with this group and teaching, but there has been very little available written information on Planet Earth concerning them. Through my extensive research I have been able to uncover some of the hidden mysteries of this most amazing group.

Modern history knows of Melchizedek through the Old Testament, for it was Melchizedek who was the spiritual teacher of Abraham. This is clearly documented. Edgar Cayce, in his channelings, says that in one of his incarnations, Jesus Christ was a man named Melchizedek.

It is important to understand here that there is a being who is Melchizedek and there is the Melchizedek priesthood. When a person achieves spiritual illumination within this order he is called a Melchizedek. *The Keys of Enoch* describes the being in the spiritual worlds who heads the Melchizedek priesthood as the Eternal Lord of Light, the Sovereign of Light in charge of organizing the levels of the heavenly worlds of YHWH (God) for transit into new creation, equal with Metatron and Michael in the resourcing, regenesis, and reeducation of worlds going through the purification of the living Light. He is in charge of the heavenly order Brotherhood of Melchizedek and the spiritual and planetary priesthood of Melchizedek:

> Jehovah (the revealed God of our universe) will prepare the world for deliverance through Melchizedek and the Order of Melchizedek. Melchizedek is a manifestation of a Son of God in the history of the planet. Melchizedek was commissioned (according to the covenant of Enoch) to prepare the true priesthood of sonship upon a planet for eschatological participation with the Sons of Light.

The clearest definition of the Order of Melchizedek is that it is in charge of the consciousness reprogramming that is necessary to link physical creation with the externalization of the Divine Hierarchy. It is a royal priesthood that receives the voice of God for the sanctification of the people of the Light. The re-administration and teaching affect the mental, emotional, physical, and spiritual states of existence and consciousness. This priesthood is visible within every generation as a scattered Brotherhood of Light. It permeates the tree of the human race.

The order of Melchizedek has the anointing power to reawaken and resurrect the righteous people of the world into the Light of the higher worlds. They are the sons of truth behind historical wisdom. They hold the keys to the true history of the planet. They gather the Light of man which they have cultivated through the teachings of the word of God. According to Enoch in *The Keys of Enoch*, the sacred library of their priesthood was moved from the temple in Jerusalem into the desert areas of Qumran to preserve the records until the end of time. It is then that the Sons of Light as the Order of Melchizedek will return to Earth to unite the scattered Brotherhood of Melchizedek and establish the Kingdom of God.

Jesus is a high priest of the Order of Melchizedek. Moses also had the keys to this priesthood of Light. When he came to the Earth, he was anointed by the priesthood of Earth as a righteous recipient of the Light. The order had been passed on from Noah to Abraham to Jethro and then to Moses. Aaron, the brother of Moses and mouthpiece for Moses and the Word of God, was commissioned along with the seventy elders of Israel to establish a priesthood that was subordinate to the Order of Melchizedek.

> The order of Melchizedek also governs quadrants of the planetary worlds where the Adamic seed has been transplanted. It is there that they administer and teach spiritual principles to these worlds. The order of Melchizedek has the ability to communicate with the other celestial communities and brotherhoods of Light throughout the universes of God, coordinating the work of the Christ in the heavens and on Earth. In the history of the Planet Earth, the Order of Melchizedek has existed in small family communities of patriarch-priests, priest-scientists, and poet-scholars who have faithfully attended to the word of God. This Light has been passed from Melchizedek to Abraham to Moses to Elijah to David and to Jesus.

This information from *The Keys of Enoch* correlates perfectly with the information given in *The Urantia Book*, according to which the Melchizedek are widely known as emergency sons and daughters of God. They call them this because whenever an extraordinary problem arises it is quite often one among the Order of Melchizedek who accepts the assignment. They fulfill this function throughout the universe, not just on Earth. A Melchizedek actually physically incarnated in the year 1973 B.C., years before the birth of Jesus. This Melchizedek's name was Machiventa Melchizedek. According to *The Urantia Book* this had been done only six times in our local universe. It took place near what was called the city of Salem in Palestine. He was first observed by mortal man when he walked into the tent of Andon, a Chaldean herder of Sumerian extraction, and said, "I am Melchizedek, Priest of El Elyon (the Most High), the one and only God. El Elyon, the Most High, is the Divine creator of the stars of the firmament and even of this very Earth on which we live, and He is also the Supreme God of heaven."

Machiventa Melchizedek gathered around himself a group of students and disciples which became the nucleus of the later community of Salem. He soon became known throughout Palestine as the Priest of El Elyon, the Most High, and Sage of Salem. (Salem eventually became the city of Jerusalem in Israel.) He lived on the Earth for ninety-four years. He taught that at some future time another son of God would come in the flesh as he had come, but that he would be born of a virgin woman. This, of course, was Jesus. The teachings of Machiventa Melchizedek were very simple because the people were very uneducated at that period of history. The spiritual Light on the planet was very dim at the time. Every person who signed or marked the clay tables of the Melchizedek Church committed to memory the following beliefs:

    1. I believe in El Elyon, the Most High God, the only universal father and creator of all things.

    2. I accept the Melchizedek covenant with the Most High, which bestows the favor of God on my faith, not on sacrifices and burnt offerings.

    3. I promise to obey the seven commandments of Melchizedek and to tell the good news of this covenant with the Most High to all men.

Even this short and simple creed turned out in actuality to be too advanced for the people of those days.

The seven commandments set up by Melchizedek were:

    1. You shall not serve any God but the Most High Creator of heaven and Earth.

    2. You shall not doubt that faith is the only requirement of eternal salvation.

    3. You shall not bear false witness.

    4. You shall not kill.

    5. You shall not steal.

    6. You shall not commit adultery.

    7. You shall not show disrespect for your parents and elders.

Melchizedek taught an elementary form of revealed truth during these ninety-four years. According to the Urantia teachings, Abraham, the father of the Jewish religion, attended this Salem school three different times. He became a convert and one of Melchizedek's most brilliant students and supporters. Melchizedek laid upon Abraham the responsibility of keeping alive the truth of the one God, as distinguished from the prevailing belief in the plural deities of that time.

In Melchizedek's covenant with Abraham, he told him, "Look, now, up to the heavens and number the stars if you are able. So numerous shall your seed be." Melchizedek told Abraham the story of the future occupation of Canaan by his offspring after their sojourn in Egypt. It was upon receiving this covenant that Abraham changed his name from Abram to Abraham. According to *The Urantia Book*, at its height there were over one hundred thousand members of this brotherhood. The Melchizedek teachings spread to Egypt, Mesopotamia, and Asia Minor.

As decades and centuries passed, these teachings spread throughout the tree of the human race. So it really was the Jewish religion and later the Christian religion that carried the initial torch of the Order of Melchizedek. After Melchizedek's passing he continued to work with prophets and seers from the inner plane to continue the teachings he had begun with Abraham.

The Melchizedek Temple Teachings of Shield and Sharula and of Earlyne Chaney

In the chapter on the hollow Earth in my third book, *Hidden Mysteries*, I mention a woman who says she comes from the underground city of Telos, two miles beneath Mount Shasta. Her name is Sharula and her husband's name is Shield. I went to a lecture they gave and was impressed with their presentation. She also says that she is something like three hundred fifty years old. My clairvoyant healer friend saw a picture of her and said her aura was totally different from that of most Earthlings. I ordered some of their material, for they are connected with the Order of Melchizedek in this underground civilization of Telos where she is a priestess in the temple. In their teachings they confirm that Melchizedek once lived on this planet. They also speak of the Order of Melchizedek as a cosmic priesthood. They speak of four levels of initiation within this priesthood:

1.   Neophyte,
2.   Initiate,
3.   Hierophant,
4.   High priest and priestess.

An interesting confirmation of Shield and Sharula's statement about the levels of initiation comes from Earlyne Chaney in her book, *Initiation in the Great Pyramid*. Earlyne, in a past life during the third dynasty in

Egypt, went through all seven levels of initiation in the Great Pyramid of Giza. The spiritual order into which she was being initiated was none other than the Order of Melchizedek. She gave the same classifications as Shield and Sharula for candidates desiring to become initiated into the hidden mysteries. It was only when Earlyne passed the seventh initiation that she was entitled to call herself a Melchizedek priestess. She also gave one more step that some Masters took after this which she called becoming a Ptah.

Edgar Cayce, in his channelings of the Universal Mind, has said that even the Essenes had their origins in this ancient order. Earlyne also spoke of studying in Heliopolis which was the same place that Jesus and John the Baptist studied. Her training was almost word for word the same as the Huna teachings of Hawaii, which is most interesting. Some of her training to become initiated into this order was also based on teachings from extraterrestrials of whom she has total recall. Their spacecraft came from other star systems and from Atlantis and the Mayan civilization where extraterrestrials were very active.

As part of her studies she was also trained in the teachings of Thoth-Hermes. I cannot emphasize strongly enough the similarity among the trainings of the Huna, the Egyptians and the Order of Melchizedek.

The following description was written by Earlyne Chaney's father who was a seventh-degree initiate in the Order of Melchizedek.

> The Order of Melchizedek existed even before time began on this miniature planet called Earth. This is the Order of the Divine Hierarchy existing among all the planets of the solar system and even beyond. This mystery school is the fountainhead of the great work. Its initiates are scattered not only on Earth but throughout the universe. . . .
>
> This divine school of the Melchizedeks is the repository of all the mysteries of God and nature, and they are preserved there in the children of the Light. All the secret societies and orders on the Earth plane are only shadows or projections of a corresponding hierarchical order in the superphysical, the supernal invisible mystery school being the generating cause, and the order on Earth the effect. . . .
>
> It possesses its own qualifications and requirements for admission. . . . The principal purpose of the Hierarchy is to project into the world, through its incarnate initiates, inspiration and motives for human enlightenment. Masters of the Hierarchy seek for initiation the most spiritually exalted of Earth's life wave. All truths penetrate into the world from this divine source, the hidden source of all spiritual communities.
>
> Since time and life began on Earth there has been this holy hierarchy, the Order of Melchizedek, of which all exterior schools are but an extension . . . its initiates include those still in flesh who possess the most capacity for Light.
>
> It confers three major degrees on selected candidates still incarnate.

The first degree is imparted solely through inspiration. Such a contact is often unrecognized even by the chosen candidate as he pursues his inspired writings, teachings, or other studies. The second opens the candidate to interior illumination through which he gains intuitive understanding and becomes aware that he is part of a spiritual community and is undergoing a process of initiation. The third, highest and final confers the opening of the entire sensorium by which the soul attains union with eternal verities. Intellectual prowess is not necessary. Some initiates are actually intellectually inferior but are spiritually harmonious with the divine purpose.

This secret community possesses knowledge of the primitive mysteries of space, of nature, and of creation. It watches over all the mystery schools and orders of Earth, superintending their development. Its three graded initiations encompass all the initiations offered in these orders, some of which confer three, some seven, and others thirty-three. But all are encompassed in the three cosmic degrees of the divine hierarchy. Any qualified initiate may be called to this holy company, uniting in love and Light with the illuminated of the community of holy angels.

Shield and Sharula are actually traveling around the country initiating people into this sacred order. Sharula apparently channels a being called Adama. Adama says that the Melchizedek teachings are guarded and protected in the underground world until that time when the outer temples can again be reestablished.

The time is now. That is why it is no accident that I am writing this chapter or that you are reading it. The goal of these teachings is to become a Melchizedek. They suggest that the people who are sincerely interested in becoming Melchizedeks petition to Shamballa three times out loud in a meditative state, asking to be placed on the conscious path of Melchizedek initiation. How you request this and what words you use do not matter. Just make the request three different times in meditation and/or before going to bed. A fully realized Melchizedek is an ascended being.

The Cosmic Order of Melchizedek

On a more cosmic level, *The Urantia Book* speak of a being they refer to as the Father Melchizedek who functions as the chief executive of our local universe. He is concerned with practical procedures of the universe and presides over special, extraordinary and emergency commissions and advisory bodies. The Melchizedek order does not function extensively outside of the local universe except when they are called as witnesses in matters pending before tribunals of the super-universe. The Melchizedeks on this more cosmic level are the first order of Divine sons to approach sufficiently close to physical life to be able to function directly in the ministry of mortal upliftment and to serve without the necessity of incarnation. They serve at the midpoint between the personalities in the material universe and the highest Divinity. The seraphic orders of angels delight to work with the Melchizedeks.

The Melchizedeks are also a self-governing order. They maintain an autonomous organization devoted to universal intelligence. They have the full confidence of all classes of intelligent beings. The Melchizedeks are close to perfect in their wisdom. The Melchizedek orders are chiefly devoted to the vast educational system and experiential training regime of the local universe.

According to *The Urantia Book* their service work embraces approximately ten million inhabited worlds in our universe alone. Besides their normal educational training work the Melchizedeks go into action whenever there is an emergency situation in the universe. When failure of some aspect of the Creator's plan is threatened, forthwith will go a Melchizedek to render assistance. It is possible for a Melchizedek to make himself visible to mortal beings and on rare occasions they do physically incarnate. The Order of Melchizedek are the versatile and volunteer emergency ministers to all orders of universe intelligences and to all systems of worlds.

Solara's Message on the Order of Melchizedek

Solara is a spiritual teacher and is deeply connected to the angelic kingdom. She has written a series of very interesting books and was particularly instrumental in making people aware of the 11:11. The 11:11, for those who don't know, is a symbol for the ascension energy. The 11:11 that occurred on January 11, 1992 (1/11/1(992) was the subsequent planetary awakening after the Harmonic Convergence.

In Solara's message from the archangels, she said that on November 11, 1991, there was the long-awaited "activation of the Order of Melchizedek" on Planet Earth. According to Solara's words, Melchizedek serves as the "overseer of the Lords of Wisdom and holders of the secret and ancient knowledge."

All the secret mysteries of the initiates are under the leadership of the Order of Melchizedek. With this activation there has been an externalization of all the secret mysteries that have been hidden. The externalization of the Hierarchy and the reappearance of the Christ are part of this process also. The esoteric mystery schools are in the process of becoming exoteric. The order of Melchizedek will rise into full activation between 1991 and 1995. Melchizedek's rod of power has been activated and it is awakening the cellular memory banks of the people of Planet Earth. This activation is part of the renewed interest in this most sacred and ancient order.

More Universal Information

As I have continued my research throughout this year, more fascinating information has come to me. According to channelings from Vywamus, the name of our Universal Logos (the being who ensouls the universe) is none other than Melchizedek. This gives a double confirmation of what was channeled in *The Urantia Book* about the Father Melchizedek.

Vywamus, in his channelings, spoke of different levels of Source. As we evolve as a planet, solar system, galaxy, and universe, we are able to gain attunement to higher levels of Source. He has referred to these as Source A and Source B. The higher-level source he referred to as Kalmelchizedek, speaking here on a universal level. The Galactic Logos and the Galactic Logos of our quadrant (Melchior) are in service to this great being.

One last piece of fascinating occult information about Melchizedek is the fact that Nikola Tesla was a soul extension or probe of the vast being we know as Melchizedek, according to Vywamus and channelings of members of The Tibetan Foundation.

Melchizedek on the Galactic Level

On the Galactic Core level there is another great and powerful being who is now very available to us on Earth to attune to, channel, and be overshadowed by. His name is none other than Melchizedek. He is a member of the governing council of this galactic section. He is a new member of this council, having recently replaced another cosmic Master who has moved on to a position on the universal level.

The galactic Melchizedek serves as a liaison between the Earth and other planets, and the galactic core of our galaxy. He has had some lifetimes on Earth. His last life on Earth of which we are aware was as a king named Melchizedek. He has overshadowed (as Lord Maitreya did with Jesus) many beings on Earth, one of whom was Enoch ("the man who walked with God").

I asked Djwhal Khul about Enoch and he told me a fascinating piece of information. He said that Enoch was none other than an incarnation of Jesus Christ. A double confirmation of this is the fact that Edgar Cayce said that Enoch had been a past life of Jesus. In his life as Enoch, with Melchizedek overshadowing him, he ascended.

The galactic Melchizedek is currently working through a number of people on Earth to bring through information about how to use Light. He is very available to be contacted and channeled.

22

The Universality of Religion

*Start the day with love. Fill the day
with love. Spend the day with love, and
end the day with love, for this is
the way to God.*

Sathya Sai Baba

What I have to share with you now is absolutely extraordinary. I have spoken of the Essene community and how it influenced and affected the life of Jesus Christ. In my research into the Edgar Cayce files I came across a statement of the Universal Mind as channeled through Edgar Cayce. The Universal Mind said that the true origins of the Essenes were with Melchizedek. Melchizedek was the great spiritual Master who lived on Earth one thousand nine hundred seventy-three years before the birth of Christ. He was called the prince of Salem and was the spiritual Master who initiated Abraham, the father and originator of the Jewish religion, into the spiritual mysteries. This fact is clearly mentioned in the Old Testament.

Melchizedek was Abraham's spiritual teacher. Melchizedek was a representative of the ancient order of the Melchizedek priesthood. The Melchizedek priesthood is a universal mystical order that is in charge of the training and education of mortal beings of all types throughout the universe. The Great White Brotherhood on our planet would be a part of this much larger order of Masters and teachers.

I knew that Jesus had had a past life as a being named Melchizedek; however, any being that goes through all seven levels of initiation in this mystical order is termed a Melchizedek priest, so I didn't give too much thought to it. My intuitive guidance told me to ask Djwhal Khul whether in Jesus' past life as Melchizedek he had been the same Melchizedek who was

Abraham's teacher and who caused him to start the Jewish religion. Djwhal Khul immediately told me it was the same person. This is extraordinary information, for what it means is that Jesus started the Essenes and then was trained by them again on his return to Earth as the baby Jesus.

This also means that the Essenes are a branch of the Order of Melchizedek, which is extraordinary. It also means that Jesus is the Master who started not only the Christian religion, but also the Jewish religion, for he was Abraham's spiritual teacher. Moreover, in later incarnations he was Joshua, who lead the Jewish people into the promised land after Moses died. We also know that he was Enoch, Jeshua, and Joseph, all major Jewish Biblical figures. To make this story even more amazing, he also was Zend, the father of the Persian Avatar Zoroaster (who had been Buddha in a past life) so he greatly influenced the beginnings of the Zoroastrian religion as well. In addition, he was one of Mohammed's spiritual teachers on the inner plane, along with the Archangel Gabriel.

It also must be remembered that Jesus was born into a Jewish family and became a Jewish rabbi. The intertwining of the Jewish and Christian religions, in truth, is amazing. We have the intertwining of Judaism, Christianity, the Essenes, and the order of Melchizedek all coming from the same source.

What is even more remarkable is Earlyne Chaney's recall of being initiated in the Great Pyramid of Giza into the Order of Melchizedek. Upon studying the teachings she was given, I was amazed to see that the Egyptian teachings were almost word for word exactly the same as the Huna teachings of Hawaii. And when I say word for word, I mean word for word. I have studied these teachings inside and out so I should know.

I was turned on to the Huna teachings by one of my first spiritual teachers, a man by the name of Paul Solomon who channels the Universal Mind in much the same manner as Edgar Cayce did. In his channelings of the Universal Mind, he said that the purest form of psychology and religion on the planet was the Huna teachings of Hawaii.

What we are seeing now is that the Order of Melchizedek, Judaism, Christianity, the Essenes, the Egyptian teachings, and the Huna beliefs of Hawaii all came from the same source; and I have only begun this discussion.

We have the Lord Maitreya, who is the head of the Spiritual Hierarchy and the Great White Brotherhood and who also helped Jesus begin the Christian dispensation by overshadowing Jesus in that lifetime. It is an occult fact that the Lord Maitreya was, in his past life, the great Hindu spiritual Master, Lord Krishna. All of Hinduism is based on his glorious teachings in the *Mahabarata*, especially the *Bhagavad-Gita*. Thus, Hinduism and the Great White Brotherhood can be added to the list of teachings that came from the same source.

Then to add to this, the scribe for the *Bhagavad-Gita* was Vyassa. Vyassa was none other than Gautama Buddha in a past life. Buddha was also Hermes-Thoth who taught the spiritual mysteries in Egypt. He was also Orpheus, who began the Grecian Mystery School. He was also Zoroaster who founded the Zoroastrian religion. Then, last but not least, he founded the Buddhist religion. The same being was involved in founding five different religions! So we can now add these to the core group, all of which come from the same source.

To add to this list further, we have Djwhal Khul, who was a Tibetan Buddhist in his life as Djwhal Khul. In a previous life he was Confucius and began the religion of Confucianism. Djwhal was also Caspar, one of the three wise men of the Christian religion, so again we have an interrelationship among Confucianism, Tibetan Buddhism, Christianity, and the Great White Brotherhood.

Then we also have the fact that the people of the inner Earth, many of whom came from Atlantis and Egypt, also follow the teachings of Melchizedek. Shield and Sharula from an underground city two miles below Mount Shasta called Telos, say that the source of their religion is the Order of Melchizedek. Earlyne Chaney's writings confirm this also.

Taoism was founded by Lao Tse. In a later life he was a God-realized Siddha Yoga Master in the lineage taught by Babaji. Again we see the correlation between Taoism and the Hindu and Yoga path.

We also have the Archangel Gabriel who has been instrumental in the founding of the Islamic religion through the prophet Mohammed as well as in the founding of Christianity. He was Mohammed's teacher and as the teacher of the Virgin Mary and Joseph, her husband (Saint Germain). So here we see the connection between the Islamic and Christian faiths.

Then we have Ascended Master El Morya who was Abraham, the father of the Jewish religion. He was also one of the three wise men in the Christian story. Here again we see the correlation of Judaism and Christianity in the Great White Brotherhood.

Then there is the Count Saint Germain. He was Joseph, the husband of the Virgin Mary, he was the Jewish prophet, Samuel, and the founder of the I Am Discourses through Godfrey Ray King. This again, ties in Christianity, Judaism, and the modern mystical occult teachings of the I Am foundation.

This brings us to the great Master Kuthumi who was Pythagoras, Saint Francis of Assisi, and John the Beloved, the disciple of Christ. And here again we have the interweaving of the Pythagorean Mystery School with the Christian dispensation. These are the past lives that clearly demonstrate and prove that which we all already intuitively knew: that all religions are one and they all come from the same source. One of my main goals is to weave this tapestry together and to show the incredible beauty of all the diverse forms of religion and yet the oneness of them all.

All the great prophets really were teaching the same truths. This will not be too hard to demonstrate, for as we have clearly seen, they are all based on the teachings of the same great beings who were just switching Earthly bodies from lifetime to lifetime.

23

Prophecies of Things to Come

Why worry when you can pray
Edgar Cayce

The most important thing to understand about prophecy is that a prophecy is really accurate only at the moment it is given. The reason for this is that we have free choice. A prophet is looking into the future from within the pattern that is extending forward in that moment. If we as people on Earth continue in that pattern then that prophecy will come true.

Prophecy was once described to me as being like a grid on a checkerboard. The grid is set and even some of the squares are filled in. Most of the squares are left open, however, and are filled in by our choices.

The reason I bring this up first thing in the chapter is that there have been a lot of prophecies by a great number of psychics and channels concerning massive Earth changes and natural disasters that will be hitting this planet. The real reason that these prophecies have been provided is so that we on Earth will use our free will and free choice to change our consciousnesses and change our world. I am very happy to say that we, as a planet, have done this to a great extent. All the sources of information that I am in contact with have said that the consciousness of people on Earth has changed enough to avoid the massive catastrophes that were once on tap for us.

Planetary karma works just like personal karma. If we, personally, get out of harmony with God's laws then we suffer. The same is true of the mass consciousness of this planet. If the mass consciousness is out of harmony with God's laws, then we will have planetary karma such as Earthquakes, economic collapses, and so on.

Djwhal Khul has stated that humanity as a whole is actually ahead of schedule. If we look at all the changes that have taken place recently, such as the transformation of the Soviet Union into a democracy and the tearing down of the Berlin Wall and reunification of Germany, then we can see the global transformation that is beginning to take place.

A lot of the fundamentalist religions are holding on to a lot of the Armageddon-type prophecies of the Bible that were given anywhere from two to five thousand years ago. When these prophecies were given, I am absolutely sure they were accurate. They were given, however, to warn us to use our free choice to change, not because they were definitely going to happen.

In the prophecies of the Virgin Mary in the early 1900's as Lady Fatima, she made a request that all of the prayers of the Catholic Church be consecrated to the Soviet Union, for she foresaw in the future a possible nuclear holocaust. I honestly believe that the prayers of the members of the Catholic Church and many other people played a big part in the transformation from Communism to a free and democratic society. If prophecy can't be changed then why did the Virgin Mary ask that all prayers be consecrated to the Soviet Union?

Sai Baba made a prediction about the Soviet Union approximately twenty years ago. He said that the people of the Soviet Union are not the Communists, they are the ones who are "coming next." Edgar Cayce predicted over forty years ago that the next great religion would come from the Soviet Union and that they would one day be the hope of the free world. These are amazing prophecies, given that just thirty years ago we were dealing with a Soviet Union under Khrushchev and a Cuban missile crisis.

The period of history in which we are living can be likened to the Earth Mother giving birth to a New Age. Planet Earth has now moved from a third-dimensional consciousness to a fourth-dimensional consciousness. We are completing a two-thousand-year cycle as we move from the Piscean age to the Aquarian age. We are also completing even larger planetary cycles of six thousand, twelve thousand, and thirty-six thousand years. We have just begun, in 1992, the last twenty-year cycle of the Mayan calendar which ends in the year 2012.

As I mentioned earlier, Vywamus has said we are right at the end of a one-hundred-year window for mass ascension which runs from the year 1995 to the year 2000. Then to top it off, the Lord Maitreya, Sai Baba, and the entire externalization of the Spiritual Hierarchy are now manifest on this planet. Add to this all the extraterrestrial activity. Djwhal Khul has said that we can now achieve as much evolution in fourteen months as previously took fourteen years.

When a mother gives birth to a child there are labor pains. The pain is a bittersweet kind of pain in that it hurts, but the mother knows that a beautiful child is coming from the pain, so it is totally worthwhile and even joyous. This is the situation we are in on this planet. The Earth Mother is giving birth to a New Age. There may be some labor pains; however, what is coming is so beautiful that the pain is really inconsequential.

We are moving toward the Golden Age on this planet. This Golden Age will have to do with a spiritualized world—spiritualized government, spiritualized economic system, and spiritualized institutions in every aspect of society, a world that manifests Christ-like principles of sharing, brotherhood, service, and the awareness that we are all our brothers' keepers.

Djwhal Khul has prophesied that in the future the churches and temples of this world will teach the process of initiation exoterically, not just esoterically. People will actually be able to take initiations in churches. The first initiation will become the most sacred ceremony of the church, he predicts.

Djwhal has also predicted that the whole field of religion will be inspired and reoriented because the Master Jesus will take hold of the Christian Church in an effort to spiritualize it and reorganize it. John the Beloved, the disciple of Christ (who is now incarnated), will release all the secrets of the Atlantean civilization from the hall of records in the Great Pyramid of Giza.

The Antichrist

There are many predictions of the appearance of the antichrist, both in the Bible and elsewhere. It is very important to understand that in reality there are many antichrists working in this world. Paul Solomon, the man whom many people call the modern-day Edgar Cayce, has said in his source channelings that the real antichrist to watch is not someone like Saddam Hussein, who is so boisterous, but rather one who claims to be a savior at first. Once he gets total power, then he will become power-driven. The real antichrist will be deceptive and cunning. He will ultimately be defeated, however. Brian Grattan says, in one of his books, that the antichrist is a thirty-three-year-old Arab (in 1993) and describes him very much as Paul Solomon does.

One of the real hot spots on the planet is, of course, the Middle East. Paul Solomon has predicted the potential for a "very limited" nuclear war between Syria and Israel. I am not saying this is going to happen for sure; however, it is a trouble spot. In his channelings, Paul Solomon has said that he sees that the war would be over very quickly, with Israel winning.

Paul Solomon has also said that another spot that could be a problem near the end of the century is the Temple on the Mount in Israel. This particular spot is one of the most holy spots in Israel for both the Arabs and the Jews. In around 1975, Paul Solomon saw a radical Israeli group trying to rebuild their temple there which would be sacrilege to the Moslems and would start some kind of holy war. A lot has happened in the world since 1975 and this may be outdated already, but it is a place to watch closely.

Crystal Technology

With the opening of the hall of records in the Great Pyramid by John of Penial, the reincarnation of John the Beloved, disciple of Christ, there will be a great upsurge in crystal technology. We will have the understanding of how to overcome the law of gravity. This is how the ancient Egyptians were able to build the pyramids of Egypt. This technology, along with the inventions of Nikola Tesla, will have a revolutionary impact on this world. We will all have antennas over our houses and businesses that will supply all the energy we need from the universal cosmic supply. Vywamus has said in a channeling through Janet McClure that as of the Harmonic Convergence, the Ashtar Command was allowed to energize crystals on the planet tenfold.

As we move into the Golden Age, there will be much more open contact with the higher, more advanced extraterrestrial civilizations. Some of the extraterrestrial civilizations in our galaxy that have been visiting us for eons of time are those from the Lyra system, the Vega system, Arcturus, Sirius, Orion, the Pleiades, and, of course, the Ashtar Command, to name just a few.

In the future, open extraterrestrial contact will be commonplace. We will be allowed to join the confederation of planets in our galaxy and universe as Earth moves into the status of being a more spiritualized planet. The extraterrestrials will be of enormous help in advancing our technologies way beyond their present scope. Space travel will be commonplace, as will Earthly flying saucers. The extraterrestrials are waiting for us to develop sufficient spiritual consciousness so we can handle these advanced technologies and not use them for warfare.

Light and Sound

Djwhal Khul has said, in the Alice Bailey books, that there would be great inventions in the future using light and sound. Some of this information was used in the healing temples of Atlantis and Lemuria. One of the results of studies in this field will be the development of much greater etheric vision for all of us. Djwhal has said that increasingly in the future, people will think and talk in terms of light.

He also said that a great discovery will take place at the end of this century or the beginning of the next involving the use of thought to direct light. Two small children, one living in the United States and one in India, will work out a formula along scientific lines which will fill in some of the existing gaps in the scale of light vibration.

Cosmic Telephones

In the future it is predicted that we will have machines that will be able to communicate with spirit beings on the inner plane. We will be able to speak to relatives who have passed on to the astral plane.

Nikola Tesla's inventions will be put into use, also, and we will be able to communicate with flying saucers and other planets using his machines.

Messiah for the Jewish People

A fascinating prophecy of Djwhal Khul's in the Alice Bailey books is that he sees a high-level initiate, other than the Lord Maitreya, who will serve as the Messiah for the Jewish people.

Cure for AIDS

It has been prophesied that there will be a cure for AIDS having to do with some kind of vaccine that will be invented in the near future.

A Smog-Clearing Machine

Paul Solomon has predicted there will be a future invention of some kind of ion generator that will collect and clear away the smog and pollution in the air.

Judgment Day

It has been prophesied by many channels and psychics that at the end of this planetary cycle of evolution we are in, there will be a type of judgment day or division of souls. The term judgment day is not used here to mean anything negative, but rather to indicate that those souls who are still of a third-dimensional consciousness will reincarnate in the future on another planet that is more suitable for their evolution. Brian Grattan has suggested that this planet will be in the Pleiades.

The Planet Earth is moving toward stabilizing a fourth-dimensional consciousness now. Those souls who are in tune with this change within their own personal evolution will continue to reincarnate on this planet.

The Future World Teacher

Djwhal Khul has predicted that when the Lord Maitreya completes his mission and moves on to his cosmic evolution, Kuthumi will take his place as the Bodhisattva, world teacher, Planetary Christ, and head of the Spiritual Hierarchy.

As many people know, Djwhal Khul was Kuthumi's senior disciple and has taken on much of his work and many of his students. Theosophical literature prophesied that the Lord Maitreya would return to Earth again in the far distant future as the Cosmic Christ.

Airships

The *I Am Discourses* prophesied that airships will be invented that will receive energy for propulsion from the atmosphere. We will also have planes and cars run by crystal energy, as they had in Atlantis.

Ronald Beasly, the spiritual Master from England, predicted that cars would eventually be run on water. Gasoline will become obsolete. Ruth Montgomery's spirit guides predict that new forms of energy will be produced by solar disks that slowly rotate in wide arcs while generating steam for power. They say that this new form of energy will also be available for cars.

The Economic System

Benjamin Creme, in his channelings, predicted that after the full declaration of the Lord Maitreya, high-level initiates with expertise in economics would revamp our whole economic system, instituting a new system based on sharing. Each country on the planet would take stock of resources and all excess would be put into some kind of pool for use by those countries that were less productive.

George Washington's Vision

One of the most fascinating prophecies and visions was given to George Washington, our first president, at Valley Forge in 1777. His ragtag army was slowly starving and freezing to death. George Washington went to his tent for solitude. A beautiful woman appeared to him (the Goddess of Liberty) and showed him three visions of the future of the United States. Each of the visions had to do with a certain peril the United States would have to face in the future.

At the end of the three visions the Goddess of Liberty said to George Washington, "Son of the Republic, what you have seen is thus interpreted: Three great perils will come upon the Republic. The most fearful is the third, but the whole world united shall not prevail against her. Let every child of the Republic learn to live for God, his land, and the union."

The three perils in his vision have been interpreted as the American Revolution, the Civil War, and a possible invasion of the United States. It is to be hoped that we people of the United States have raised our consciousnesses enough so that the third vision will not need to come to pass. It is my belief that we have passed this cornerstone. Either way, the Goddess of Liberty said that the United States would prevail.

One interesting note about George Washington: In a later life in this century he incarnated as Godfrey Ray King, the channel for the *I Am Discourses* of Saint Germain. These were Saint Germain's great teachings brought forth in the 1930's and 1940's. Saint Germain actually physically materialized himself to Godfrey Ray King at Mt. Shasta, California.

Another interesting point is that Saint Germain, in a past life, was Columbus. So the founder of America and the first president of the United States teamed up again in this century to bring forth inner freedom for the United States through the *I Am* teachings.

Edgar Cayce's Return

Edgar Cayce was told in a reading of the Universal Mind that he would reincarnate again in 1998 as a world liberator, if he so desired, to help bring about the New Age. In another dream of Edgar Cayce's, he was born in the year 2100 in Nebraska. As a child in the dream, he told his elders that he had been Edgar Cayce in the early twentieth century. He said that people traveled in long cigar-shaped metal ships which moved at high speeds through the air. (This sounds like Atlantean technology.) He also said that houses were made of glass.

A Testing Period from 1958 to 1998

Cayce said that the world would be going through a testing period from 1958 to 1998. A very interesting day to mark on our calendars is May 5th of the year 2000. Paul Solomon, in his source channelings, has said that this day, astrologically, is called a grand alignment. All the planets will be lined up, one behind the other. When this happens, an energy beam will run right down the center of all the planets. If the Earth is still unstable it could cause an axis shift. Djwhal Khul, again, has stated that we have learned this lesson by grace instead of by karma. It still should be a very interesting day, however. A grand alignment happens extremely rarely in terms of cosmic astrology.

The Prophecies of Earlyne Chaney

Earlyne Chaney, again, is the originator of Astara, the mystery school in Upland, California. Her teachers are Kuthumi, Zoser, and the Virgin Mary. Her teachings are very much in tune with Djwhal Khul's teachings, which is not surprising. She has made a great many wonderful and exciting prophecies.

Earlyne sees, in the future, a rediscovering of the Ark of the Covenant. This term was recently popularized by the movie Raiders of the Lost Ark. Earlyne says that the arks of the covenant were actually brought by extraterrestrials and were special instruments with crystals attached to them that were used to create light beams similar to our lasers. She says they were used in Atlantis and later in Egypt to build the pyramids.

The arks of the covenant could cut stone and could be used to defy gravity and actually levitate large stones. Earlyne says that these arks were also used to build the great underground tunnels. Earlyne says that a small extraterrestrial spacecraft is stored in a chamber not yet found, far beneath the Great Pyramid.

Earlyne sees automobiles run by solar batteries, photo batteries, and superelectric batteries containing strange rods, coils, and magnets. She says we will not need to drive in for gas anymore, we will only need to get recharged.

Earlyne predicts that satellites in the future will contain vast cities, and she sees one satellite actually housing our criminals. Earlyne predicts the formation of a psychic FBI in which the workers will be trained to leave their bodies and travel to secret meetings of other countries to gain classified information.

She predicts the invention of brain implants on which entire subjects will be recorded and filed on biochips to enable one to learn a subject overnight. She says the brain implants will pour knowledge into the mind, giving an individual the equivalent of a college education in a few hours.

She sees the much greater use of sound and color in combination with crystals for healing. She is prophesying the discovery of more planets in our solar system. She says that we will eventually find twelve planets orbiting our sun. She also sees a moving planet or spaceship that resembles a glowing white moon. She says that she thinks it is coming from Orion or the Pleiades. Earlyne predicts that holographic science will eventually include three-dimensional movies and television. Won't that be fun!

Other Prophecies and Spiritual Tidbits from Vywamus

Vywamus, in a channeling through Janet McClure, said that an asteroid that was a mile to a mile and a half in diameter was heading toward the Earth. He said it should arrive around 1994 or 1995. From a consciousness point of view, he said, it could actually be a very positive thing, a new kind of energy being integrated into the Earth's system. He said the asteroid would be carrying a great amount of spiritual energy. If humankind has gotten to the point where it can use this energy the asteroid won't be destructive, although it could cause some Earthquakes if it does actually hit the Earth. It is apparently bringing with it some kind of energy of integration.

Vywamus, in another reading, has said that there are ninety-five people who basically control the Earth; they are part of the Trilateral Commission. These ninety-five men and their families are very involved with the banking conglomerates and holding companies. The Trilateral Commission and the secret government on this planet are connected with thirty-five other planets in our galaxy. This makes the Trilateral Commission a galactic problem, not just a planetary problem as most people are assuming.

These thirty-five planets are, however, very disorganized in their functioning because of their negative egotistical consciousnesses, and this is going to be their downfall. Vywamus has said that their power will be coming to an end soon. He also said that the invasion by these negative extraterrestrials did not begin in 1947 with the Roswell crash, when the United States actually found physical proof of the existence of extraterrestrials, but has been going on for over five hundred years.

Vywamus also said that the physical health problems of the Grays stem from the fact that they came from another universe. Each universe has its own unique energy matrix because each universe has its own unique source that governs it. The reason they are sick is that they are trying to live in the wrong universe.

Vywamus says that their energy matrix must be changed for them to survive. He is amazed they have survived as long as they have, given what they are trying to do. He said the Grays could be healed if the Spiritual Masters from the Galactic Core were invoked. They have the ability to change the energy matrix but they must be asked for this help before they step in and give it.

Prophecy of Brian Grattan

Brian Grattan, in an article I read in a wonderful magazine called *Sedona Journal of Emergence*, has said that there is a spiritually accelerated window, of sorts, on the Earth from the year 1988 (the anchoring of the Mahatma energy) to the year 2028. During this forty-year period of spiritual acceleration on this planet, he said we would accomplish more spiritual growth than in the previous 3.2 billion years of our Cosmic Day.

A Cosmic Day lasts for 4.3 billion years, so we have 1.1 billion years left in the cosmic day of our section of God's infinite universe. Just think about this: In this forty-year span of time we will make more progress than we have made in the past 3.2 billion years. It is an amazing time to be incarnated on this planet!

24

Mantras, Names of God, and Words of Power

*Holy, Holy, Holy, is the Lord
God of Hosts*
The Keys of Enoch

In my opinion, next to meditation, repetition of the names of God and the use of mantras and words of power may be the most important spiritual practice you can use in your daily life. There is not a single spiritual teacher or Master of any path or religion who has not recommended this practice in some form. In this chapter I am going to include an eclectic and universal collection of names of God, mantras, and words of power which are guaranteed to fill you with God intoxication if you use them with any regularity.

The benefits of this practice are unbelievable. Gandhi chanted the name of God as Rama constantly throughout his life and he said it was one of the absolute keys to his success. The *Bhagavad-Gita* says that where you go when you die depends in the last thought in your mind; Gandhi's last word as he was assassinated was "Rama." Sai Baba says repeating of the name of God and visualizing His form is one of the main keys to spiritual success. The idea is to not just do it in meditation but to do it throughout your day, while standing in line at the bank, doing laundry, vacuuming, showering, walking.

The law of the mind is that thoughts create reality. Energy follows thought. When you chant the name of God, you eventually become that which you are chanting. If you say the name of God enough times it has the effect of cleansing your physical, emotional, mental, and etheric bodies to the point that they reflect only God.

One of the biggest problems of people on the path is a wandering mind; "an idle mind is the devil's workshop." The chanting of the name of God keeps your mind focused on God. If your mind isn't on God then it is likely to float back to the lower self and negative ego. In India everyone chants the name of God. In the West it is not prescribed in the same way and this is unfortunate.

Any time you feel negative emotions coming on or if you are feeling depressed or angry, try chanting the name of God, and visualizing your favorite form of God. You will find that this will pull you right out of it. It is a way of pulling you from your lower self to your higher self. You don't have to use just one name; you can switch around if you like variety. This chapter will provide you with hundreds of choices. Experiment and see which ones feel best. You will have a spiritual arsenal that will provide for every need and circumstance; visualization will increase the power. Repetition of the name of God is really an antidote to all challenges of life.

As well as actual names of God you can also use mantras that are sacred sounds. An example is Aum. Sai Baba says that Aum is the arrow and Brahman is the target. Aum takes you straight to Brahman. It is the mother of all mantras.

The amazing thing about mantras is that many of them actually exist in the highest dimensions and have been brought forth to humanity by the ancient Indian rishis or seers. They have actually heard these mantras claraudiently by being able to tune in to the higher dimensions. The power of mantras is unbelievable. God created the universe by saying a mantra. As you evolve into cosmic levels of spiritual you will be able to create planets and even solar systems with the power of a mantra.

You recognize the power of words. Look at the evidence of the power of words. Jesus said, "Lazarus, arise!" and Lazarus arose from the dead. Look at the effect of Hitler's words on Nazi Germany. Words of power can be used by a white magician or a black magician. Most people have no idea of the tremendous power they wield when they speak.

There are studies being done now with sound, in which certain frequencies of sound are beamed to cancer cells and the cancer is completely healed. The human voice is the ultimate instrument for the making of sound. Sound in conjunction with the meaning of the words or the names of of God can heal all problems.

The Lord's Prayer and the Great Invocation are obviously powerful. Another interesting thing about the use of mantras, names of God, and words of power is that the more they are used, the more powerful they become. They take on a collective spiritual force of their own. When you use, let's say, the rosary of the Virgin Mary, you are tapping into a group consciousness as well as your own personal God-connection.

Mantras and names of God can be chanted out loud, whispered, said silently in your mind, or written down. Each has its own unique effect. The idea is to not become too mechanical in their recitation. Say each mantra as a type of worship and devotion to God. The name of God in mystical Judaism was so sacred that in certain aspects of Jewish tradition people weren't even allowed to say the name. This is also why the Bible also says to never use the Lord's name in vain.

The chanting of a mantra or a name of God builds spiritual force and purifies, cleanses, and heals all your bodies. When you chant the name of God you are programming perfection into your subconscious mind. This creates perfection in your physical, emotional, mental, and spiritual bodies.

The chanting of mantras or names of God helps to build your Light-body which is the body you will use in your ascended state. The more you chant God's name, the more that name becomes the center of your consciousness. The mantra is like a seed that will eventually grow into a beautiful tree. The tree is symbolic of God-realization. The mantra and name of God protect you from glamour, illusion, maya, and negative energies. They also attract to you that which you are chanting.

If you chant the Divine word "Elohim" which means "All that God Is," then you are attracting to yourself all that God is. Chant God's name as you are falling asleep and you will float in your soul body to the dimension and consciousness of the name you are reciting, since where you go when you fall asleep depends on the last thought in your mind.

The ultimate purpose of reciting the names of God or mantras is to blend your individual consciousness with God-consciousness. The name of God or mantra helps you to become aware of your true nature as the eternal self, awakens your higher faculties, and raises your consciousness to the level of that particular mantric resonance.

The constant practice of this most holy spiritual discipline builds enormous spiritual force and power in your aura which can then be used as a blessing upon every person you meet throughout your day. The mind is an incredibly powerful tool. Jesus said that if you have the faith of a mustard seed you could literally move a mountain. Paul Solomon said, in his channeling of the Universal Mind, that Jesus Christ's use of free choice was so powerful he actually changed the positions of stars in the universe. Edgar Cayce said that the sunspots on the sun are actually created by man's negative thinking.

Can you imagine how you would feel if you could harness the tremendous force of your mind and channel it into a spiritual focus only? Imagine if you used your mind constantly, twenty-four hours a day, to chant the names of God, mantras, and words of power: your every thought, word, and deed would be of Divine origin. This is the ideal — to let your entire life on

Earth be an affirmation of God which is who you really are. The reason more of you don't do this is that you have not been educated in the need to do it or given the tools and methods. That is the purpose of this chapter and this book in general.

Each of you has one or several particular mantras, names of God, and words of power to which you will respond strongly. There may be many or just a few. There is no right or wrong. Let your intuition guide you. Experiment and have fun. You will be amazed at the results you receive in the form of the tremendous joy, love of God, love of people, and Light that are generated.

When you are not chanting mantras and names of God throughout your day, then do your other spiritual disciplines such as meditation, prayer, spiritual reading, affirmations, journal writing, and physical fitness. Repeating the name of God and mantras can be the glue that connects them all together throughout your day.

It is also incredibly powerful to sing the names of God. In India they call this the singing of bhajans or kirtans. In the West we call them devotional songs. Adding the emotional body to the chanting of the names of God and mantras makes them even more powerful. Make up your own melodies and songs if you like, or buy tapes. Another great tool is to make or buy tapes that already have mantras and names of God on them. You can play them as background music. This is a receptive rather than an active practice. One of the interesting things that begins to happen when you are doing this consistently is that your subconscious and inner nature begin to say the mantras without your conscious mind even being involved. It begins to happen automatically. You begin doing it in your dreams. Your life inwardly and outwardly begins to become filled with the Divine music and song of God.

It is also appropriate, if you like, to set aside certain times for chanting or singing. It can be done in meditation or, if you like, you can use mala beads as is common in India. You have a string of one hundred eight beads (one hundred eight is a holy number) made of sandalwood or rudraksha seeds. As you say your mantra or name of God, you count a bead or seed with your fingers. There are usually some kind of little marker beads that let you know you have completed a certain number of repetitions or have finished a complete circle. Mantras may be done in sets, such as seven times around the string of beads. It is good to know that each set of repetitions not only assists your own spiritual growth but is helping humanity and the Earth as well. Using mala beads is very much like using rosary beads. Buddhists have a similar practice. Hold a crystal while you chant and it will become even more powerful yet. I can't recommend stongly enough that you do this throughout your day. The more you chant the name of God and His Divine mantras, the more you will become like Him.

This practice will clean out your subconscious mind and help you develop tremendous powers of concentration. It will lead to stilling the mind, calming the emotions, and healing the physical body. It will eventually lead to being in the Christ consciousness at all times and not in the negative ego consciousness at all.

It is important to create variety, for you do not want to make this drudgery. You want to make it your greatest joy. Interest can be maintained by using different names of God and mantras and also by using different speeds or tempos of chanting. You can go slow or fast, loud or soft, with melody or without melody. The most important thing is to chant with enthusiasm and great devotion and love; you are worshiping and making love to God.

Just as you want to feed your physical body good, healthful food, repeating the name of God is feeding good food to your mind and spirit. One of the keys to spiritual and worldly success is understanding the importance of where you put your attention. Where your attention lies is literally where you live. Repeating the name of God and His mantras keeps your attention where it needs to be. It will attract spiritual and material wealth to you, for does not the Bible say, "Seek ye the kingdom of God, and all things shall be added unto thee."

Every mantra will lead to God-realization and to the top of the spiritual mountain; however, each one will take a different path up the mountain. There are mantras and words of power for every purpose in life. Some are for healing, some for raising the dead, some for the manifestation of prosperity. I also want to make it clear that you don't have to change your religion to use a universal and eclectic assortment of mantras. Sai Baba has said that "Any name or form of God you chant or worship, I will respond to." This is the New Age religion of the future. All names and all forms lead to the same place. Choose the ones that you resonate with the best. At different times in your life you may feel you want to focus on different ones, and that is fine.

Chanting the name of God also helps you practice being conscious of the presence of God in your daily life. The biggest problem is forgetting. If you are constantly chanting the name of God then this will not happen. This practice will also help to build positive God-habits, instead of negative, lower-self habits. Dedication to this practice cannot help but invoke a response from God Himself. God cannot resist a pure, loving, and devoted heart.

Repeat the name of God any time you are afraid or start to worry, and the fear will disappear. "If God be for you, who or what can be against you?" Think about the effect of advertising on the general public. I refer here to all the slogans, catchy words, and tunes. Look how the public buys the advertisers' products. Use this same method but chant God's name and you will buy only "God's product." When you are starting to get into a fight with your spouse, begin chanting, silently, the name of God in your mind and see what the effect is.

The more you practice your names of God and mantras, the deeper the seed will become implanted in the soul of your subconscious mind, and the deeper the roots will grow. Ultimately, it will unify your entire consciousness in the service of your soul and monad until you become the monad, and, hence, ascend. Was it not Saint Paul who said, "Pray without ceasing"?

Names of God, Mantras, and Words of Power

Mantras from the Mystical Jewish Tradition

1. Elohim (This is the Divine Mother aspect of God; it means All that God Is. In my personal opinion, this is one of the most powerful mantras there is.)
2. Yod Hay Vod Hay or Yod Hay Wah Hay (This is the Divine Father aspect of God; it could also be chanted using Christian terminology: Jehovah.)
3. Adonai (This is the Earth aspect of God; in the Kabbalah it means Lord.)
4. Eh Hay Eh (This is the I Am. Another version that may be even more powerful is Ehyeh Asher Ehyeh which means I Am that I Am. This was the name given to Moses by God when he spoke to the burning bush.)
5. YHWH (This is the living, revealed name of God behind all the creator gods.)
6. El Shaddai (God Almighty)
7. Ha Shem (the name; or Baruch Ha Shem, meaning Blessed is the Name)
8. Shekinah (Holy Spirit)
9. El Eliyon (The Most High God)
10. Sh'Mah Yisrael Adonai Elohainu Adonai Chad (Hear, oh Israel! The Lord our God, the Lord is One!)
11. Barukh Ata Adonai (Blessed is the Lord)
12. Qadosh, Qadosh, Qadosh, Adonai Tzeba'oth (Holy, Holy, Holy is the Lord God of Hosts)
13. Eli Eli (My God, My God)
14. Ruach Elohim (Spirit of the Godhead)
15. Ribono Shel Olam (Lord of the Universe)

16. Shekinah Ruach Ha Quodesh (Divine Presence of the Holy Spirit)

17. Ain Sof Ur (Limitless Light of the Absolute)

18. Layoo-esh Shekinah (Pillar of Light of the Holy Spirit)

19. Ehyeh Metatron (I Am Metatron. Metatron is an Archangel who is the representative of God in the outer universe; often called the Garment of Shaddai; the visible manifestation of deity and creator of the outer worlds; creator of the electron.)

20. Yahweh Elohim (Divine Lords of Light and Learning)

21. Yeshua Michael (Jesus and Archangel Michael)

22. Shaddai El Chai (the Almighty Living God)

23. Adonai H'artez (Lord of the Earth)

24. Moshe Yeshua Eliahu (Moses, Jesus and Elijah)

25. Shalom (Peace)

26. Hyos Ha Koidesh (Highest Servants of the Ancient of Days)

Hindu Mantras

1. Aum or Om (the mother of all mantras)

2. Brahma, Vishnu, Shiva (the Hindu trinity: Creator, Preserver, and Destroyer).

3. So Ham (I Am He or I Am the Self. This is the mantra of Sai Baba and Baba Muktananda. It is the sound as God listens to the breath of humans. At night while humans sleep the sound becomes Aum, according to Sai Baba. Say this mantra in accordance with your breath: when you breath in, say "So," when you breath out, say "Ham." Let the breath lead the meditation and mantra; say the mantra however the breath wants to move.)

4. The Gayatri Mantra (This is the holiest mantra of the Hindu religion. It is the equivalent of the Lord's Prayer in Christianity.)

> Bhur bhuvah svah,
> Tat-savitur varenyam
> Bhargo devasya dhimahi
> Dhiyo yo na pracodayat.

> Translation:

bhur(h)	Earth (body)
bhuvah	atmosphere (breath)
svah	heavens (cosmic mind)
tat-savituh(r)	of that source
varenyam	sacred (to be revered)
bhargo (gah)	light
devasya	effulgent, radiant
dhimahi	we meditate on

dhiyo (yal)   our thoughts
yo (yah)   which
na ᐧ our
pracodayat   should propel, urge, direct

Om Earth, atmosphere, heavens,
We meditate on the sacred light of that effulgent source
which should direct (be the impulse for) our thoughts.

5. Sai Baba or Sai Ram or Om Sri Sai Ram (these will attract Sathya Sai Baba)

6. Hare Krishna, Hare Krishna, Krishna, Krishna, Hare, Hare. Hare Rama, Hare Rama, Rama, Rama, Hare Hare.
(Hail to Krishna, Hail to Krishna, Krishna, Krishna, Hail, Hail. Hail to Rama, Hail to Rama, Rama, Rama, Hail, Hail.
This is the Hare Krishna chant. It is used to disperse the negativity that covers our true nature.)

7. Om Namah Sivaya (This invokes the Supreme Guru who is the Self of all. This is the mantra of Baba Muktananda and Swami Sivananda.)

8. Om Sri Dattatreya Namaha (Om, Honor the name of Dattatreya; Dattatreya is the incarnation of Brahma, Vishnu, and Shiva living in the same body. Sai Baba has said he is the incarnation of the Lord Dattatreya.)

9. Om Shanti (Mantra of Peace)

10. Om Tat Sat (Thou art the Inexpressible Absolute Reality)

11. Hari Om Tat Sat (Om, the Divine Absolute Reality)

12. Hari Om (This is a healing mantra; Hari is a name for Vishnu, the healing aspect of Lord Krishna.)

13. Om Sri Rama Jaya Rama Jaya Jaya Rama (Victory for the Spiritual Self)

14. Yesu Christu (Jesus Christ, in Hindi)

15. Rama (a name of God: He who fills us with abiding joy)

16. Krishna (a name of God: He who draws us to Him)

17. Tat Twam Asi (That and This of One)

18. Hong Sau (I Am He or I Am the Self; this mantra is done following the breath in the same manner as the So Ham and Ham Sa mantras are done. This was Paramahansa Yogananda's mantra.)

19. Lam (first chakra)

20. Vam (second chakra)

21. Ram (third chakra)

22. Yam (fourth chakra)

23. Ham (fifth chakra)

24. Om (sixth chakra)

25. Aum (seventh chakra)

26. Sat Nam (mantra of the Sikhs and of Guru Nanak)

27. Eck Ong Kar Sat Nam Siri Wha Guru (The Supreme is One, His Names are Many)

28. Sivo Ham (I Am Shiva)

29. Aham Brahmasmi (I Am Brahman or I Am God)

30. Om Ram Ramaya Namaha (O Lord Ram, I Bow Down To You)

Islamic Mantras

1. Allahu Akbar (God is Great)

2. Bismillah Al-Rahman, Al-Rahim (In the name of Allah, the Compassionate, the Merciful)

3. Ya-Rahman (God, the Beneficent)

4. Ya-Salaam (The Source of Peace)

5. Ya-Mutakabir (God, the Majestic)

6. Ya-Ghaffar (God, the Forgiver)

7. Ya-Fattah (God, the Opener)

8. Ya-Hafiz (God, the Preserver)

9. Ya-Sabur (God, the Patient)

Western Mantras

1. I Am that I Am

2. I Am God

3. I Am

4. I Will

5. I Love

6. Be Still and Know I Am God

7. Areeeooommm (Edgar Cayce's Mantra of Universal Mind)

Egyptian Mantras

1. Nuk-Pu-Nuk (I Am He I Am)

2. Au-U Ur-Se-Ur Au-U (I Am the Great One, Son of the Great One, I Am)

3. Ra (Egyptian Sun God)

4. Ra-Neter-Atef-Nefer (The Divine God, Ra is Gracious)

5. Nefer-Neter-Wed-Neh (The Perfect God Grants Life)

6. Osiris

7. Isis

8. Erta-Na-Hekau-Apen-Ast (pronounced Err-Tai No Che-kah-oo O-pen Ost) (May I be given the words of power of Isis)

9. Heru-Udjat (Eye of Horus)

Christian Mantras

1. Jesus Christ (This is one of the most powerful mantras you can possibly say.)
2. God, Christ, Holy Spirit
3. The Lord's Prayer:

    Our Father, Who art in heaven, Hallowed be Thy name. Thy Kingdom Come, Thy Will be done on Earth as it is in heaven. Give us this day our daily bread, and forgive us our debts as we forgive our debtors. And lead us not into temptation, but deliver us from evil. For Thine is the Kingdom and the Power and the Glory, for ever. Amen

4. Ave Maria (Hail Mary)
5. Hail Mary, Full of Grace! The Lord is with Thee. Blessed are Thou amongst women, and blessed is the fruit of thy womb, Jesus. Holy Mary, Mother of God, Pray for us sinners, now and at the hour of our death.

Word Mantras

Peace, Joy, Love, Equilibrium, Personal Power, Forgiveness, Humility, Humbleness, Even-Mindedness, Balance, Centeredness, Bliss, Compassion, Service, Good Will, Altruism, Loving Kindness, Oneness

The Tibetan Foundation Chakra Mantras

O	(First Chakra)
Shu	(second chakra; pronounced shuck)
Ya	(third chakra)
Wa	(fourth chakra; pronounced yawn)
He	(fifth chakra)
Hu	(sixth chakra; pronounced hue)
I	(seventh chakra)

Buddhist Mantras

1. Om Mani Padme Hum (the Jewel (of compassion) in the Lotus (of the heart); one of the most powerful mantras in use in the world today)
2. Om Ah Hum (Come toward me, Om)
3. Padme Siddhi Hum (Come to me, O Lotus Power)
4. Buddha
5. Quan Yin, Avalokitesvara, Chenrazee

Djwhal Khul's Mantra

The soul mantra is the mantra to activate the help of your soul and higher self. It is the mantra of the Great White Brotherhood. This is one of the most powerful mantras I have ever found. I have never met anyone who has not been profoundly affected by using it.

I Am the Soul (or I Am the monad),
I Am the Light Divine,
I Am Love,
I Am Will,
I Am Fixed Design.

Chanting the Names of the Masters

Chant the name of any Masters with whom you want to attune and blend. As you chant their names, see their forms in your crown, in your heart, or just in front of you. Some of the names of the Masters you might chant are:

El Morya, Saint Germain, Serapis Bey, Hilarion, Kuthumi, Lord Maitreya, Paul the Venetian, Sanat Kumara, Vywamus, Buddha, Sai Baba, Jesus, Baba Muktananda, Paramahansa Yogananda, Guru Nanak, Ramakrishna, Ramana Marharshi, Sri Aurobindo, Swami Vivekananda, Isis, Virgin Mary, Quan Yin, Avalokitesvara, Patanjali, Krishna, Rama, Osiris, Melchizedek, Metatron, Sandalphon, Enoch, Thoth, Djwhal Khul, Mother Teresa, Appolonius of Tyanna, Shirdi Sai Baba, Sri Sankara, Swami Nityananda, Kabir, Confucius, Lao Tse, Mohammed, Mahavira, Adonis, Ganesha, Hanuman, Babaji, Meishu-Sama, Mahatma Gandhi, the Holy Mother, Lahiri Mahasaya, Sri Yukteswar, Helios, Zoroaster, Pallas Athena, the Seven Mighty Elohim (Hercules, Apollo, Heros, Purity, Cyclopia, Peace, Arcturus), Archangels (Michael, Jophiel, Chamuel, Gabriel, Raphael, Uriel, Zadekiel), the Mahatma, Avatar of Synthesis, Allah Gobi, Portia, Vista, Lady Nada, the Great Divine Director, Melchior . . . to name a few.

The Great Invocation

From the point of Light within the mind of God
Let Light stream forth into the minds of men.
Let Light descend on Earth.
From the point of love within the heart of God
Let love stream forth in to the hearts of men.
May Christ return to Earth.
From the center where the will of God is known
Let the purpose guide the little wills of men—
The purpose which the Masters know and serve.
From the center which we call the race of men
Let the plan of love and Light work out
And may it seal the door where evil dwells.
Let Light and love and power restore the plan on Earth.

This invocation was brought forth by Djwhal Khul in the Alice Bailey books from the Lord Maitreya himself.

Prayers of the Rosary of the Virgin Mary

The following is a traditional rosary that can be used in any way or form you see fit. It is an extraordinarily powerful prayer. Some of the words in the prayer are written in a traditional Catholic language which bothers some people. For this reason I have also included a New Age rosary which I found in Earlyne Chaney's book, *A Book of Prophecy.*

The Sign of the Cross

In the name of the Father and of the Son and of the Holy Spirit. Amen.

The Apostles' Creed

I Believe in God, the Father Almighty, Creator of heaven and Earth; and in Jesus Christ, His only Son, our Lord; who was conceived by the Holy Spirit, born of the Virgin Mary, suffered under Pontius Pilate, was crucified, died, and was buried. He descended into hell; the third day He arose again from the dead; He ascended into heaven, to sitteth at the right hand of God the Father Almighty; from thence He shall come to judge the living and the dead. I believe in the Holy Spirit, the Holy Catholic Church, the communion of Saints, the forgiveness of sins, the resurrection of the body, and life everlasting. Amen.

The Our Father

Our Father, who art in heaven, hallowed be Thy name. Thy kingdom come. Thy will be done on Earth as it is in heaven. Give us this day our daily bread and forgive us our trespasses as we forgive those who trespass against us. And lead us not into temptation, but deliver us from evil. Amen.

The Hail Mary

Hail Mary, full of grace; the Lord is with thee. Blessed art thou among women, and blessed is the fruit of thy womb, Jesus. Holy Mary, Mother of God, pray for us sinners, now and at the hour of our death. Amen.

Glory Be to the Father

Glory be to the Father and to the Son and to the Holy Spirit; as it was in the beginning, is now, and ever shall be, world without end. Amen.

The Hail, Holy Queen

Hail, holy Queen, Mother of Mercy! Our life, our sweetness, and our hope! To thee do we cry, poor banished children of Eve; to thee do we send up our sighs, mourning, and weeping in this valley of tears. Turn, then, most gracious Advocate, thine eyes of mercy toward us; and after this our exile show unto us the blessed fruit of thy womb, Jesus; O clement, O loving, O sweet Virgin Mary.

    V.   Pray for us, O holy Mother of God.

    R.   That we may be made worthy of the promises of Christ.

Let Us Pray

O God, whose only begotten Son, by His life, death, and resurrection has purchased for us the rewards of eternal life, grant, we beseech Thee, that meditating upon these mysteries in the most Holy Rosary of the Blessed Virgin Mary, we may imitate what they contain, and obtain what they promise: through the same Christ our Lord. Amen

A New Age Rosary

The following is from Earlyne Chaney's *A Book of Prophecy*.

The Flame of Love Rosary

First make the sign of the cross five times, honoring our Lord's five wounds. Then on the large beads, say:

> Sorrowful and Immaculate Heart of Mary, pray for us who seek refuge in thee.

On the small beads, say:

> Holy Mother, save us through your Immaculate Heart's Flame of Love.

At the end, hold the cross and say three times:

> Glory be to the Father, etc.

Close the rosary by saying:

> Mother of God, send down your grace through your Immaculate Heart's Flame of Love to the whole human race, now and at the hour of our death.

How It Was Received

She was Sister Faustina Kowalska. Born near Lodz in Poland in 1905, she was one of ten children and received little education. She entered the congregation of the sisters of Our Lady of Mercy at the age of twenty. Our Lord first appeared to her in 1931. She began to keep a record of all he told her. Among many other revelations, he gave her the Chaplet of Divine Mercy, which can be prayed on rosary beads.

On September 13, 1935, Sister Faustina wrote in her record book, "I saw an angel who was the executor of God's wrath." Her own prayers were without power to hold back a terrible punishment, which the angel was about to pour out upon a segment of humanity. Suddenly the Holy Trinity appeared before her. She heard a voice speaking to her, asking her to pray to God for the world with these words:

> Eternal Father-Mother God, I offer you the Body and Blood, the Soul and Divinity of your dearly beloved Son, Our Lord Jesus Christ, in atonement for our sins and the sins of the whole world. For the sake of his most sorrowful Passion, have mercy on us and the whole world.

As Sister Faustina kept repeating these words, the angel became powerless to carry out the ordained punishment.

The next day, as she was entering the chapel, Sister Faustina received instructions on how most effectively to recite the prayer she had heard. She also heard Jesus tell her to recite the prayer on rosary beads:

> First, say the Our Father, the Hail Mary, and the Credo. Then on the large beads, say:
>
>> Eternal Father-Mother God, I offer you the Body and Blood, the Soul and Divinity of your dearly beloved Son, Our Lord Jesus Christ, in atonement for our sins and for the sins of the whole world.
>
> On the small beads, say:
>
>> For the sake of his sorrowful Passion, have mercy on us and on the whole world.
>
> In conclusion, say three times:
>
>> Holy God, Holy Omnipotent One, Holy Immortal One, have mercy on us and on the whole world.

25

Golden Keys to Achieving Ascension in this Lifetime

God equals man minus ego

Sathya Sai Baba

One of the main purposes of all my books is to make the vast amount of spiritual and esoteric information that you are bombarded with easy to understand. In this chapter I have formed what might be called an "ascension checklist." I have listed over one hundred key spiritual practices to achieve liberation and ascension.

Very often you get involved in certain tangents and forget about the basic meat and potatoes (or should I say vegetables and potatoes for the vegetarians?) of the spiritual path. This is a very universal and eclectic list and it applies to whatever religion or particular spiritual path you have chosen.

I am sure you are already doing many of these things; other items on this list may remind you about something you have forgotten. I have purposely not gone into great detail, for that would have defeated the purpose of the chapter. For greater detail all you have to do is read all four volumes of *The Easy-to-Read Encyclopedia of the Spiritual Path*.

These are the golden nuggets I personally consider to be the absolute keys to realizing the self as God in this lifetime. As you read this list I would suggest doing an inventory of yourself, with devastating honesty, to determine your strengths and to note which practices need more of your focus and concentration. The key to self-realization is always well-rounded development.

The average disciple is usually very well developed in some areas and very weak in others. Never forget there are three levels to the spiritual path—the spiritual, the psychological, and the physical or Earthly levels. All three levels must be mastered separately and distinctly before full integration, synthesis, and union can take place.

As you go through this list, check off your strengths and weaknesses. Then set up a "battle plan," a routine and a spiritual regime for the development of those areas in which you are weak. If the list seems overwhelming, then set up a plan for the next five- or ten-year cycle in your life. For example, maybe every three months you can work on developing another aspect of self.

Djwhal Khul has said that it is possible for a person to move from the third initiation to the sixth initiation in six years during this most accelerated planetary cycle. This, of course, would take a 100% commitment. There is no limit to how fast you can grow; it is all based on your commitment. The most important thing is to be organized in the approach to your overall development.

With this brief introduction I bring you the one hundred and forty-seven golden keys checklist to achieving spiritual liberation and ascension in this lifetime.

1.   The single most important golden key, in my opinion, is to see every person, animal, plant, and mineral as God visiting you in physical form. See everyone and everything, including yourself, as an incarnation of the Eternal Self.

2.   The first golden key then leads you to golden key number two which is to "love the Lord your God with all your heart and soul and mind and might and to love your neighbor as you love yourself." It is easy to practice unconditional love when you remember that God is embodied in all forms.

3.   Golden key number three is the famous definition of God given by His Holiness, the Lord Sai Baba: "God equals man minus ego." Negative ego is the mountain range that stands between you and self-realization. Die to your lower self and you will realize the higher self. In the beginning stages of the path the negative ego is in control. In the middle stages there is a tremendous battle for control. In the later stages, the negative ego which is embodied as the dweller on the threshold (glamour, illusion, and maya) has been mastered and subjugated.

4.   Meditate daily. Prayer is talking to God; meditation is listening to and experiencing God.

5.   Pray daily for help from God, the Ascended Masters, and your angels. God and the God force can help only if you ask. Why do it all yourself when there is so much help available? The Higher Forces evolve only by being of service, so they are eager and most delighted to help; however, because of humanity's free will they need an invitation.

6. Learn to channel. This spiritual practice will accelerate your spiritual progression one-thousandfold. It doesn't necessarily have to be voice channeling, but definitely learn how to consciously channel spiritual energy in as many forms and ways as are suited to your unique and individual spiritual path.

7. Learn to keep your mind steady in the Light. This means keeping your mind focused on the soul and spirit. Most aspirants and disciples are definitely attuned to the soul, but aren't able to hold themselves there. This is the real work.

8. Learn to master your physical body and all its appetites. This is the golden key for passing the first initiation.

9. Learn to master your emotional and desire body. This is the golden key to passing the second initiation. Don't let your emotions push you around. You are God and must learn to choose your own emotions. When this golden key is mastered you will have longer and longer periods of sustained inner peace, tranquillity, and joy.

10. Learn to master your mental body. You are not your mind. Your mind is your tool for creating your reality. This is the golden key for passing the third initiation which leads to soul merge and a fully integrated personality.

11. Eliminate all desire except the desire for liberation, ascension, and God-realization. Material desire is one of the major stumbling blocks for aspirants and disciples on the spiritual path.

12. Make a lifelong practice of repeating the name or names of God in your daily life. As you do this, also visualize the form of God you are chanting. This is one of the most important practices for achieving self-realization. Do this throughout your day as you walk or stand in line at the grocery store or in meditation. Whatever your challenges in life, this is your spiritual antidote.

13. Never give your personal power to anyone or anything ever again. Don't give it to other people. Don't give it to the Ascended Masters of God. Don't give it to your subconscious mind, inner child, negative ego, desires, five senses, or physical, emotional, or mental body. This lesson may be the single most important lesson of all. Your spiritual path begins when you start to own your personal power. Without personal power you will be a total victim in life, and you will be completely dysfunctional. Without personal power you can't even be loving or really do any of the other practices. This point cannot be emphasized strongly enough.

14. The next golden key follows in line with the last one. Use your personal power only in the service of unconditional love, in the service of God and humanity. This is why you don't have to be afraid to own it 100%.

15. Be sure to acknowledge that you have an inner child and learn to parent it properly. Many spiritual people get so involved with God and spiritual realities that they forget they have an inner child who needs to be taken care of and loved. God and the Masters will not do this for you. This is your job. This is part of being integrated as a person. Talk to your inner child and see that it is getting its needs met. The ideal is to treat your inner child with firmness and love.

16. Dedicate your life to the service of humanity. Be sure you are self-actualized first, however, so you are serving out of wholeness and not emptiness.

17. Read spiritual scriptures and books of all religions and spiritual paths. Spiritual reading sometimes gets a bum rap by many on the spiritual path and this is not valid. It is a very important spiritual practice.

18. Remain balanced at all times. Learn to live in the Tao. The Tao is like surfing a wave. You don't want to get ahead of the wave or you will get dumped. You don't want to go too slowly and get behind the wave or you will miss it. Learn to live in the Tao and in the harmony of life at all times. Be moderate in all things. Let go of extremism. Follow the middle way.

19. Practice attitudinal healing. When you start feeling bad, examine the attitudes and beliefs that are causing you to feel that way. Never forget that it is your thoughts that cause your reality, and this includes your emotions. "As a man thinketh, so is he." "Be it done to you as you believe." Practice affirmations and positive visualizations.

20. Stay grounded and connected to Mother Earth. Many spiritual people get ungrounded and are not properly integrating the Earthly and material face of God. God lives as much in matter as He does in the higher dimensions. The idea is to bring heaven to Earth.

21. Learn to balance the feminine and masculine aspects of self. This is a prerequisite for ascension.

22. Learn to integrate your three minds. All three must be utilized and integrated, with full power at each level. Don't overly rely on just one mind.

23. Demonstrate and practice all that you know, and more will be given. Many people are filled with book knowledge, but they don't practice or demonstrate what they are learning. What you learn is useless if you don't demonstrate and apply it in your life.

24. Do some form of protective prayers, visualizations, or affirmations every day as a standard spiritual practice throughout your life. This is just a basic simple practice that all people on the path need to do.

25. Learn to balance your four bodies—physical, emotional, mental, and spiritual. This is another prerequisite for ascension.

26. Get some form of physical exercise every day or at a minimum every

other day. Being spiritual does not mean that you can stop your physical disciplines.

27. Forgive everything and everyone, including yourself. As *A Course in Miracles* says, "Forgiveness is the key to happiness." Grudges hurt only yourself and are just binding you to the reincarnational process.

28. Transcend duality. This means learning to remain even-minded, and in a state of equanimity whether you have profit or loss, pleasure or pain, sickness or health, victory or defeat, whether people praise or criticize you. This is the consciousness of the God-self. It is a consciousness of remaining in inner peace, happiness, and joy, regardless of what is going on outside of yourself. Outside things don't make you feel anything. It is your attitude toward outside events that make you feel everything.

29. Cultivate preferences and not attachments. As Buddha said, "All suffering comes from your attachments."

30. Learn to develop self-love. If you don't love yourself you will end up seeking love, worth, approval, and acceptance from other people, which will throw you totally out of balance.

31. When you physically die, even if you have ascended, let the only thought in your mind be to merge with the clear Light of God. As you die let the last thought on your mind be the name of God. Where you go when you die, as the *Bhagavad-Gita* says, is determined by the last thought in your mind. When you leave this physical body, leave through your crown chakra.

32. Be vigilant for God and His kingdom. This is another crucial key. Too many people operate on automatic pilot and are not vigilant enough over the thoughts and energies they allow to enter their minds.

33. "To have all, give all to all." When you hold back giving to any aspect of creation, in truth you are holding back from yourself. You are all of creation, for your identity is the Eternal Self, not your physical body.

34. See with your spiritual eyes, not your physical, egotistical eyes. You see life either through your Christ mind or your negative ego mind. There are no other choices. What you see is a mirror of what you are giving to yourself. You will not realize God unless you see your brothers and sisters as God. What you see in others is what you are seeing in yourself. What you give to your brothers and sisters is what you are giving to yourself and to God.

35. Cultivate compassion. Never forget that another person's suffering is, in truth, your suffering. This is not just flowery talk. If you are the Eternal Self which is the consciousness of ascension, then you live as much in the physical body of your brothers and sisters as you do in your own physical body. The Eternal Self or the Christ lives within all people. There is only one Eternal Self. God has only one son, and we are

all part of that sonship.

36. Release all consciousness of separation, fear, and selfishness for this is the cancer of negative ego.

37. Take extremely good care of the physical body for spiritual growth on Earth becomes very difficult once it begins to break down. The physical body is the temple for the soul and spirit you are.

38. Become a renunciate. This is the key to passing the fourth initiation which is liberation from the wheel of rebirth. What this means is to renounce material desire and attachment to the material world. It means to live in this world but not be of this world. It is the vow to live in life with total detachment, yet still be involved in service and in demonstrating God.

39. The spiritual path is really very simple. If you want to be with God in heaven, then act like Him. Be God. Be Christ. Be the Buddha, the Atma, the Eternal Self on Earth.

40. Cultivate a flawless character and embody virtue in everything you do.

41. Purify all four of your bodies of physical toxins, emotional toxins, mental toxins, and energetic toxins.

42. Love your enemies.

43. See only perfection. When anything other than perfection occurs, pray to your mighty I Am Presence to heal and remedy the situation or do an affirmation that affirms the true perfection of the situation as God sees it. This state of consciousness causes you to be a healing presence and consciousness wherever you may be.

44. Be the total cause and creator of your reality. Do not be a victim or at the effect of anything.

45. Call forth the twelve rays throughout your day, choosing whatever quality and color energy you need at a given moment. The rays and energy come the second you call them, but they must be requested.

46. In every situation of life, especially when you get into a sticky situation, ask yourself, "Do I want God or do I want my ego in this situation?" It is only by giving into the negative ego that you can be taken out of oneness, unconditional love, joy, and the realization of God. You can, in truth, never be taken out of oneness with God. However, you can be taken out of the realization of your oneness with God and your brothers and sisters if you choose the negative ego.

47. Look at all mistakes as just learning experiences. Gain the golden nugget of wisdom. Forgive yourself and move forward. Don't waste time with guilt and regret. Mistakes are positive, not negative. You don't go out of your way to make them; however, when they happen they are good learning opportunities.

48. Practice a religion based on a universalistic premise. This means

that all religions and paths are equal, and they all lead to the same place. No competition or comparison among paths is needed or necessary.

49. Be eclectic in your spiritual education. God is too vast and limitless to be understood in just one form.

50. Transcend carnal sexuality. Pornography is of the lower self. Learn to practice moderation in your sexual habits and learn to raise the energy to the higher chakras.

51. Help the poor, sick, and disabled. It is only by the grace of God that you are not in that position.

52. Give up all attack thoughts. Attack is not of God. It stems from fear which is the essence of the negative ego. An attack, in truth, is a call for love.

53. Completely surrender your life to God while simultaneously owning your power.

54. Keep a journal and write down your dreams every morning upon waking. They are guidance from your subconscious and superconscious minds.

55. Keep your inner and outer environments clean.

56. Every night before bed, ask to be taught on the inner plane by your soul, monad, and the Ascended Masters. Take advantage of your sleep time for accelerating your path of ascension.

57. Give up all drugs, coffee, liquor and artificial stimulants and cut down on sugar and sweets. Just as we are striving for even-mindedness on the psychological level, we are all striving for evenness in our physical body's energy throughout the day.

58. Fulfill your dharma and mission in this lifetime. Don't let the negative ego and other people take you on side roads that your soul and monad would not have you follow. This lifetime is too precious and important.

59. Seek to balance your karma by building only good karma in your every thought, word, and deed.

60. As Edgar Cayce said, "Why worry when you can pray?"

61. Have implicit faith, trust, and patience in God and in God's laws.

62. Never forget that it is your mind that creates bondage and your mind that creates liberation.

63. Transcend all beliefs that you are superior or inferior to anyone else. All are the Eternal Self in truth, regardless of their level of initiation.

64. Seek to cooperate and never to compete. Never compare yourself with others, only compare yourself with yourself.

65. Never forget your worth comes from God. Could what God created not be worthy? You are the Eternal Self. Of course you are worthy. The negative ego will tell you that you have to do something to have worth. Don't believe it.

66. "Judge not that ye be not judged." "Let he that hath no sin cast the first stone." "Don't try and take the speck out of the eye of your brother when you have a log in your own eye."

67. "Hands that help are holier than lips that pray."

68. Create a spiritual shrine in one corner of your home for prayer, meditation, and devotional practices.

69. Get rid of your bad habits now so you don't carry them to the inner plane when you pass on to the spirit world.

70. Constantly ask yourself, "Who am I?" (I am the Eternal Self, I am Brahman, I am God.)

71. Drink six to eight big glasses of water a day, get lots of sunshine and fresh air.

72. Constantly discriminate between the real and the unreal, between that which is permanent and impermanent, between truth and illusion, between physical appearances and the true reality behind all form.

73. Cultivate constant remembrance of God.

74. Spiritualize all activities, which means seeing yourself as an instrument in the hands of the Lord. You are God's hands, eyes, mouth, and feet in action on the Earth. You are God interacting with God. You are the Eternal Self serving and administering the Eternal Self in form.

75. Practice loving kindness toward all sentient beings.

76. Take responsibility for being the elder brother or sister and spiritual guide for the animal, plant, and mineral kingdoms.

77. Cultivate an absolutely burning desire to achieve ascension and liberation so you can be of greater service to all sentient beings.

78. Practice humility. Jesus Christ said, "If anyone give you a slap on one cheek, show him the other cheek also."

79. Bless the person who curses you.

80. Transmute a good amount of your sexuality into Ojas Shakti (brain illumination).

81. Take the vow of physical immortality.

82. Take the vow of Bramacharya (purity of thought word and deed).

83. Eat a sattvic physical diet (more bland, organic, and natural food).

84. Give yourself an intense daily time of self-analysis, intro- spection, and self-examination, especially before bed.

85. Be a love-finder, not a fault-finder.

86. Keep logs and charts of your spiritual development as you would keep an accounting of your budget and taxes.

87. Serve your fellow man with an attitude of indifference to the fruits of your actions.

88. Chant the Om mantra at every appropriate available opportunity. (The *Bhagavad-Gita* says that he who meditates on and chants the Om at the

time of death attains the supreme state.)

89. Take the vow of nonviolence.

90. Say the So Ham mantra in coordination with your breath throughout your day. Also chant the Om mantra.

91. Practice denial and affirmation. As *A Course in Miracles* says, "Deny any thought not of God to enter your mind." Then switch your attention to a positive or Christ-like thought or image.

92. Build your antakarana to your soul, your monad, and then all the way up to God.

93. Learn to soul-travel consciously and cultivate the ability of lucid dreaming.

94. Intensely study the exact workings of the seven levels of initiation.

95. Master and subjugate the dweller on the threshold (glamour, illusion, maya).

96. Practice being an Ascended Master and God-realized being even though you have not taken that initiation yet. Fake it till you make it.

97. Discover the ray structure of your monad, soul, personality, mind, emotions, and body to more fully understand your exact mission in this lifetime and your ashramic connection.

98. Call forth your higher chakras to become anchored in your crown chakra.

99. Remove all sense of separation from your consciousness on all levels.

100. Be politically active on some level as an integral part of your spiritual practices.

101. Recognize that extraterrestrial life on all the planets in God's infinite universe are as brothers and sisters in a universal family.

102. Honor and revere Pan and the Nature spirits as you do the Ascended Masters and God.

103. As you pass the third initiation (the soul merge), begin polarizing your consciousness into your monad (the I Am Presence), upper spiritual triad, and upper three permanent atoms. As you evolve and go through the initiation processes, you become polarized at a higher and higher level after each initiation.

104. Have all your extraterrestrial implants cleared. (Terri Sue Stone can perform that service for you within one hour and I can't recommend strongly enough that you have this done either by her or by some other qualified person.)

105. Never forget that you are the soul and monad living in your body on Earth.

106. Live with absolute supreme integrity, for to cheat another

person is to literally cheat God and yourself which are all one.

107. Seek and find a spiritual teacher, or spiritual teachers, on this plane or on the ascended plane or both. I am not recommending here a guru but rather a teacher. There is always someone above us we can learn from and beneath us whom we can serve. This is the true spiritual hierarchy of life.

108. Affirm that you are creating within your physical body and vehicle the twelve strands of DNA that are appropriate to your ascended self.

109. Visit holy places and spiritual power spots on the planet.

110. Develop "equal vision," no matter what it is that you see.

111. Take a vow of silence for a certain part of every day and practice speech control. In the mystery school of Pythagoras (Kuthumi) at Crotona, disciples had to remain silent for three years before they were even allowed to be initiated into the hidden mysteries. We can certainly practice this a little bit each day.

112. When temptations arise turn your consciousness from them and turn your attention back to God. Sin is not being without temptation, but rather being tempted and not acting upon it.

113. Give up arguing. You must ask yourself, "Do I want love, or do I want to win?" You can't have both.

114. Eat lightly. Eat to live, don't live to eat.

115. Identify yourself with your higher self and die to your lower self. This is the way to God.

116. Make spiritual vows and commitments and stick to them once you make them. This is one of the spiritual practices that will accelerate your path of ascension the most quickly. Spiritual vows take all choice out of the situation and lock you in, so your consciousness is free to work on the next level of refinement and purification.

117. Develop absolute one-pointedness in your spiritual quest for ascension and liberation, and you will achieve your goal in due time.

118. Develop the quality of being a courageous "spiritual warrior" in life. You are in truth a great spiritual warrior battling against glamour, illusion, and maya, and seeking only the self.

119. Keep satsang (company) with uplifting spiritual people. Spend your time going to uplifting spiritual classes, lectures, and seminars. Go to see saints and sages when they come into town. Avoid bad company and people who are run by their lower selves. When you are around those types of people, put up your protection and psychic self-defenses.

120. Don't waste a single moment of time or energy. Death is around the corner for everyone and can happen at any time. Don't waste time on those things that are impermanent. Can hedonistic sensuous pleasure

compare with the reality of realizing God?

121. Simplify your life. Reduce your wants and needs.

122. Think of God the first thing as you wake up in the morning, and let the thought of God be the last thought in your mind as you go to bed. (If you really want to accelerate your path of ascension, let God be the only thought in your mind throughout your day.)

123. Be much more discriminating about your mental, emotional, and spiritual diet. Don't waste your time reading trashy novels, seeing violent movies, watching meaningless or violent television shows. Everything you experience creates an impression on your subconscious mind. Life is too short and too precious. Most definitely enjoy yourself; however, do it in the context of being about the Father's business. Ascension takes a total commitment, twenty-four hours a day, even while you sleep. Once the habit of this type of consciousness is developed it is not even hard to do. It is actually fun, for true pleasure is serving God.

124. Give 10% of your salary, money or energy to some charitable cause. You must be generous with others if you expect the universe to be generous to you.

125. To everything that happens in life say, "Not my will, but thine. Thank you for the lesson."

126. Remain the same in consciousness whether people criticize you or flatter you. If you give in to either you are back in the negative ego system instead of transcending the negative ego. Never forget: "After pride cometh the fall."

127. Know thyself, which really means know God, for that is who you are.

128. Your spiritual practices should be steady, gradual, full of sincerity, common sense, and perseverence.

129. Do not use the Lord's name in vain; give up all swearing.

130. Remove the blemish of selfishness and negativity from your consciousness.

131. Set up a spiritual routine and regimen for yourself that is not too hard and not too easy and then stick to it. This includes your physical disciplines such as physical exercise, diet, and so on as well as your spiritual practices.

132. Never forget there are only two emotions: love and fear. There are no neutral thoughts. All reality stems from one or the other.

133. Avoid looking at people with lustful thoughts. See the Eternal Self and Christ first before seeing people with your physical eyes.

134. "Unceasing effort," no matter what the obstacles, is the key. "Seek and ye shall find." "Knock and the door shall be opened."

135. Remain obedient to God and God's laws. It is through this

understanding that you avoid suffering.

136. Your salvation is up to you, not up to God. God has already given you everything. The question is, what are you willing to give yourself?

137. Be positive and optimistic in all things.

138. "Be still and know I Am God."

139. Call forth the golden twelfth ray and the energy of the Mahatma, for they are the two highest frequencies that are available to us on Earth.

140. Work with the MAP team (Medical Assistance Program of the Ascended Masters) to upgrade your physical health on a regular basis. (See my book on soul psychology for more information.)

141. Constantly affirm that your pituitary gland has stopped producing the death hormone and is producing only the life hormone.

142. On a daily basis call forth an axiatonal alignment as described in *The Keys of Enoch* to balance your entire meridian system and spiritual and electrical fields.

143. Call forth your fifth-dimensional ascended self (who has already achieved ascension in non-time and non-space realities) to merge its consciousness with your consciousness and aura throughout your day.

144. Call forth the Mahatma on a daily basis to infuse and blend His energy and aura with yours on Earth. This is a sure-fire method to accelerate your path of ascension literally one-thousandfold.

145. See yourself as the monad and your teacher now as God. The monad or I Am Presence is no longer up above you. The consciousness of ascension is that you are the monad. You are the I Am Presence on Earth.

146. Do the ascension meditation and treatment I have provided in this book on a daily basis. If you do this meditation on a regular basis for three months you will see yourself become completely transformed.

147. In your meditations and prayer sessions, call forth and attune to the Galactic Core and the Galactic Teachers. This level has just been made available to humanity and is guaranteed to help You fully anchor your body of Light into the physical level, not just the mental, emotional, and spiritual levels. Two of the teachers on this galactic level that you can attune to are Melchizedek and the Master Averran. Tapping into the Galactic Core level will help your ability to teleport, instantly manifest, and communicate with the language of Light.

26

The Cutting Edge of Ascension: Information and Techniques

As of September 1994 there were five hundred Ascended Masters on the surface of Planet Earth who had completed their ascension. I mention the surface of the Earth here, for there are another three hundred added to this accounting if you include the Ascended Masters in the hollow Earth. There is a grand total of somewhere between one thousand eight hundred and two thousand five hundred Ascended Masters if you include the etheric Ascended Masters who no longer retain physical vehicles; this number includes many of the Ashtar Command and Ascended Masters in the spiritual government on the inner plane who are currently focused on the Earth's surface.

Of the five hundred Ascended Masters who are physicalized and on the surface, thirty of them have just recently completed their ascension and are students of Djwhal Khul or members of his ashram.

It is important to understand here that there is a big difference between what might be termed a kindergarten Ascended Master and an Ascended Master who has completed his ascension. This can be explained by the fact that there are seven major initiations that all who travel the spiritual path must traverse. These seven major initiations were delineated quite clearly by the Theosophical movement headed by Madam Blavatsky and in the Alice Bailey books written by the Ascended Master Djwhal Khul. This information was further expanded by the Tibetan Foundation which was headed by the phenomenal channel, Janet McClure. My wife Terri and I and my dear friend and spiritual sister Marcia Dale Lopez have connections with all three movements, and our current work is to bring forth a part of the next dispensation of information from Djwhal Khul and the Spiritual Hierarchy as we mutually anchor Djwhal's ashram on the East and West Coasts.

Of the five thousand Ascended Masters predicted for Wesak (May 1995), approximately 2,500 will be completing their sixth and the other 2,500 of the kindergarten variety, which means again just taking the beginning of the sixth. Melchizedek told us that there would be approximately 30,000 Ascended Masters on the planet by the year 2000 of both the completed and kindergarten variety. After the year 2000, there is the potential for this number to jump at a much larger rate.

By the year 2000, Melchizedek said there could be 5,000 to 10,000 completed seventh degree initiates on the planet.

I also asked about walkins. I was given a figure of there being 250,000 walkins on the planet. I would take these numbers with a grain of salt, because the future is always changing as we use our free choice, however they do provide some perspective and ball park figures for the planetary ascension process.

I used to be confused about why the masters called ascension the sixth initiation rather than the seventh. The reason for this is that you achieve ascension at the sixth initiation, but you don't complete ascension until taking the seventh sublevel between the sixth and seventh major initiations. In other words, there are seven sublevels between each of the seven major initiations. A kindergarten Ascended Master has just taken the sixth initiation. This signifies complete freedom from the wheel of rebirth, and in the past it meant the death of the physical vehicle. In more recent times, most kindergarten Ascended Masters have usually remained on Earth to serve. Upon evolving through the seven sublevels of the sixth initiation they officially complete their ascension. Shortly thereafter, they take their seventh initiation, which marks total completion of the ascension, the sixth initiation.

The seventh initiation is the final and last initiation that can be taken on the physical plane. When you first take the seventh, you are considered a kindergarten seventh degree initiate. There are seven sublevels you must evolve through to complete this initiation. Upon reaching the seventh sublevel of the seventh initiation, all initiations stop until you leave the physical plane. You cannot take the eighth initiation without losing the physical vehicle.

In some systems of spiritual growth there has been reference to three sublevels between each of the seven major initiations. This is the system used by Brian Grattan in *Mahatma I & II.* He speaks of twelve initiations rather than seven. Djwhal told Marcia and me that the two systems of looking at the initiation process are the same up to the sixth initiation. The seventh, eighth, and ninth initiations in Brian's system are the three sublevels of the sixth initiation I spoke of. Initiations ten, eleven, and twelve are the three sublevels of the seventh initiation. In other words, full completion of the seventh initiation in Djwhal Khul's system would be the same as the twelfth initiation in Brian Grattan's system. I share this so there may be greater unification and understanding between these two useful systems.

The seventh initiation is full merger with the logoic, or seventh, plane of reality. I use the term plane here, rather than dimension, for the seventh initiation is the merging with the sixth dimension of reality. Ascension is the merging with the fifth dimension of reality. It is the seventh initiation at which the advanced ascension skills such as teleportation, walking on water, and materialization are potentially, but not automatically, acquired. Djwhal Khul has also told us that the highest Light quotient you can hold without losing the physical vehicle is 98%. At the completion of the seventh initiation you retain this level of Light quotient until leaving the Earthly plane. The seventh degree initiate is usually a teacher on a more global scale, which is not necessarily true of a sixth degree initiate.

The Earth is also in the same initiation process and when she completes her seventh initiation, she will actually disappear and ascend also and take her eighth initiation on the inner plane.

This issue of building your Light quotient is one of the most important factors in attaining the advanced initiations. For the sake of review, the third initiation requires a minimum of 56% Light quotient; the fourth initiation requires 62% Light quotient; the fifth initiation requires 75% Light quotient; the sixth initiation, or ascension, requires 80% to 83% Light quotient; the seventh initiation requires a minimum of 92% Light quotient.

In finishing up this discussion on the process of how to complete your ascension and move on to the seventh initiation, there are a few other interesting pieces of information I would like to share. There has been almost no information on the seventh initiation available on this plane. The little we do have is from Djwhal Khul through Alice Bailey. However, Djwhal wrote most of those books as a fifth degree initiate and inner plane sixth degree initiate. The information of fifty years ago was very sketchy.

The seventh initiation is merger with the Planetary Logos and Shamballa, the will aspect of the Creator of Planet Earth. It is full merger with the monad whereas ascension is only 80% to 83% merger. It is the seventh initiation that begins the process of transcending physical laws. There is a core group of people in Djwhal's ashram who are now preparing to take this initiation.

The seventh initiation creates a complete implosion of energy in the heart chakra. It creates a whole new unified chakra system which, metaphorically, is like the creation of a new star system. The seventh initiation is a complete commitment to service, to group consciousness, and to the relinquishment of negative ego and separateness. You become a concentrated point of living Light. It gives you the right to come and go in the courts of Shamballa. It has been referred to esoterically as the initiation of resurrection. Lord Maitreya took his seventh on the cross at the death of the Master Jesus. As an initiate, you have found your way back to your originating source, or that state of existence known as Shamballa. You have officially become a seventh degree Melchizedek. At the taking of the seventh initiation an even higher electrical force is transmitted by Sanat Kumara through his rod of initiation, which signifies full completion. You do not complete your seventh initiation until you stabilize your Light quotient at the 97% to 98% level. Djwhal said that you aren't really in the seventh until you are at the 94% Light quotient level. You touch the very edges of it as early as the 89% level of Light quotient; however, you aren't fully in the seventh until the 94% level.

There are five thousand people scheduled to complete their ascension as of Wesak, the festival of the Buddha at the full moon of May of 1995. At that time there will be five hundred people on the Earth who will have completed their seventh initiation. In September of 1994 there were two hundred people on the surface of the Earth who had completed the seventh initiation. Sanat Kumara and the Hierarchy have earmarked as many as five hundred thousand people to complete their ascension by the year 2000 which is close to but not at the end of the ascension window of which Vywamus has spoken.

I want to make it clear that these higher initiations occur in groups or waves. It can be likened to a sports team. Even though there may be star players on any team who score more points than the others, all get the same championship award if the team wins. The gains of one are shared by all. This removes all sense of competition or comparing. The process can also be likened to a puzzle. All have a part to play; even though some of you might have a bigger puzzle piece than others, the puzzle cannot be completed unless each of you plays your part. Another example Djwhal has used is an emergency room: the ambulance driver, receptionist, orderlies, nurses, and doctors all must do their parts in perfect cooperation. In terms of the initiation process, all will take the same initiation, even though one job may be more glamorous than another.

The Masters are not looking for glamour but rather for each initiate to do his or her job for the greater ashramic work and the fulfillment of the Divine Plan. My job, for example, is to write books and teach. My wife's job is to channel. Marcia's job is to run Djwhal Khul's ashram in New York. Each of you has your own part to play and there are many others who are a part of the puzzle upon whom you rely as much as they rely on your doing your part. The fastest path to ascension and completion of the seventh initiation is to play your Divine part perfectly!

Ascension Techniques

The following ascension techniques are some of the most advanced, cutting-edge ascension techniques you will find anywhere on Planet Earth. They are exciting additions to the twenty techniques listed in Chapter 4. Practice them with regularity and I personally guarantee you extraordinary results. I can say this based on both theoretical and experiential knowledge.

Ascension Technique Number Twenty-one

One of the most extraordinary pieces of information I have come across in my continuing research is the existence of actual ascension seats on Planet Earth and throughout the universe. The following list includes the ones I have uncovered so far.

A. The golden chamber of Melchizedek in the universal core;

B. Lenduce's ashram ascension seat at the galactic level;

C. The ascension seat in Melchior's ashram in the galactic core;

D. The ascension seat in the solar core in the chamber of Helios;

E. The ascension seat in Shamballa, the home of Sanat Kumara;

F. The ascension seat on the Arcturian spacecraft called the Light Synthesis Chamber;

G. The ascension seat in Table Mountain, Wyoming, called the Atomic Accelerator;

H. The ascension seat in the Great Pyramid of Giza in the king's chamber;

I. The ascension seat in Mount Shasta;

J. The ascension seat in Telos, the underground city one mile below Mount Shasta;

K. The ascension seat on Commander Ashtar's ship;

L. The ascension seat in Africa in an underground exterrestrial craft;

M. The ascension seat in the center of the middle Earth in Melchizedek's Golden Chamber;

N. The ascension seat in Serapis Bey's ascension retreat in Luxor.

These fourteen ascension seats are, in my opinion, truly one of the golden keys to achieving and completing your ascension. Use them as much as possible. All you have to do is ask very simply in meditation to be taken to the ascension seat of your choosing and you are instantly there in your spiritual body. You will immediately feel a subtle and sometimes not-so-subtle spiritual current running through your entire four-body system. The ascension seats will help strengthen your grid system, revitalize your molecules, build your Light quotient, and accelerate your ascension.

The Ascended Masters have given us a variety of seats to prevent boredom and to spice up our spiritual exploration. I would recommend using the first three ascension seats on the list primarily after you ascend. Working with ascension seats on the galactic and universal levels before you have even ascended is getting a little ahead of yourself. You are certainly welcome to experiment with them a little bit, however. Use the other ascension seats for your regular, ongoing meditation work.

The only ascension seat on this list that I have ever before seen in a book is the one called the Atomic Accelerator, which Saint Germain spoke of in his wonderful books, the *I Am Discourses*. The rest have all been channeled from spirit and are truly a divine dispensation for humanity at this most wondrous time.

Ascension Technique Number Twenty-two

Call forth from Sanat Kumara, Vywamus and your own mighty I Am Presence a firing of all your fire letters, key codes, and sacred geometries from the twelve dimensions of reality. Upon your doing this, infinitesimally small fire letters, key codes, and sacred geometric shapes will come pouring through your crown chakra and begin flowing through your entire meridian system. The higher you go in spiritual evolution, the more key codes and fire letters are available for activation and anchoring.

Ascension Technique Number Twenty-three

Call forth the Microtron from Metatron. The Microtron is a type of microchip and energy latticework that is laid in and that allows for the availability of the highest level of ascension energy you can potentially receive.

Ascension Technique Number Twenty-four

Call forth directly and specifically the ascension energies to come down through your crown chakra. Djwhal Khul has told us that they can be seen as golden-white Light. It is a good idea to start every meditation by invoking this energy to make the ascension connection.

Ascension Technique Number Twenty-five

Call forth a Light shower from Archangel Metatron, the Mahatma, and Melchizedek. Begin a dedicated focus of intent to build your Light quotient every day, ultimately to the 80% to 83% needed to ascend.

Ascension Technique Number Twenty-six

Call forth from Vywamus and Djwhal Khul the matrix-removal program. This is a most wonderful, divine dispensation recently received by humanity from Sanat Kumara and the Spiritual Hierarchy. I first learned about it from my compatriot in Djwhal Khul's ashram, Marcia Dale Lopez.

My knowledge was then increased further through channelings by my wife Terri during a recent workshop we held at our home.

The basic concept here is that the Spiritual Hierarchy has now been given permission to actually pull the fear-based programs right out of your subconscious minds and four-body systems. This is done in the way a gardener pulls weed out of the earth. The fear-based programs actually look like dark weeds with many roots when you look at them clairvoyantly. This matrix-removal program has never been available to humanity before this time; it is brand new. Ask Djwhal Khul and Vywamus to be set up in this program on the inner plane. Also, just request in your meditations that all your fear-based programs be removed. It helps if you can be specific. This work can be done when you are in an emotional crisis or when you are feeling good and just want to do some refining work.

In a recent workshop, Djwhal Khul told us that in one weekend, 45% of our core fear had actually been removed, pulled out, and completely erased from the soul records. This is quite extraordinary, as I am sure you will agree. It is available to you for the asking.

Ascension Technique Number Twenty-seven

Call on Archangel Metatron for a 100% Light quotient increase. This is one of my favorite ascension techniques and I use it all the time. I use it not only in meditation but also while watching television with my wife late at night. Believe it or not, my best Light quotient building has occurred during these times. I am a firm believer in time management. Some of my best ascension work is done while standing in line at the bank or grocery store or while running errands. Metatron is a most glorious being and has great abilities in the area of Light technology.

Ascension Technique Number Twenty-eight

Go to the Golden Chamber of Melchizedek and request to be initiated into the Order of Melchizedek by the Universal Logos Melchizedek himself. Whatever level of initiation you have achieved is irrelevant; just ask to begin this process and ask for his blessing. Melchizedek is the being who ensouls the entire universe, and it is the Order of Melchizedek that is the core, essence, and antecedent of all spiritual teachings on Planet Earth. Who better to initiate you into this order than Melchizedek himself?

Ascension Technique Number Twenty-nine

Call forth to your own mighty I Am Presence for the spinning of all your electrons at the same frequency as the electrons of the Ascended Masters.

Ascension Technique Number Thirty

Every day, go for what I refer to as an ascension walk. This is another one of my favorite spiritual practices and is actually one of my favorite parts of the day. Begin your walk by invoking one of the ascension seats or a Light shower from Metatron, Mahatma, Melchizedek or all three. Then just walk and try to remain a little more receptive than normal. If you get too masculine, or active, in your thinking you can disconnect the energies a bit. No harm done; you can just call them in again if this begins to happen. This particular ascension technique is also good practice for bilocating when you are using the ascension seats. By this I mean part of you will be in the ascension retreat and part of you will be walking. It is good to begin practicing doing two things at once even prior to your ascension.

I do want to say here that it is possible to do too much ascension seat activity. The physical body needs some time during the day to run its own natural current. Practice a lot but do take a break. The energies will usually stop on their own during meals, driving, and more masculine, yang activities.

Ascension Technique Number Thirty-one

This ascension technique I call the ascension buddy system. It is not essential that you do this with another, but it can greatly accelerate your personal ascension to team up with a friend or group of friends for your ascension practice. I do this with my wife Terri, with Marcia, and with my dear friend Karen. Recently, this core ascension group has grown even larger. Djwhal has said that this works sometimes like the positive and negative poles of a battery. We spark each other and channel forth different rays of the Creator. Two or more people become almost a group entity. A group mind is formed and the acceleration of any one member is automatically translated to the entire group. This further erases all competition and comparison, for the Masters tend to initiate simultaneously groups of people working together at a similar level of evolution. Did not Jesus also speak of "two or more" being "gathered in my name." Meditations always are more powerful when done in a group.

I spend a lot of time meditating with friends over the telephone. Marcia and I spend a couple of hours a week doing this, even though she lives in New York and I live in Los Angeles. I seem to meditate much longer when I do it with a friend. Time passes more quickly and it is more fun.

Ascension Technique Number Thirty-two

Call forth from Melchior, Lenduce, Vywamus and Sanat Kumara an anchoring of the Light packets of information from the higher university on Sirius. These are actually like metaphysical Light envelopes that are programmed into your computer banks and four-body systems. Ask every night before bed to travel to Sirius while you sleep to attend the higher university.

Ascension Technique Number Thirty-three

Do these meditations especially at the full moon of each month and during other special astrological configurations such as Wesak, Christmas, December 31st, on spiritual occasions such as the 11:11 or the 12:12, during meteor showers, on saints' birthdays, and so on. These times allow for special openings, gateways and downpourings of spiritual energies. They can provide quantum leaps of energy that many weeks of meditating can sometimes not provide.

Ascension Technique Number Thirty-four

Call forth from Vywamus, Sanat Kumara, Djwhal Khul and your own mighty I Am Presence for the anchoring of your monadic blueprint body. Ask that this body now replace the previous, tainted blueprint you have previously been working from through all your past lives. This will provide you with a perfect blueprint for your physical vehicle to work from. Many people never recover from chronic physical health problems because of this issue. Also call in the MAP Healing Team and the Etheric Healing Team to repair any damage in the etheric vehicle that needs repairing from all your past lives and your present life. The value of this simple ascension technique cannot be overestimated. Call to the Arcturians and ask to be taken to the Mechanism Chamber any time you need physical healing.

Ascension Technique Number Thirty-five

Call to your mighty I Am Presence, Vywamus and Djwhal Khul and ask that your monad (your spirit or mighty I Am Presence) be permanently anchored into your physical vehicle. This can be done for you upon request. It will greatly accelerate the merger of your personality, soul, and monad which is, in truth, what ascension really is.

Ascension Technique Number Thirty-six

Before bed every night, ask to be enrolled in teleportation classes on the inner plane. Your spiritual body will receive all necessary information, which will be stored up until that time when you are ready to really do it. Djwhal Khul has told us that realistically you need to have almost completed your seventh initiation and be up to the 96% to 98% Light quotient to actually do this. Teleportation, of course, is the actual moving of the physical body from one location to another. Teleportation is not a requirement for completing the seventh initiation, but it is an option.

Ascension Technique Number Thirty-seven

Request, either in meditation or before bed, to be enrolled in Djwhal Khul's second ray Light quotient building program on the inner plane. This program is orchestrated by Djwhal Khul and is much like an intravenous needle giving nutrients to a hospital patient. While you are sleeping, the Light quotient is "dripped" at a gradual and safe rate into those who are enrolled in the program. Regardless of whether you are personally connected to Djwhal Khul's ashram, you are welcome. The chohans of the seven rays send most of their students for training to Djwhal's ashram. It is good to take advantage of the different programs going on in all seven ashrams — those of El Morya, Kuthumi and Djwhal Khul, Serapis Bey, Paul the Venetian, Hilarion, Jesus, and Saint Germain.

Ascension Technique Number Thirty-eight

Call forth from Vywamus and Djwhal Khul the permanent anchoring of the cosmic heart. This invocation speaks for itself as to its intent and purpose.

Ascension Technique Number Thirty-nine

Call forth to Vywamus, Archangel Michael, and Djwhal Khul to place a golden dome of protection around you at all times. Request that Vywamus bring forth his golden hands moving them through your fields to remove all alien implants, elementals, negative entities, imbalanced energies, and etheric mucus.

Ascension Technique Number Forty

Call forth in the place where you meditate or hold classes a permanent ascension column to be set up by the Ascended Masters. If necessary, set up two of them, one in your meditation room and one in the room where meetings are held. As you evolve, your ascension column will evolve. All who enter it will be helped and accelerated.

Ascension Technique Number Forty-one

At the end of your meditation, call forth what I am calling here mini-tornadoes to help blend your higher bodies with your four-body system (your physical, mental, emotional, and spiritual bodies) on Earth. The mini-tornadoes are infinitesimally small tornadoes that blend and merge the higher bodies with lower bodies. These tornadoes almost sew the two bodies together. They can be seen clearly by those who are clairvoyant. Those of you who are not clairvoyant can trust that they are there and will anchor at your slightest invocation.

Ascension Technique Number Forty-two

Call forth from Helios the anchoring and activation of your ascension healing module. This ascension healing module is a specific type of merkabah that, upon request, can be programmed for ascension activation. It can also be extremely helpful in facilitating the anchoring and firing of all the fire letters, key codes, and sacred geometries I spoke of earlier.

Ascension Technique Number Forty-three

Call forth from the Mahatma and your own mighty I Am Presence for a widening of your antakarana, or rainbow bridge, on both a personal and a cosmic level so that a greater amount of God-current can flow into your field.

Ascension Technique Number Forty-four

Call forth from your own might I Am Presence and monad an anchoring and activation of your unified chakra. When you ascend, the seven chakras become one elongated chakra. This can be invoked and set into place before you ascend.

Ascension Technique Number Forty-five

Call forth from the Earth Mother and Archangel Sandalphon and Khamel an alignment of your personal kundalini with the planetary kundalini. This will facilitate a greater influx of energy through your feet chakras, root chakra and grounding core.

Ascension Technique Number Forty-six

Call forth to Vywamus, Djwhal Khul and the Earth Mother that your personal energies be integrated and aligned with the twelve Elohim computers in the Earth that are in the process of firing and activating over the next five years. As these Elohim computers fire, there will be a corresponding activation within your own being.

Ascension Technique Number Forty-seven

Call forth to Melchizedek to purify your entire being with his golden flame and sacred ash to remove all impurities in your four-body system and to remove all blemishes of negative ego, separateness, and fear-based reactions.

Ascension Technique Number Forty-eight

Call to the seven Ray Masters to shine through the third eye center and connect the force of the rainbow bridge and antakarana, into the light of the ascension column. Request that this be done through the entire chakra column, through the soul all the way back to the monad.

Summation

As you can see, these are extraordinary ascension tools and techniques. Practice them as much as possible. Share them with your friends and send them around the country and around the globe.

27

Ascension Meditation
and Treatment

*I choose now to accept and invoke a deep
penetration of the Mahatma energy into
my entire energy matrix, thereby allowing
a full, open radiation of my divine self
in service to all that is*

Vywamus

In beginning this meditation, find a comfortable place to sit where you will not be bothered. Face eastward, for the spiritual current is strongest in that direction. This ascension meditation and treatment can be done out loud or silently. It can also be put on an audio tape and listened to before bed at night. Those who are highly motivated might consider taping it and putting it on an auto-reverse tape recorder so you can play it while you sleep.

This is an extraordinarily complete and comprehensive meditation. It is guaranteed to invoke the ascension energies. It is a meditation and treatment I would recommend working with every day, either once or twice a day, on a consistent and ongoing basis. I will guarantee you that this meditation and treatment will completely transform your consciousness, your four-body system, and your reality.

Ascension Meditation and Treatment

Beloved God, Christ, Holy Spirit, Beloved Mighty I Am Presence, my Monad, I Am that I Am, Beloved Mahatma, the Avatar of Synthesis, Seven Mighty Elohim, Melchior, our Galactic Logos, Ashtar Command, Archangels Michael, Jophiel, Chamuel, Gabriel, Raphael, Uriel, Zadkiel, Metatron, Helios, our Solar Logos, Sanat Kumara, our Planetary Logos, Lord Maitreya, the Planetary Christ, the Manu, Allah Gobi, the Mahachohan, Sathya Sai Baba, beloved Chohans of the Seven Rays, El Morya, Kuthumi, Serapis Bey, Paul the Venetian, Hilarion, Master Jesus, and Saint Germain, Lords of Karma, Djwhal Khul, Buddha, Vywamus, Virgin Mary, Quan Yin, Isis, Babaji, the Great Divine Director, Enoch, the Great White Brotherhood MAP Healing Team (Pan, Overlighting Angel of Healing, Ascended Masters and Monad), Order of Melchizedek, Spiritual Hierarchy, Great White Brotherhood, Masters of Shamballa!

I Am the Monad, I Am the Light Divine, I Am Love, I Am Will, I Am Fixed Design! I hereby ask and pray for your collective help in the following ascension meditation. I hereby call forth an all-powerful tube of cosmic Light substance to serve as an invincible shield of protection throughout this meditation and throughout my life in general. I ask that this tube of Light be absolutely invulnerable and invincible to all that is not of God and the Christ Light.

Within this large tube I now visualize a smaller tube the circumference of my head now moving upward from my crown chakra, up through my soul, up through my monad or I Am Presence, and then continuing up through all three hundred fifty-two levels of the cosmic being known as the Mahatma or the Avatar of Synthesis, and then all the way up to God Himself.

This tube of Light is your antakarana, or rainbow bridge. When you are connected through all levels in your mind's eye, then bring this tube down through the seven chakras, or chakra column, and send it down into the center of the Earth. Your antakarana now goes from the center of the Earth all the way up to God.

Now attune yourself to the presence of God. Chant the sacred sound of Aum seven times and send it up the antakarana through the soul, monad, and Mahatma, back to God. Remain silent for a few moments to experience the effects.

Now call forth from God and the God Force a pillar of God's Light which is now flowing down your antakarana and your tube of protection. Let this Light first fill your physical body, then your etheric body, emotional body, mental body, and spiritual bodies.

Now call forth in your mind's eye the Mahatma energy, which is a group consciousness that embodies all three hundred fifty-two levels back to God. Call forth this Mahatma and Avatar of Synthesis energy and let it first fill every cell in your physical body.

Let it now fill every physical organ with cosmic Light. Let it fill your pineal gland, your pituitary gland, your thyroid gland, your thymus gland, your adrenal glands, and your gonadic and sexual glands. Let the Mahatma energy fill your seven bodies with cosmic Light. The Mahatma energy is the highest cosmic energy that is available to us on Earth, according to Vywamus. Let this energy bathe your entire being.

Beloved God and Beloved Mahatma, I choose now to accept and invoke a deep penetration of the Mahatma energy into my entire energy matrix, thereby allowing a full, open radiation of my Divine self in service to All That Is, now.

I now call forth from God and the God Force a series of golden balls of Light. These large golden balls of Light are coming down from God and my mighty I Am Presence and moving down my chakra column, entering my seven chakras.

I let the golden ball of Light enter my first chakra. I now fully open and activate my first chakra. I Am that I Am. Aum!

I Let the golden ball enter my second chakra. I now fully open and activate my second chakra. I Am that I Am. Aum!

I now fully open and activate my third chakra. I Am that I Am. Aum!

I now fully open and activate my fourth chakra. I Am that I Am. Aum!

I now fully open and activate my fifth chakra. I Am that I Am. Aum!

I now fully open and activate my sixth chakra. I Am that I Am. Aum!

I now fully open and activate my seventh chakra. I Am that I Am. Aum!

Now, call forth your Mighty I Am Presence and Archangel Michael and the Great White Brotherhood Medical Assistance Program (MAP) team (composed of Pan, Ascended Master healers, angels of healing, and your own monad) to enter each chakra and perfectly balance and attune it, removing any unwanted energies or cords of energy that are not for your highest God purpose and of your true Divine monadic blueprint. Take about fifteen seconds or more for each chakra to fully invoke cleansing, perfect healing, and balancing for each chakra. Once you have perfectly purified, cleansed, healed, and balanced each chakra with God's healing Light, then request an activation for the perfect integration and balancing of your chakras so they function as one unified chakra.

Now call forth the violet flame of Saint Germain to bathe your entire being in his violet transmuting flame. Let this beautiful violet energy flowing down from God transmute any and all negativity into the purity and perfection of God. After bathing in this energy for about fifteen to thirty seconds, then call forth the golden twelfth ray and allow it to bathe your entire being in the energy of the Christ consciousness. See your entire being and all seven bodies being filled with this luminous golden energy pouring down from God, your Mighty I Am Presence and the Ascended Masters. Bathe in this twelfth ray golden Light for another fifteen to thirty seconds.

Now request God and the God force to be placed within your living Light merkabah vehicle. See the merkabah vehicle as a double-terminated crystal that surrounds your entire body, with another horizontal double-terminated section coming out the front and back of the vertical part. The merkabah vehicle will help to accelerate and quicken your overall vibrational frequencies. It is also a vehicle in which you can soul travel during meditation or while you sleep at night. Place yourself fully within the merkabah vehicle now and allow it to spin clockwise. This spinning allows you to become even more attuned to the cosmic pulse and frequencies of God and the God Force.

I am now ready for the ascension process to begin! (The ascending process is really the descending process of spirit into matter.) Beloved God and God force, I now call forth my soul to fully descend into my consciousness and four-body system if it has not done so already. I Am that I Am. Aum!

I call forth my glorified Lightbody to now descend into my consciousness and four-body system. I Am that I Am. Aum!

I call forth the Ascension Flame to descend and enter my consciousness and entire four-body system. I Am that I Am. Aum!

I call forth the full activation of my Alpha and Omega chakras! I Am that I Am. Aum! I call forth the Amrita, fire letters, sacred geometries, and key codes from the Keys of Enoch to now become fully activated. I Am that I Am. Aum!

I now call forth the full activation and creation of my full potential twelve strands of DNA within my physical vehicle. I Am that I Am. Aum!

I now call forth the full activation of my pituitary gland to create only the life hormone and to stop producing the death hormone! I Am that I Am. Aum!

I now call forth and fully activate my monadic Divine blueprints in my conscious, subconscious, and superconscious minds and four-body system. I Am that I Am. Aum!

I now call forth and fully activate my kundalini energy as guided by my monad and Mighty I Am Presence. I Am that I Am. Aum!

I now call forth a matchstick-sized spark of Cosmic Fire from the presence of God Himself to illuminate and transform my entire being into the light of God. I Am that I Am. Aum!

I now call forth a full axiatonal alignment as described in *The Keys of Enoch* to perfectly align all my meridian flows within my consciousness and four-body system! I Am that I Am. Aum!

I now call forth and fully claim my physical immortality and the complete cessation of the aging and death process. I am now youthing and becoming younger every day. I Am that I Am. Aum!

I now call forth the full opening of my third eye and all my psychic abilities and channeling abilities, that I may use them in the glory and service of the Most High God and my brothers and sisters in Christ on Earth. I Am that I Am. Aum!

I now call forth perfect radiant health to manifest within my physical, emotional, mental, etheric, and spiritual bodies. I ask and command that these bodies now manifest the health and perfection of Christ. I Am that I Am. Aum!

I now call forth my sixteenth chakra to descend, moving all my chakras down my chakra column until my sixteenth chakra resides in my seventh, or crown chakra. I Am that I Am. Aum!

I now call forth my fifteenth chakra to descend and enter my sixth, or third eye chakra. I Am that I Am. Aum!

I now call forth my fourteenth chakra to descend and enter my throat chakra. I Am that I Am. Aum!

I now call forth my thirteenth chakra to descend and enter and reside in my heart chakra. I Am that I Am. Aum!

I now call forth my twelfth chakra to descend and enter and reside in my solar plexus chakra. I Am that I Am. Aum!

I now call forth my eleventh chakra to descend and enter and reside in my second chakra. I Am that I Am. Aum!

I now call forth my tenth chakra to descend and enter and reside in my first chakra. I Am that I Am. Aum!

I now see the rest of my chakras, nine through one, descend down my legs and into the Earth in a corresponding fashion. I Am that I Am. Aum!

I now call forth the complete stabilization of my new fifth-dimensional chakra grid system within my consciousness and four-body system now. I Am that I Am. Aum!

I now call forth and see my chakra column lighting up like a Christmas tree with my first chakra becoming a large ball of pearl-white Light.

My second chakra now becomes a large ball of pink-orange Light.

My third chakra now becomes a glowing ball of golden Light.

My heart chakra now lights up with a pale violet-pink Light.

My fifth chakra now lights up with a deep blue-violet Light.

My third eye chakra now lights up with a large ball of golden-white Light.

My crown chakra now lights up with violet-white Light.

My entire chakra column has now been ignited with the fifth-dimensional ascension frequency. I Am that I Am. Aum!

I now call forth with all my heart and soul and mind and might the collective help of my eleven other soul extensions in my ascension process. I Am that I Am. Aum!

I now call forth the combined collective help of the one hundred forty-three other soul extensions of my monadic group in my ascension process, now. I Am that I Am. Aum!

I now call forth the complete descending and integration into my being of the raincloud of knowable things! I Am that I Am. Aum!

I now call forth the trinity of Isis, Osiris, and Horus, and all pyramid energies that are aligned with Source to now descend into my consciousness and four-body system and to become fully activated now.

I also call forth the Ascended Master Serapis Bey and his Ascension Temple energies from Luxor to descend and become fully activated within my consciousness and four-body system now. I Am that I Am. Aum!

I now call forth an ascension column of Light to surround my entire being. I Am that I Am. Aum!

I now call forth the complete balancing of all my karma from all my past and future lives. I Am that I Am. Aum!

I now call forth the raising of my vibrational frequencies within my physical, astral, mental, etheric, and spiritual bodies to the fifth-dimensional frequencies. I Am that I Am. Aum!

I now call forth the Light of a thousand suns to descend into my being and raise my vibrational frequencies one-thousandfold. I Am that I Am. Aum!

I now call forth the sacred sound of Aum to descend and reverberate through my consciousness and four-body system. I Am that I Am. Aum!

I now call forth a complete and full baptism of the Holy Spirit. I Am that I Am. Aum!

I call forth the perfect attunement and completion of my dharma, purpose, and mission in this lifetime in service of God's plan. I Am that I Am. Aum!

I call forth to descend now my Christed overself body. I Am that I Am. Aum!

I call forth my fifth-dimensional ascended self, who is already ascended within the understanding of simultaneous time, to now meld its consciousness with my unified field and aura. I Am that I Am. Aum!

I call forth my spiritual teacher, (insert name), to descend through my crown chakra and meld his or her ascended consciousness and Light into my consciousness and four-body system. I Am that I Am. Aum!

I hereby call forth the great God Flame to now descend and integrate and blend its greater flame with my lesser flame on Earth. I Am that I Am. Aum!

Lastly, I call forth my monad, my mighty I Am Presence and spirit to now fully descend into my consciousness and four-body system and transform me into Light and the Ascended Master I truly am. I Am that I Am. Aum!

Take a few moments of silence to allow the complete ascension to fully take place while remaining on Earth. Upon complete merger with the Light in consciousness and in your four body system, recite the following affirmations of truth:

Be still and know I Am God! I Am that I Am. Aum!

I Am the resurrection and the life! I Am that I Am. Aum!

I Am the mighty I Am Presence on Earth forever more! I Am that I Am. Aum!

I Am the Ascended Master (insert your full name)! I Am that I Am. Aum!

I am God living in this body as (insert name)! I Am that I Am. Aum!

The mighty I Am Presence is now my real self! I Am that I Am. Aum!

I Am the ascension in the Light. I Am that I Am. Aum!

I Am the Truth, the Way, and the Light. I Am that I Am. Aum!

I Am the open door which no man can shut. I Am that I Am. Aum!

I Am Divine perfection made manifest now. I Am that I Am. Aum!

I Am the revelation of God. I Am that I Am. Aum!

I Am the Light that lights every man that cometh into the world. I Am that I Am. Aum!

I Am the cosmic flame of cosmic victory. I Am that I Am. Aum!

I Am the ascended being I wish to be now. I Am that I Am. Aum!

I Am the raised vibration of my full Christ and I Am potential. I Am that I Am. Aum!

I Am the Aum made manifest in the world. I Am that I Am. Aum!

I Am a full member of the Great White Brotherhood and Spiritual Hierarchy. I Am that I Am. Aum!

I Am the realized manifestation of the eternal self. I Am that I Am. Aum!

I Am the embodiment of Divine love in action. I Am that I Am. Aum!

I live within all beings and all beings live within me. I Am that I Am. Aum!

I Am now one with the monadic plane of consciousness on Earth! I Am that I Am. Aum!

I Am now living in my glorified body of Light on Earth. I Am that I Am. Aum!

I now affirm my ability to transform my four bodies into Light and travel anywhere in God's infinite universe. I Am that I Am. Aum!

I call forth to Helios, the Solar Logos, to now send forth into my consciousness through my crown chakra, the sixty-four Keys of Enoch in all five sacred languages so they are fully integrated into my being on Earth. I Am that I Am. Aum!

I fully affirm my identity as the Eternal Self, the Christ, the Buddha, the atma, the monad, the I Am Presence on Earth in service of humankind. I Am that I Am. Aum!

I fully affirm that I Am physically immortal and I can, if I choose, remain on Earth indefinitely without aging! I Am that I Am. Aum!

I see every person, animal, and plant as the embodiment of the Eternal Self, whether they are aware of their true identity or not. I Am that I Am. Aum!

I am now the perfect integration of the monad, soul, and personality on Earth. I Am that I Am. Aum!

In this holy instant has salvation come. I Am that I Am. Aum!

I Am one self united with my Creator. I Am that I Am. Aum!

I Am the Light of the world. I Am that I Am. Aum!

I Am now a fully ascended being who has chosen to remain on Earth to be of service to all sentient beings! I Am that I Am. Aum!

Kodoish, Kodoish, Kodoish, Adonai Tsebayoth! (Holy, Holy, Holy, is the Lord God of Hosts!) Kodoish, Kodoish, Kodoish, Adonai Tsebayoth! (Holy, Holy, Holy, is the Lord God of Hosts!) Kodoish, Kodoish, Kodoish, Adonai Tsebayoth! (Holy, Holy, Holy, is the Lord God of Hosts!) I Am that I Am. Aum!

Bibliography

Bailey, Alice A. *The Rays and the Initiations*, Vol. 5. New York: Lucis Publishing Co., 1960.
——. *Esoteric Psychology*, Vol. I. New York: Lucis Publishing Co., 1936.
——. *Esoteric Psychology*, Vol. II. New York: Lucis Publishing Co., 1942.
——. *Ponder on This*. New York: Lucis Publishing Co., 1971.
——. *Initiation, Human and Solar*. New York: Lucis Publishing Co., 1922.
——. *The Soul, the Quality of Life*. New York: Lucis Publishing Co., 1974.
——. *The Reappearance of the Christ*. New York: Lucis Publishing Co., 1948.
——. *Serving Humanity*. New York: Lucis Publishing Co., 1972.
——. *The Externalization of the Hierarchy*. New York: Lucis Publishing Co., 1957.
——. *Glamour, a World Problem*. New York: Lucis Publishing Co., 1950.
——. *Death: The Great Adventure*. New York: Lucis Publishing Co., 1985.

Bey, Serapis *Dossier on the Ascension*. Livingston, MT: Summit University Press, 1967.

Burmester, Helen S. *Seven Rays Made Visual*. Marina del Rey, CA: DeVorss & Co., 1986.

Carey, Ken *The Starseed Transmissions*. San Francisco: Harper, 1982.
——. *Starseed: The Third Millennium*. San Francisco: Harper, 1991.

Carter, Mary Ellen. *Edgar Cayce on Prophecy*. New York: Warner Books, 1968.

Cayce, Edgar Evans. *Edgar Cayce on Atlantis*. New York: Warner Books, 1968.

Chaney, Earlyne. *Beyond Tomorrow*. Upland, CA: Astara's Library of Mystical Classics, 1985.
——. *The Mystery of Death and Dying*. York Beach, Maine: Samuel Weiser, Inc., 1988.

Cherry, Joanna. *Ascension for You and Me*. Mt. Shasta, CA: Ascension Mastery International, 1985.

Creme, Benjamin. *Maitreya's Mission*. Amsterdam: Share International Foundation, 1986.
——. *The Reappearance of the Christ and the Masters of Wisdom*. London: Tara Press, 1980.

Crowley, Brian & Esther. *Words of Power: Sacred Sounds of East and West*. St. Paul, MN: Llewellyn Publications, 1992.

Easwaran, Eknath. *Mantram Handbook*. Petaluma, CA: Nilgiri Press, 1977.

Furst, Jeffrey. *Edgar Cayce's Story of Jesus*. New York: Berkley Books, 1976.

Giri, Swami Satyeswarananda. *Babaji: The Divine Himalayan Yogi*. San Diego, CA: Satyeswarananda Giri, 1984.

Govindan, Marshall. *Babaji and the Eighteen Siddha Kriya Yogis.* Montreal: Kriya Yoga Publications, 1991.

Grattan, Brian. *Mahatma I & II.* Sedona, AZ: Light Technology Communications, Inc., 1991.

Hurtak, J.J. *The Book of Knowledge: The Keys of Enoch.* Los Gatos, CA: Academy for Future Science, 1977.

Jurriaanse, Aart. *Prophecies by D.K.* South Africa: World Unity & Service, 1977.
——. *Bridges.* South Africa: Sun Centre, 1978.

Kittler, Glenn D. *Edgar Cayce on the Dead Sea Scrolls.* New York: Warner Books, 1970.

Leadbeater, C.W. *The Masters and the Path.* Adyar: Theosophical Publishing House, 1925.

Levi. *The Aquarian Gospel of Jesus the Christ.* Marina del Rey: DeVorss, 1907.

Marciniak, Barbara. *Bringers of the Dawn: Teachings from the Pleiadians.* Santa Fe, NM: Bear & Company, 1992.

McClure, Janet. *The Story of Sanat Kumara: Training a Planetary Logos.* Sedona, AZ: Light Technology Publishing, 1990.

Montgomery, Ruth. *A World Beyond.* New York: Fawcett Crest, 1971.

——. *The World Before.* New York: Fawcett Crest, 1976.

Prophet, Elizabeth Clare. *The Lost Years of Jesus.* Livingston, MT: Summit University Press, 1984.

Radha, Swami Sivananda. *Mantras: Words of Power.* Porthill, ID: Timeless Books, 1980.

Read, Anne. *Edgar Cayce on Jesus and His Church.* New York: Warner Books, 1970.

Robinson, Lytle. *Edgar Cayce's Story of the Origin and Destiny of Man.* New York: Berkley Books, 1972.

Roeder, Dr. Dorothy. *Reach for Us!* Sedona, AZ: Light Technology Publishing, 1991.

Sedona Journal of Emergence! Sedona, AZ: Love Light Communications, Inc.

Sivananda, Sri Swami. *Sadhana.* Delhi: Motilal Banarsidass, 1958.

Stubbs, Tony. *An Ascension Handbook.* Livermore, CA: Oughten House Publications, 1991.

Two Disciples. *The Rainbow Bridge.* Danville, CA: Rainbow Bridge Productions, 1975.

Urantia Foundation. *The Urantia Book.* Chicago, 1955.

Yogananda, Paramahansa. *Autobiography of a Yogi.* Los Angeles, CA: Self-Realization Fellowship, 1946.

About the Author

Dr. Joshua David Stone has a Ph.D. in transpersonal psychology and is also a licensed marriage, family and child counselor in Los Angeles, California. He is licensed by the state of California in the practice of hypnosis and is also a minister.

He works very closely with his wife, Terri Sue Stone, who is a claraudient voice channel for the Ascended Masters, most specifically for the Ascended Master Djwhal Khul, of Alice A. Bailey fame.

Joshua and Terri teach classes, workshops, and seminars in Los Angeles and around the country, disseminating the teachings and spiritual practices of the Ascended Masters.

The prime focus of their work is the path of ascension and initiation. They have recently opened a center in Los Angeles to further their work, called The Center for Ascension in the Light. Those people interested in Joshua's and Terri's workshops, classes, lectures, and tapes can contact them through the publisher.

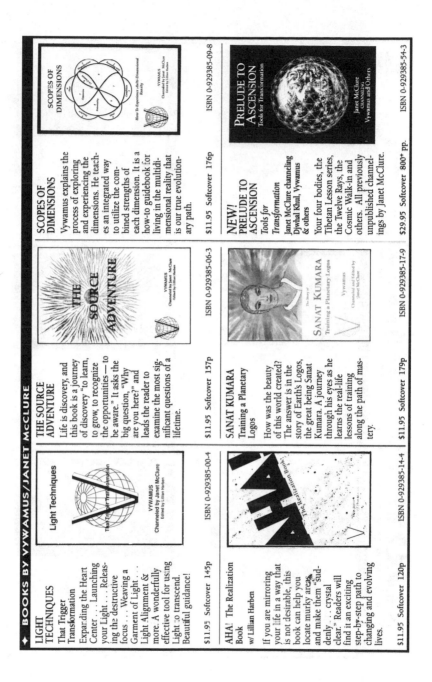

BOOK MARKET

A reader's guide to the extraordinary books we publish, print and market for your enLightenment.

◆ BOOKS BY LYNN BUESS

CHILDREN OF LIGHT, CHILDREN OF DENIAL

In his fourth book Lynn calls upon his decades of practice as counselor and psychotherapist to explore the relationship between karma and the new insights from ACOA/ Co-dependency writings.

$8.95 Softcover 150p

ISBN 0-929385-15-2

NUMEROLOGY FOR THE NEW AGE

An established standard, explicating for contemporary readers the ancient art and science of symbol, cycle, and vibration. Provides insights into the patterns of our personal lives. Includes life and personality numbers.

$11.00 Softcover 262p

ISBN 0-929385-31-4

NUMEROLOGY: NUANCES IN RELATIONSHIPS

Provides valuable assistance in the quest to better understand compatibilities and conflicts with a significant other. A handy guide for calculating your/his/her personality numbers.

$12.65 Softcover 239p

ISBN 0-929385-23-3

◆ EILEEN ROTA

THE STORY OF THE PEOPLE

An exciting history of our coming to Earth, our traditions, our choices and the coming changes, it can be viewed as a metaphysical adventure, science fiction or the epic of all of us brave enough to know the truth. Beautifully written and illustrated.

$11.95 Softcover 209p

ISBN 0-929385-51-9

◆ GUIDE BOOK

THE NEW AGE PRIMER

Spiritual Tools for Awakening

A guidebook to the changing reality, it is an overview of the concepts and techniques of mastery by authorities in their fields. Explores reincarnation, belief systems and transformative tools from astrology to crystals.

$11.95 Softcover 206p

ISBN 0-929385-48-9

◆ GABRIEL H. BAIN

LIVING RAINBOWS

A fascinating "how-to" manual to make experiencing human, astral, animal and plant auras an everyday event. Series of techniques, exercises and illustrations guide the reader to see and hear aural energy. Spiral-bound workbook.

$14.95 Softcover 134p

ISBN 0-929385-42-X

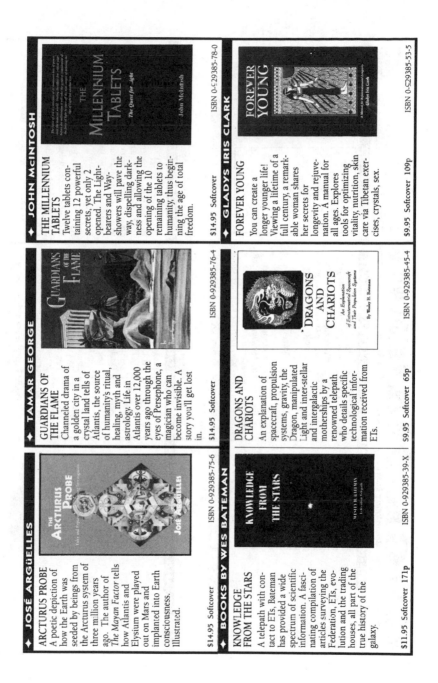

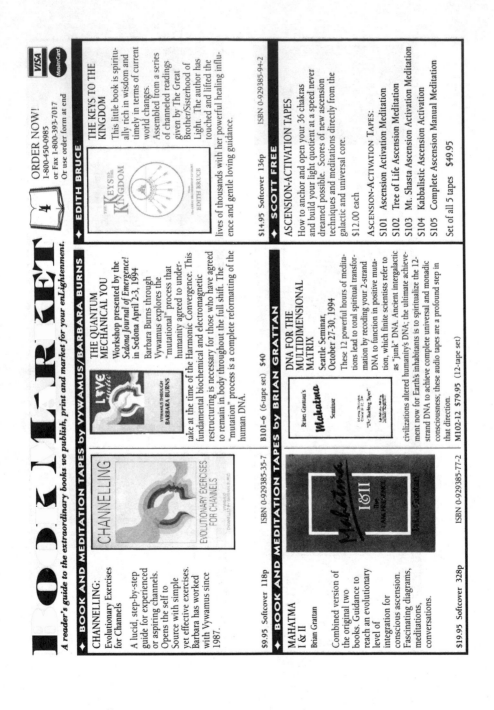

BOOK MARKET 4

A reader's guide to the extraordinary books we publish, print and market for your enLightenment.

ORDER NOW!
1-800-450-0985
or Fax 1-800-393-7017
Or use order form at end

VISA MasterCard

◆ BOOK AND MEDITATION TAPES by VYWAMUS/BARBARA BURNS

CHANNELLING: Evolutionary Exercises for Channels

A lucid, step-by-step guide for experienced or aspiring channels. Opens the self to Source with simple yet effective exercises. Barbara has worked with Vywamus since 1987.

$9.95 Softcover 118p   ISBN 0-929385-35-7

THE QUANTUM MECHANICAL YOU

Workshop presented by the *Sedona Journal of Emergence!* in Sedona April 2-3, 1994

Barbara Burns through Vywamus explores the "mutational" process that humanity agreed to undertake at the time of the Harmonic Convergence. This fundamental biochemical and electromagnetic restructuring is necessary for those who have agreed to remain in body throughout the full shift. The "mutation" process is a complete reformatting of the human DNA.

B101-6 (6-tape set) $40

◆ EDITH BRUCE

THE KEYS TO THE KINGDOM

This little book is spiritually rich in wisdom and timely in terms of current world changes. Assembled from a series of channeled readings given by The Great Brother/Sisterhood of Light. The author has touched and lifted the lives of thousands with her powerful healing influence and gentle loving guidance.

$14.95 Softcover 136p   ISBN 0-929385-94-2

◆ BOOK AND MEDITATION TAPES by BRIAN GRATTAN

MAHATMA I & II
Brian Grattan

Combined version of the original two books. Guidance to reach an evolutionary level of integration for conscious ascension. Fascinating diagrams, meditations, conversations.

$19.95 Softcover 328p   ISBN 0-929385-77-2

DNA FOR THE MULTIDIMENSIONAL MATRIX

Seattle Seminar, October 27-30, 1994

These 12 powerful hours of meditations lead to total spiritual transformation by recoding your 2-strand DNA to function in positive mutation, which finite scientists refer to as "junk" DNA. Ancient intergalactic civilizations altered humanity's DNA; the ultimate achievement now for Earth's inhabitants is to spiritualize the 12-strand DNA to achieve complete universal and monadic consciousness; these audio tapes are a profound step in that direction.

M102-12 $79.95 (12-tape set)

◆ SCOTT FREE

ASCENSION-ACTIVATION TAPES

How to anchor and open your 36 chakras and build your light quotient at a speed never dreamed possible. Scores of new ascension techniques and meditations directly from the galactic and universal core.

$12.00 each

ASCENSION-ACTIVATION TAPES:

S101 Ascension Activation Meditation
S102 Tree of Life Ascension Meditation
S103 Mt. Shasta Ascension Activation Meditation
S104 Kabbalistic Ascension Activation
S105 Complete Ascension Manual Meditation

Set of all 5 tapes $49.95

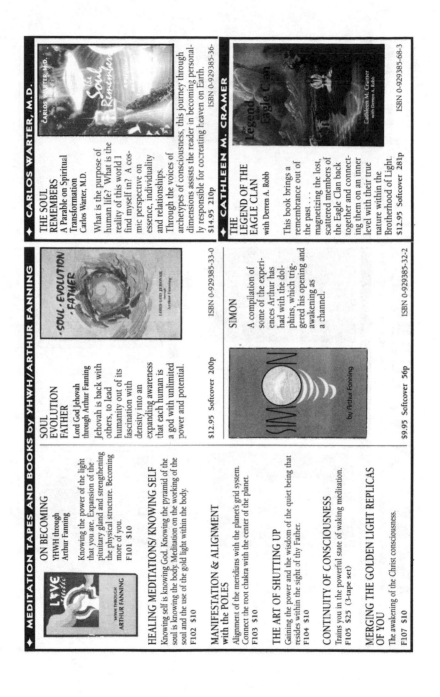

BOOK MARKET 7

A reader's guide to the extraordinary books we publish, print and market for your enLightenment.

◆ RICHARD DANNELLEY

THE SEDONA VORTEX GUIDEBOOK

200-plus pages of channeled, never-before-published information on the vortex energies of Sedona and the techniques to enable you to use the vortexes as multidimensional portals to time, space and other realities.

$14.95 Softcover 236p   ISBN 0-929385-25-X

◆ AI GVHDI WAYA

NEW!
PATH OF THE MYSTIC

The author shares her own journey through Native American stories of her discovery — and how you can access the many teachers, too. Walk the path of the mystic daily and transform from chrysalis into butterfly. "Our best teachers are inside ourselves."

$11.95 Softcover 114p   ISBN 0-929385-47-0

◆ NANCY ANNE CLARK, Ph.D.

EARTH IN ASCENSION

About the past, present and future of planet Earth and the role humans will play in her progress. Nothing can stop Earth's incredible journey into the unknown. You who asked to participate in the birthing of Gaia into the fifth dimension were chosen!

$14.95 Softcover 136p   ISBN 0-9648307-6-0

◆ ELLWOOD NORQUIST

WE ARE ONE:
A Challenge to Traditional Christianity

Is there a more fulfilling way to deal with Christianity than by perceiving humankind as sinful, separate and in need of salvation? Humanity is divine, one with its Creator, and already saved.

$14.95 Softcover 169p   ISBN 0-9646995-2-4

◆ RICH WORK & ANN GROTH

AWAKEN TO THE HEALER WITHIN

An empowerment of the soul, an awakening within and a releasing of bonds and emotions that have held us tethered to physical and emotional disharmonies. A tool to open the awareness of your healing ability.

$16.50 Softcover 330p   ISBN 0-9648002-0-9

◆ NICOLE CHRISTINE

TEMPLE OF THE LIVING EARTH

An intimate true story that activates the realization that the Living Earth is our temple and that we are all priests and priestesses to the world. A call to the human spirit to celebrate life and awaken to its cocreative partnership with Earth.

$16.00 Softcover 150p   ISBN 0-9647306-0-X

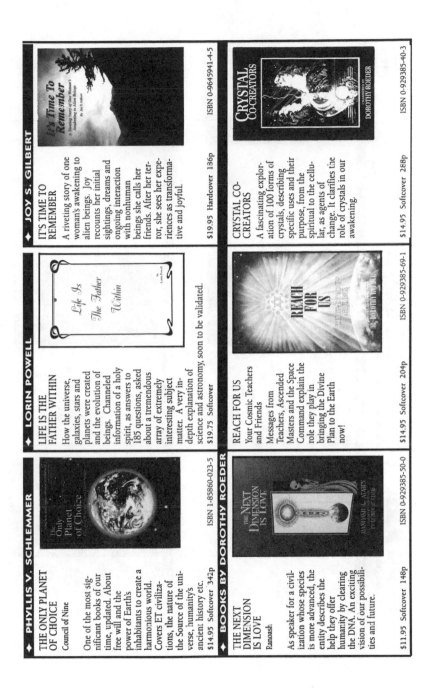

BOOK MARKET

A reader's guide to the extraordinary books we publish, print and market for your enLightenment.

◆ NANCY FALLON

ACUPRESSURE FOR THE SOUL

A revolutionary vision of emotions as sources of power, rocket fuel for fulfilling our purpose. A formula for awakening transformation with 12 beautiful illustrations.

$11.95 Softcover 150p   ISBN 0-929385-49-7

◆ JOSÉ ARGÜELLES

THE TRANSFORMATIVE VISION

Reprint of his 1975 tour de force, which prophesied the Harmonic Convergence as the "climax of matter," the collapse of materialism. Follows the evolution of the human soul in modern times by reviewing its expressions through the arts and philosophers.

$14.95 Softcover 364p   ISBN 0-9631750-0-9

◆ BOOKS BY RUTH RYDEN

THE GOLDEN PATH

"Book of Lessons" by the master teachers explaining the process of channeling, Akashic Records, karma, opening the third eye, the ego and the meaning of Bible stories. It is a master class for opening your personal pathway.

$11.95 Softcover 200p   ISBN 0-929385-43-8

◆ JERRY MULVIN

OUT-OF-BODY EXPLORATION

Techniques for traveling in the Soul Body to achieve absolute freedom and experience truth for oneself. Discover reincarnation, karma and your personal spiritual path.

$8.95 Softcover 87p   ISBN 0-941464-01-6

LIVING THE GOLDEN PATH

Practical Soul-utions to Today's Problems Guidance that can be used in the real world to solve dilemmas, to strengthen inner resolves and see the Light at the end of the road. Covers the difficult issues of addictions, rape, abortion, suicide and personal loss.

$11.95 Softcover 186p   ISBN 0-929385-65-9

◆ CHARLES H. HAPGOOD

VOICES OF SPIRIT

The author discusses 15 years of work with Elwood Babbit, the famed channel. Will fascinate both the curious sceptic and the believer. Includes complete transcripts.

$13.00 Softcover 350p   ISBN 1-881343-00-6

STARCHILD PRESS

BOOK MARKET

A reader's guide to the extraordinary books we publish, print and market for your enLightenment.

— A DIVISION OF LIGHT TECHNOLOGY PUBLISHING

1-800-450-0985
or Fax:
1-800-393-7017
Or use order
form at end

9

✦ BRIAN GOLD

CACTUS EDDIE

Imaginative and colorful, charmingly illustrated with 20 detailed paintings by the artist author. The tale of a small boy who when separated from his family has more adventures than Pecos Bill. Printed in large 8½" by 11" format.

$11.95 Softcover 62p
ISBN 0-929385-74-8

✦ TONI SIEGEL

SPIRIT OF THE NINJA

Returning as a dog, a Spiritual Warrior gains love and peace with a young woman in Sedona. Profoundly moving tale for all ages.

$7.95 Softcover 67p
ISBN 0-9627746-0-X

✦ LOU BADER

THE GREAT KACHINA

A warm, delightful story that will help children understand Kachina energy. With 20 full-color illustrations, printed in 8½" by 11" format to dramatize the artwork.

$11.95 Softcover 62p
ISBN 0-929385-60-8

IN THE SHADOW OF THE SAN FRANCISCO PEAKS

Collection of tales about those who shaped the frontier and were changed by it. A young boy's experiences with people and the wilderness is fascinating reading for all ages.

$9.95 Softcover 152p
ISBN 0-929385-52-7

✦ DOROTHY McMANUS

SONG OF SIRIUS

A truthful view of modern teens who face drugs and death, love and forgiveness. Guided by Ecknita of Sirius, they each find their destiny and desires.

$8.00 Softcover 155p
ISBN 0-929686-01-2

✦ ALOA STARR

I WANT TO KNOW

Inspiring responses to the questions of Why am I here? Who is God? Who is Jesus? What do dreams mean? and What do angels do? Invites contemplation, sets values and delights the young.

$7.00 Softcover 87p
ISBN 0-929686-02-0

A CIRCLE OF ANGELS
A workbook. An in-depth teaching tool with exercises and illustrations throughout.
$18.95 ISBN 0-929385-87-X

THE 12 UNIVERSAL LAWS
A workbook for all ages. Learning to live the Universal Laws; exercises and illustrations throughout.
$18.95 ISBN 0-929385-81-0

ALL MY ANGEL FRIENDS
A coloring book and illustrative learning tool about the angels who lovingly watch over us.
$10.95 ISBN 929385-80-2

WHERE IS GOD?
Story of a child who finds God in himself and teaches others.
$6.95 ISBN 0-929385-90-X

HAPPY FEET
A child's guide to foot reflexology, with pictures to guide
$6.95 ISBN 0-929385-88-8

WHEN THE EARTH WAS NEW
Teaches ways to protect and care for our Earth.
$6.95 ISBN 0-929385-91-8

THE ANGEL TOLD ME TO TELL YOU GOOD-BYE
Near-death experience heals his fear.
$6.95 ISBN 0-929385-84-5

COLOR ME ONE
Lessons in competition, sharing and separateness.
$6.95 ISBN 0-929385-82-9

ONE RED ROSE
Explores discrimination, judgment, and the unity of love.
$6.95 ISBN 0-929385-83-7

WHO'S AFRAID OF THE DARK?
Fearful Freddie learns to overcome with love.
$6.95 ISBN 0-929385-89-5

THE BRIDGE BETWEEN TWO WORLDS
Comfort for the "Star Children" on Earth.
$6.95 ISBN 0-929385-85-3

EXPLORING THE CHAKRAS
Ways to balance energy and feel healthy.
$6.95 ISBN 0-929385-86-1

CRYSTALS FOR KIDS
Workbook to teach care and properties of stones.
$6.95 ISBN 0-929385-92-5

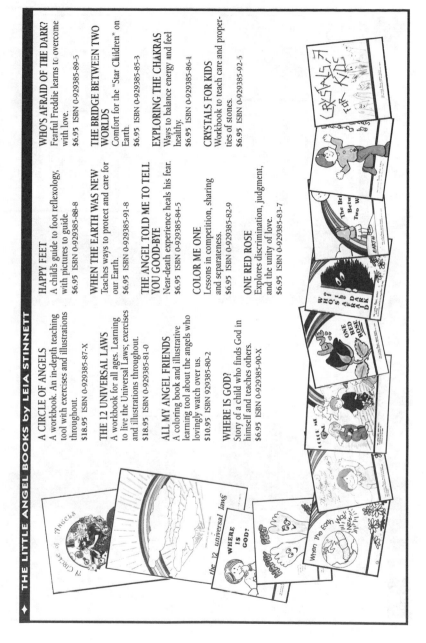

BOOK MARKET

A reader's guide to the extraordinary books we publish, print and market for your enLightenment.

10 ORDER NOW!
1-800-450-0985
or Fax 1-800-393-7017
Or use order form at end

◆ 4 BOOKS by MSI

ASCENSION!
An Analysis of the Art of Ascension as Taught by the Ishayas

Clearly explains the teachings of the Ishayas, an ancient order of monks entrusted by the Apostle John to preserve the original teachings of Christ until the third millennium. An invitation to awaken the innermost reality of your wonderful, exalted soul!

$11.95 Softcover 194p   ISBN 0-931783-51-8

FIRST THUNDER
An Adventure of Discovery

This riveting tale of discovery and adventure contains a secret teaching that is changing our world. Tells how to rise above stress and self-defeating beliefs and experience life Here and Now! A vital book that can lead you away from the past into a bright new future of joy and wonder.

$12.95 Softcover 282p   ISBN 0-931783-07-0

SECOND THUNDER
Seeking the Black Ishayas

A fascinating visionary story of Universal Consciousness, expressing the highest aspirations of our souls. Continues the adventures of discovery of *First Thunder*. Beautifully illustrated with pen and ink drawings.

$17.95 Softcover 390p   ISBN 0-931783-08-9

ENLIGHTENMENT
The Yoga Sutras of Patanjali
A New Translation and Commentary

The Yoga Sutras of Patanjali are verses that show the way to Divine Union or Enlightenment. This new translation shows how other translations make it seem difficult when it is actually simple. Makes Yoga effortless and natural.

$15.95 Softcover 338p   ISBN 0-931783-17-8

◆ 2 BOOKS by BARBARA MARCINIAK

BRINGERS OF THE DAWN
Teachings from the Pleiadians

Imparts to us the wisdom of the Pleiadians, a group of enlightened beings who have come to Earth to help us discover how to reach a new stage of evolution. Startling, intense, intelligent and controversial, these teachings offer essential reading.

$12.95 Softcover 288p   ISBN 0-939680-98-X

EARTH
Pleiadian Keys to the Living Library

More teachings from the Pleiadians. Explore the corridors of time, sacred sites and ancient civilizations. Once again the work is challenging, controversial, humorous and brilliant, awakening our deepest rememberings.

$12.95 Softcover 288p   ISBN 1-879181-21-5

◆ BOOK MARKET ORDER FORM ◆

BOOKS PUBLISHED BY LIGHT TECHNOLOGY PUBLISHING

	No. Copies	Total
ACUPRESSURE FOR THE SOUL	$11.95	$ ___
ARCTURUS PROBE	$14.95	$ ___
BEHOLD A PALE HORSE	$25.00	$ ___
CACTUS EDDIE	$11.95	$ ___
CHANNELLING: EVOLUTIONARY . . .	$ 9.95	$ ___
COLOR MEDICINE	$11.95	$ ___
FOREVER YOUNG	$ 9.95	$ ___
GUARDIANS OF THE FLAME	$14.95	$ ___
GREAT KACHINA	$11.95	$ ___
KEYS TO THE KINGDOM	$14.95	$ ___
LEGEND OF THE EAGLE CLAN	$12.95	$ ___
LIVING RAINBOWS	$14.95	$ ___
MAHATMA I & II	$19.95	$ ___
MILLENNIUM TABLETS	$14.95	$ ___
NEW AGE PRIMER	$11.95	$ ___
PATH OF THE MYSTIC	$11.95	$ ___
POISONS THAT HEAL	$14.95	$ ___
PRISONERS OF EARTH	$11.95	$ ___
SEDONA VORTEX GUIDE BOOK	$14.95	$ ___
SHADOW OF SAN FRANCISCO PEAKS	$ 9.95	$ ___
THE SOUL REMEMBERS	$14.95	$ ___
STORY OF THE PEOPLE	$11.95	$ ___
THIS WORLD AND THE NEXT ONE	$ 9.95	$ ___
ROBERT SHAPIRO/ARTHUR FANNING		
SHINING THE LIGHT	$12.95	$ ___
SHINING THE LIGHT — BOOK II	$14.95	$ ___
SHINING THE LIGHT — BOOK III	$14.95	$ ___
SHINING THE LIGHT — BOOK IV	$14.95	$ ___

	No. Copies	Total
ROBERT SHAPIRO		
THE EXPLORER RACE	$25.00	$ ___
ETs AND THE EXPLORER RACE	$14.95	$ ___
EXPLORER RACE ORIGINS . . .	$14.95	$ ___
EXPLORER RACE PARTICLE PERSON...	$14.95	$ ___
ARTHUR FANNING		
SOUL, EVOLUTION, FATHER	$12.95	$ ___
SIMON	$ 9.95	$ ___
WESLEY H. BATEMAN		
DRAGONS & CHARIOTS	$ 9.95	$ ___
KNOWLEDGE FROM THE STARS	$11.95	$ ___
LYNN BUESS		
CHILDREN OF LIGHT, CHILDREN . . .	$ 8.95	$ ___
NUMEROLOGY: NUANCES . . .	$12.65	$ ___
NUMEROLOGY FOR THE NEW AGE	$11.00	$ ___
RUTH RYDEN		
THE GOLDEN PATH	$11.95	$ ___
LIVING THE GOLDEN PATH	$11.95	$ ___
DOROTHY ROEDER		
CRYSTAL CO-CREATORS	$14.95	$ ___
NEXT DIMENSION IS LOVE	$11.95	$ ___
REACH FOR US	$14.95	$ ___
HALLIE DEERING		
LIGHT FROM THE ANGELS	$15.00	$ ___
DO-IT-YOURSELF POWER TOOLS	$25.00	$ ___
JOSHUA DAVID STONE, PH.D.		
COMPLETE ASCENSION MANUAL	$14.95	$ ___
SOUL PSYCHOLOGY	$14.95	$ ___

	No. Copies	Total
BEYOND ASCENSION	$14.95	$ ___
HIDDEN MYSTERIES	$14.95	$ ___
ASCENDED MASTERS	$14.95	$ ___
COSMIC ASCENSION	$14.95	$ ___
VYWAMUS/JANET MCCLURE		
AHA! THE REALIZATION BOOK	$11.95	$ ___
LIGHT TECHNIQUES	$11.95	$ ___
SANAT KUMARA	$11.95	$ ___
SCOPES OF DIMENSIONS	$11.95	$ ___
THE SOURCE ADVENTURE	$11.95	$ ___
PRELUDE TO ASCENSION	$29.95	$ ___
LEIA STINNETT		
A CIRCLE OF ANGELS	$18.95	$ ___
THE TWELVE UNIVERSAL LAWS	$18.95	$ ___
ALL MY ANGEL FRIENDS	$10.95	$ ___
WHERE IS GOD?	$ 6.95	$ ___
HAPPY FEET	$ 6.95	$ ___
WHEN THE EARTH WAS NEW	$ 6.95	$ ___
THE ANGEL TOLD ME . . .	$ 6.95	$ ___
COLOR ME ONE	$ 6.95	$ ___
ONE RED ROSE	$ 6.95	$ ___
EXPLORING THE CHAKRAS	$ 6.95	$ ___
CRYSTALS FOR KIDS	$ 6.95	$ ___
WHO'S AFRAID OF THE DARK	$ 6.95	$ ___
THE BRIDGE BETWEEN TWO WORLDS	$ 6.95	$ ___

BOOKS PRINTED OR MARKETED BY LIGHT TECHNOLOGY PUBLISHING

Title	Price		Title	Price		Title	Code	Price	
Access Your Brain's Joy Center	$14.95	$____	The Pleiadian Agenda	$15.00	$____	Earth		$12.95	$____
Awaken to the Healer Within	$16.50	$____	The Transformative Vision	$14.95	$____	**MSI**			
Earth in Ascension	$14.95	$____	Voices of Spirit	$13.00	$____	Ascension!		$11.95	$____
Galaxy Seven	$15.95	$____	We Are One	$14.95	$____	First Thunder		$12.95	$____
Innana Returns	$14.00	$____	**Lee Carroll**			Second Thunder		$17.95	$____
It's Time To Remember	$19.95	$____	Kryon—Book I, The End Times	$12.00	$____	Enlightenment		$15.95	$____
I Want To Know	$7.00	$____	Kryon—Book II, Don't Think Like...	$12.00	$____	**Preston B. Nichols with Peter Moon**			
Life Is The Father Within	$19.75	$____	Kryon—Book III, Alchemy of...	$14.00	$____	Montauk Project		$15.95	$____
Life On the Cutting Edge	$14.95	$____	Kryon—The Parables of Kryon	$17.00	$____	Montauk Revisited		$19.95	$____
Look Within	$9.95	$____	**Richard Dannelley**			Pyramids of Montauk		$19.95	$____
Mayan Calendar Birthday Book	$12.95	$____	Sedona Power Spot/Guide	$11.00	$____	Encounter in the Pleiades...		$19.95	$____
Medical Astrology	$29.95	$____	Sedona: Beyond The Vortex	$12.00	$____	**Lyssa Royal and Keith Priest**			
Our Cosmic Ancestors	$9.95	$____	**Tom Dongo: Mysteries of Sedona**			Preparing For Contact		$12.95	$____
Out-Of-Body Exploration	$8.95	$____	Mysteries of Sedona — Book 1	$6.95	$____	Prism of Lyra		$11.95	$____
Principles To Remember and Apply	$11.95	$____	Alien Tide — Book II	$7.95	$____	Visitors From Within		$12.95	$____
Song of Sirius	$8.00	$____	Quest — Book III	$9.95	$____	**Amorah Quan Yin**			
Soul Recovery and Extraction	$9.95	$____	Unseen Beings, Unseen Worlds	$9.95	$____	The Pleiadian Workbook		$16.00	$____
Spirit Of The Ninja	$7.95	$____	Merging Dimensions	$14.95	$____	Pleiadian Perspectives on...		$14.00	$____
Temple of The Living Earth	$16.00	$____	**Barbara Marciniak**						
The Only Planet Of Choice	$14.95	$____	Bringers of the Dawn	$12.95	$____				

ASCENSION MEDITATION TAPES

Joshua David Stone, Ph.D.

Title	Code	Price		Title	Code	Price	
Ascension Activation Meditation	S101	$12.00	$____	**YHWH/Arthur Fanning**			
Tree of Life Ascension Meditation	S102	$12.00	$____	On Becoming	F101	$10.00	$____
Mt. Shasta Ascension Activation Meditation	S103	$12.00	$____	Healing Meditations/Knowing Self	F102	$10.00	$____
Kabbalistic Ascension Activation	S104	$12.00	$____	Manifestation & Alignment w/ Poles	F103	$10.00	$____
Complete Ascension Manual Meditation	S105	$12.00	$____	The Art of Shutting Up	F104	$10.00	$____
Set of ALL 5 Tapes		$49.95	$____	Continuity of Consciousness	F105	$25.00	$____
Vywamus/Barbara Burns				Merging the Golden Light Replicas of You	F107	$10.00	$____
The Quantum Mechanical You (6 tapes)	B101-6	$40.00	$____	**Kryon/Lee Carroll**			
Taka				Seven Responsibilities of the New Age	K101	$10.00	$____
Magical Sedona through the Didgeridoo	T101	$12.00	$____	Co-Creation in the New Age	K102	$10.00	$____
Brian Grattan				Ascension and the New Age	K103	$10.00	$____
Seattle Seminar Resurrection 1994 (12 tapes)	M102	$79.95	$____	Nine Ways to Raise the Planet's Vibration	K104	$10.00	$____
				Gifts and Tools of the New Age	K105	$10.00	$____
				Jan Tober			
				Crystal Singer	J101	$12.00	$____

BOOKSTORE DISCOUNTS HONORED — SHIPPING 15% OF RETAIL

NAME/COMPANY _____

ADDRESS _____

CITY/STATE/ZIP _____

PHONE _____ FAX _____

E-MAIL _____

All prices in US$. Higher in Canada and Europe. Books are available at all national distributors as well as the following international distributors:

CANADA: Dempsey (604) 683-5541 Fax (604) 683-5521 • ENGLAND/EUROPE: Windrush Press Ltd. 0608 652012/652025 Fax 0608 652125
AUSTRALIA: Gemcraft Books (03) 888-0111 Fax (03) 888-0044 • NEW ZEALAND: Peaceful Living Pub. (07) 571-8105 Fax (07) 571-8513

SUBTOTAL: $ _____

SALES TAX: $ _____
(8.5% – AZ residents only)

SHIPPING/HANDLING: $ _____
($4 Min.: 15% of orders over $30)

CANADA S/H: $ _____
(20% of order)

TOTAL AMOUNT ENCLOSED: $ _____

❑ CHECK ❑ MONEY ORDER
CREDIT CARD: ❑ MC ❑ VISA

_____
Exp. date: _____
Signature: _____

(U.S. FUNDS ONLY) PAYABLE TO:
LIGHT TECHNOLOGY
PUBLISHING
P.O. BOX 1526 • SEDONA • AZ 86339
(520) 282-6523 Fax: (520) 282-4130
1-800-450-0985
Fax 1-800-393-7017

BOOKSTORE DISCOUNTS HONORED — SHIPPING 15% OF RETAIL

NAME/COMPANY _____

ADDRESS _____

CITY/STATE/ZIP _____

PHONE _____ FAX _____

E-MAIL _____

All prices in US$. Higher in Canada and Europe. Books are available at all national distributors as well as the following international distributors:

CANADA: Dempsey (604) 683-5541 Fax (604) 683-5521 • ENGLAND/EUROPE: Windrush Press Ltd. 0608 652012/652025 Fax 0608 652125
AUSTRALIA: Gemcraft Books (03) 888-0111 Fax (03) 888-0044 • NEW ZEALAND: Peaceful Living Pub. (07) 571-8105 Fax (07) 571-8513

SUBTOTAL: $ _____

SALES TAX: $ _____
(8.5% – AZ residents only)

SHIPPING/HANDLING: $ _____
($4 Min.: 15% of orders over $30)

CANADA S/H: $ _____
(20% of order)

TOTAL AMOUNT ENCLOSED: $ _____

❑ CHECK ❑ MONEY ORDER
CREDIT CARD: ❑ MC ❑ VISA

_____
Exp. date: _____
Signature: _____

(U.S. FUNDS ONLY) PAYABLE TO:
LIGHT TECHNOLOGY
PUBLISHING
P.O. BOX 1526 • SEDONA • AZ 86339
(520) 282-6523 Fax: (520) 282-4130
1-800-450-0985
Fax 1-800-393-7017

Notes

Notes